3-18-64
8-7-64

synods

(05-210877)

PRELUDE TO YORKTOWN

PRELUDE TO YORKTOWN

THE SOUTHERN CAMPAIGN OF NATHANAEL GREENE 1780-1781

by M. F. Treacy

THE UNIVERSITY OF NORTH CAROLINA PRESS

CHAPEL HILL

PRINTED BY THE SEEMAN PRINTERY, DURHAM, N. C.

ACKNOWLEDGMENTS

Space does not permit my thanking all those who have been of assistance to me in this work. I should like, however, to take the opportunity of mentioning a few of many. The members of my dissertation committee at the University of Utah were unfailingly helpful. Dr. Philip C. Sturges, chairman, cheerfully submitted to many off-hour questionings over problems arisen. Drs. Leland H. Creer and David E. Miller of the history department offered useful constructive criticism, as did Dr. W. Harold Dalgliesh, head of the department. To Dr. Robert Anderson of the anthropology department I am indebted for my first information that the William L. Clements Library at the University of Michigan contained many of Nathanael Greene's papers pertinent to the southern campaign. Dr. Charles E. Dibble of the anthropology department never failed of encouragement.

Drs. Myrtle Austin and Clarice Short of the English department, although in no way connected with my committee, nevertheless gave valuable aid in matters of style and construction. Dr. L. H. Kirkpatrick and the staff of the University of Utah Library were most helpful and patient.

I am particularly indebted to the staff of the William L. Clements Library, University of Michigan, Ann Arbor, Michigan, without whose courteous assistance this task could not have been accomplished. Mr. Howard H. Peckham, director, provided me with information as to work being done in my field long before my arrival in Michigan. Mr. William Ewing and graduate assistant Robert Keyes in the Manuscript Room of the library have my sincere gratitude, as do all other staff members, for aiding in a useful and productive five weeks in the summer of 1961.

Personnel of the New York Public Library and the Butler Hall Library, Columbia University, were also most kind and efficient. I wish in addition to thank the staff of the National Park Service, Guilford Battleground National Monument, for their assistance to me on a very hot day in July, 1961.

My father knows that I appreciate his enabling me to come to New York last summer. My husband, Colonel Kenneth W. Treacy, was of much assistance on matters military. He also suffered with forebearance disruptions and untidiness of domestic arrangements during the course of my research.

Mrs. Carol Stout and her charming son and daughter cheerfully endured the tedious task of proofreading.

This book is dedicated to three ancestral ladies: Stella Bainbridge Kimball, Genevieve Bainbridge Foreman and Mabel Bainbridge Hyde, who had a great thirst for universal knowledge but who were born into generations which believed that women should be versed only in the homely and graceful arts. In these they lacked nothing.

Lastly, I wish to acknowledge all those people and things which—without seeming malevolence or malice aforethought —contrived nevertheless to throw obstacles in the way of accomplishment and thus afford the necessary spur to ambition.

CONTENTS

LIST OF MAPS

PRELUDE TO YORKTOWN

THE SETTING AND THE
CLIMATE

In the eighteenth century the traveler, or the soldier, moving south from the Virginia line came shortly into a different world. Gone were the green fields and the groves of deciduous oak and hickory. In their place were low, yellow sand hills, moving inland like frozen waves, and as difficult to traverse. The sandy soil of these barrens supported tall stands of long-leafed loblolly pine. Above the mouths of tidal rivers and creeks were swampy areas and stretches of rich black earth, smelling of rot. Few of the rivers were bridged, although in their upper courses there were fords passable at low water. Farther south the pines gave way to palmetto palms with their rough, squat, ugly trunks and fan-shaped leaves. The air became increasingly hot and humid. Rivers and streamlets and broad expanses, half-mud, half-water, were everywhere.

This is the low country of the Carolinas and Georgia. In climate it is listed with the humid subtropics, which means, among other things, that it is only too well watered. In summer it steams, and even the nights are breathless with only the slightest cooling toward dawn. Insects abound. There are mosquitoes and flies and tiny black gnats that settle on the eyelids of infants, and of all those who are wounded or sick or helpless, to suck at the oils at the roots of the eyelashes. In the eighteenth century the mosquitoes and flies were considered a nuisance because of their sting, but the secret life cycle of the malarial plasmodium which the mosquito injected into the bloodstream was unknown. Fevers were believed to come from a mysterious effluvia or miasma rising from the swamps. That the swamp was a breeder of fever was clear enough, but the carrier was not recognized.

Back from the coast in this country, one hundred miles or so, above the fall line of the rivers, the character of the landscape changes to the rolling, wooded hills of the Piedmont with their red clay soil. Beyond is the rugged escarpment of the Blue Ridge, higher in North than South Carolina, diminishing to hills in Georgia. In the high lands back from the coast, the climate is cooler, but still humid with abundant rainfall. In winter in the Carolinas and Georgia, the days at noon are often so warm that one can sunbathe a naked baby, but at night hoar frost forms on trees and grass; puddles skim with ice; precipitation takes the form of chilling rain, or needles of sleet, or snow, which quickly melts to slush with the coming of day and turns the frozen ruts of red clay roads to churned morasses under the bleeding feet of shoeless soldiers. It is a miserable country in which to fight a war.

Yet a bitter, partisan, dog-eat-dog kind of war was fought there. On the southern seaboard the American Revolution was more a civil war than it was in any of the northern colonies. For one thing the Tory and Whig elements were more evenly divided, and many of the members of both groups were lawless men, accustomed to settling their own disputes in blood without recourse to government of any kind.

Not all of the Tories were similarly motivated. Among them were persons conscientiously opposed to every sort of war and violence. Of these the Quakers were an outstanding example. They were numerous in North Carolina at the period of the Revolution. Another group, caring nothing for the principles involved, believed in letting well enough alone—"A little tax on tea won't hurt us." Others sincerely believed that the fleets and armies of Britain were invincible; defeat and ruin must follow on rebellion. Still others, with an eye to gain, remained loyal in the hope of reaping a golden harvest from the confiscated estates of rebelling Whigs. Lastly, there was a group composed of rogues, robbers, and outlaws, shrewd enough to see a field well suited to their tastes and talents where they could plunder as they wished under the sanction of law and authority.[1] This group of course was the most dangerous. Its members were not above changing sides as the wind veered, so that "packs of rogues and scoundrels," as Lord Cornwallis termed them, could be found among Whigs as well as among Tories.

No doubt varying types of Tories existed in all of the thirteen colonies. However, some of the peculiarities of the divisions of loyalties in the Carolinas were the result of the special nature of the colonial history of the area and of the history of the Revolution in those states up to 1780.

As has been frequently pointed out, the Carolinas were never a unit geographically, politically or culturally. The group of 150 men and women who disembarked on Albemarle Point on the west bank of the Ashley River in April, 1670, comprised not only colonists from England but transplanted colonials from the West Indian islands, especially Barbados.[2] By 1680 these people had deserted the first little village on Albemarle and founded a new Charleston (Charles Town, they called it, after their king) on its present site between the Ashley and Cooper rivers. The city grew and prospered. By 1700 the scant population of the province consisted of five thousand people, most of them living within a few miles of Charleston.[3] Therefore, insofar as the opinion of many of their Charlestonian descendants was concerned, Charleston *was* South Carolina. It was *The City*, the seat of government, of wealth, of culture. Serene in the conviction of supremacy, its citizens regarded it as only proper that all possible revenues be centered in that place, despite derisive hoots from the back country suggesting that since everybody must come to Charleston to transact any business, legal or otherwise, perhaps everybody should be required to come there to answer the calls of nature as well.[4]

The Barbadians, who formed almost half of the total English population of South Carolina in the 1700's, brought the institution of slavery with them. The nature of the coastal semitropical country and the direction of their tastes, acquired in the West Indian environment, led them early to the development of the *latifundia*. This is the agricultural, one-crop type of economy which is absolutely dependent on the exploitation of a submerged laboring mass—in this case black slaves working the rice and indigo plantations—by a superior master class. By the time of the Revolution enslaved Negroes constituted two-thirds of the population of South Carolina.[5] Even this figure is misleading, however, for the slaves were concentrated on the low-lying coastal plain. The farming population of the back country Piedmont was almost wholly white. Consequently, in the large plantation area Negroes outnumbered their white masters by two, three, or even more, to one.

The evils latent in the situation were recognized by intelligent heads from 1710—when the great increase in Negroes became evident—onwards. The dangers of slave insurrection caused frequent reference to these "internal enemies" as distinguished from external enemies in the form of Spanish, French and Indians on the borders. Many of the slaves were fresh from Africa; the "country-born" Negro was still in the minority. The kings of Dahomey and Ashanti, from whence many of the Negroes came, habitually used the barracoon of the slave trader as a convenient means of disposing of dynastic competition in the person of relatives with claims to the throne. Hence, not a few of the imported Negroes may have been possessed of qualities of religious and military leadership.[6]

That the witch doctor was present seems evident from the fact that in 1761, and at other times as well, there was a rash of poisonings of white masters by house servants. The house servant was selected, naturally, from the most intelligent and teachable of the slaves. In 1765, after scores of runaways where the fugitives in some instances set up armed camps, a general insurrection was so feared that Indians were brought in from the civilized Cherokee tribes to terrorize the Negroes, and the whites of the back country were alerted to march to the coast.[7]

In addition to such immediate dangers, the economic menace was already felt. The small farmer, the artisan, and the indentured white could not compete with slave labor.[8] The yeoman was losing the battle and was either leaving the country, thus decreasing the white population, or sinking into hopeless poverty. Hence the poor white was spawned before the Revolution. But:

The standing tragedy of Southern life was already disclosed. Men saw the peril they were creating for themselves and their posterity, but were morally unable to take the obvious course for permanent well being. Only a society of philosophers could have resisted the temptation, and they probably only if legislating for some society other than their own. The immediate gain to the planter outweighed the permanent interests of the State, as is the custom when the class receiving the benefits holds the power.[9]

Another ethnic group of the South Carolina seaboard was the French Huguenots. Arriving in increasing numbers after the revocation of the Edict of Nantes in 1685, some of them settled in Charleston and its environs. Others took up lands between the Cooper and Wando rivers and on the southern bank of the Santee some forty miles from Charleston. These people were of an exceptional moral and intellectual fiber, although by no means all nobility, as has sometimes been pictured. In some cases desperately poor when they arrived, they were hard working and thrifty, and the more fortunate members took care of their own, so that a Huguenot name is almost unknown on the rolls of public charity. By the time of the Revolution, most of the Huguenots had been assimilated through intermarriage into the English population. A majority, with French adaptibility, became Anglican in faith. Their descendants bore some of the most respected and distinguished names in South Carolina history. Isaac Huger, one of Greene's generals, was of Huguenot descent, as was Francis Marion.

Although originally all of the territory granted by Charles II to the eight proprietors had been known simply as Carolina, by 1712 North Carolina had become a separate entity under a separate governor. The two regions had little in common and were prevented from easy communication with each other by a stretch of uninhabited forests and swamps. North Carolina about Albemarle and Pamlico sounds had been settled largely by colonists from Virginia with a sprinkling of Germans and French Huguenots. Its trading interests were with the colonies to the northward while those of South Carolina were with the West Indies and Europe. The institution of slavery, which took such early root in South Carolina, developed slowly in North Carolina. Tobacco became the money crop around Albemarle Sound and in the counties on the Virginia border, but agriculture tended to be diversified with emphasis on maize, beans, wheat, peas and potatoes. Plantations were smaller than in South Carolina. Few planters owned more than fifty slaves.

Nevertheless, by 1750, there had developed on the coast of both Carolinas a planter class, a gentry predominantly land owners but including also wealthy merchants, professional men, the ministry and successful mechanics.[10] It was a class highly conscious of its social position and tenacious of its presumed right to govern. These people controlled the assemblies and were able to dictate the systems of representation and taxation. An aristocracy, however, can only maintain itself through the veneration, or at least the tolerance, of others.

Consequently when in the quarter of a century or so before the Revolution there was an enormous influx of a non-slave-holding white population of small farmers into the back country of the Piedmont in both Carolinas, there was trouble. The back country, largely, was not settled from the coast. Furthermore, these newcomers were not homogeneous among themselves. In the majority were Scotch-Irish from western Pennsylvania, staunch Presbyterians all. There were also Palatine Germans newly arrived from Germany[11] and Pennsylvania Dutch from the north. Numbered among them were various faiths—Moravians, Lutherans, and Reformed Church people. There were Quakers and Baptists and short-lived little sects who believed their leaders to be God enfleshed until circumstances proved the contrary.[12]

North Carolina was in addition colorfully invaded by Highland Scots, complete with kilts, bagpipes, broadswords and skean dhus, who settled mainly in the Cross Creek area (modern Fayetteville). Stubbornly loyal they were to the House of Hanover, for they had given their word in exchange for their lands. It was a transfer of allegiance from the Jacobites and the clans, which were no more and had not been since Culloden. The Highlanders were men of word.

These diverse peoples had two things in common—a love of personal liberty (although how they individually would have defined the word is certainly debatable) and (the reasons for this also are as various as their origins) a complete and profound disbelief in the natural superiority of the coastal aristocracy.

One of the immediate grievances of the back country dwellers was the need to travel long distances for even minor business or legal reasons. Hence the sarcastic comment, mentioned earlier, that they might as well go to the coast for every necessity. They also objected to the imposition upon them of illegal fees and excessive taxes by dishonest court officials, sheriffs, and tax collectors appointed by the colonial governors. They objected violently to taxation without representation.

There were Regulator movements in both the Carolinas but with a difference. Both areas suffered from the fact that they had little or no representation in the colonial legislatures. However, while the South Carolina back country folk were so lacking in judges, sheriffs, or law officers of any sort as to be obliged to repair to Charleston for any kind of legal redress, the North Carolinians of the Piedmont were plagued by a plethora of appointive, unsalaried county officials who used the opportunities of office to line their pockets with large percentages of the fees and tax monies which in theory they should have remitted to the provincial capital. The Regulators in South Carolina obtained promise of some of the things they asked but not enough to make them trust the planter aristocracy. The Regulators in North Carolina were defeated by Governor Tryon at the Battle of the Alamance in 1771. Twelve of their leaders were tried for treason. Six of the twelve were hanged. Sixty-four hundred of their comrades subsequently laid down their arms and received pardons from the king. A sufficient number of these remained loyal to the king, when the Revolution came four years later, to make things awkward in the back country.

An estimated one thousand families, left the country in disgust in the years between 1771 and 1775 and went over the mountains to Tennessee where they set up their own government and attended to their own affairs without worrying about taxes on tea or anything else until they began to worry about Major Patrick Ferguson some nine years later.

In 1775 the seacoast assembly invited the Regulator

group in South Carolina to make war on their king over the matter of taxation without representation. The situation struck the Regulators as little short of farcical. To their way of thinking it was the seacoast assembly which had taxed *them* without representation while it was the king who had granted them their lands. Therefore, many of them remained Loyalists. So likewise did the Germans in the back country of Orangeburg, Saxe-Gotha, and Dutch Fork. They were occupied in clearing lands lately received in the king's name. They were enjoying a freedom unknown to them in the old country and could not be expected to understand that this king was violating ancient principles of liberty with which they were entirely unfamiliar. An expedition sent to them from the coast to enlighten them was a complete failure.[13]

It was a very complex situation in which an aristocracy, which had long called England "home," which had educated its sons there, and which held other men in bondage, was now up in arms against George III, while a yeomanry which had struggled for generations against authority remained loyal to an authority overseas because they could abide it better than the disdainfully assertive authority of their statesmen.

Complex as it was, this was the climate in which the war had to be fought. We may try to understand it. It is doubtful whether many of the principal participants of the regular armies on either side understood its significance very well. They merely had to cope with it. Colonel Otho Williams, commander of Greene's light troops, was frankly bewildered: "They [the back country riflemen] cannot fast with good grace. . . . They say they are Volunteers and should be treated with distinction."[14]

Cornwallis perhaps comprehended the least. The "noble earl," as Sir Henry Clinton was given to referring to him, spent much time, energy, shoe leather, and human life marching up and down the countryside in search of what he called "our friends." Tories and Whigs fought one another willingly and mercilessly in partisan bands, but the Tories were reluctant to join the royal arms when their presence was announced by proclamation. This was partly because Cornwallis had an unfortunate propensity for arriving at places when the wrong side was on top. In the end he said in an abortive attempt at self-justification: "The idea of our friends arising in any number and to any purpose totally failed, as I expected."[15]

Nathanael Greene, to whom performance and outcome were ever more important than specific personality, said that the back country militia were formidable, but the others were not. He asked for back country men when he was able.[16] His humanity was shocked by the animosity between the Whigs and the Tories: "There is not a day passes but there are more or less who fall a sacrifice to this savage disposition. The Whigs seem determined to extirpate the Tories and the Tories the Whigs. . . . If a stop cannot be put to these massacres, the country will be depopulated . . . as neither Whig nor Tory can live."[17]

AFTER CHARLESTON FELL

"By this very important acquisition," wrote Sir Henry Clinton, "there fell into our hands seven generals, and a multitude of other officers, belonging to ten Continental regiments, and three battalions of artillery, which with the militia and sailors doing duty in the siege amounted to about 6000 men in arms. The rebel lieutenant governor and the council and other civil officers became also our prisoners."[1]

Sir Henry had reference to the surrender of Charleston on May 12, 1780, by Major General Benjamin Lincoln. The Continental regiments Clinton mentioned included, among others, the entire Continental establishment of North and South Carolina and Georgia. Thenceforward the three southernmost states had no regular army forces in the field, only militia and partisan bands.

The formal surrender of the Charleston garrison took place on May 12. It had been preceded by much haggling back and forth between Clinton and Lincoln. The final two points upon which negotiations reached a seeming stalemate on May 9 appear to moderns trivial to absurdity if not to tears. Lincoln demanded that the garrison be permitted to march out with the honors of war, with colors unfurled and drums beating a British march. Clinton, the British Army commander, and Admiral Arbuthnot, the Royal Navy com-

mander, would accept neither flying colors nor a British nor
an American march.

Hostilities were therefore resumed. After a furious night
bombardment from both sides in which the British set many
houses in the city on fire, the now terrified populace begged
Lincoln to petition for surrender, which he did on May 10.
On May 12 the Continentals marched out of the city with
colors decorously cased and drums beating a Turkish march.[2]
Somehow, from somebody's point of view, certain amenities
had been observed.

The hard facts remained. The Continental troops
marched away as prisoners of war. The militia, together with
the armed citizens of Charleston, were regarded as prisoners
on parole. The militia were allowed to go to their homes
under this stipulation. This surrender constituted a loss of
6000 men to the infant United States. In the last weeks of
May, the militia around Beaufort, the rebels at Camden and
those in the Ninety Six district (Andrew Pickens among
them) also asked to be accepted on this status, that is "as
prisoners on parole; which parole, as long as they observe,
shall secure them from being molested in their property by
the British troops."[3] Clinton accepted the paroles of these
people, and thousands more men were effectually im-
moblized.

South Carolina was virtually a conquered state. Un-
doubtly a considerable portion of the population welcomed
the situation. Those who did not seemed to accept it as
inevitable. They had little apparent choice. Their army was
annihilated, and their only civil government consisted of a
"peripatetic governor in headlong flight."[4] Governor Rutledge, at Lincoln's request, had fled Charleston before it
capitulated but could hardly be effective in his present circumstances.

Briefly, life appeared to return to a peaceful normality.
Wagon trains from the mountains resumed trade with

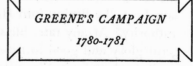

GREENE'S CAMPAIGN
1780-1781

Charleston. English money lifted the economy from the chaos into which worthless Continental paper had plunged it.[5] For a little while things seemed to be not too bad, although certain inhabitants, particularly in the Charleston neighborhood, were unhappy over the loss of property valued at £300,000 "requisitioned" under the guise of military necessity by the British.[6]

The British continued their work of reconstituting the "province," as they considered it. Lord Cornwallis, Clinton's military second in command and presumed successor, sent Lieutenant Colonel Banastre Tarleton in pursuit of a retreating column of 350 Virginia Continentals under Colonel Abraham Buford. This force had been intended for the relief of Charleston but had failed to arrive in time.

Tarleton's British Legion was made up of American Tories from New York and Pennsylvania. Only the commander was Liverpool-born, and he was suspect as not quite a gentleman, being the son of a family which had made its money in trade. The cavalry horses of the Legion had all died on the long, stormy voyage from New York. Tarleton's dragoons were mounted for the most part on horses taken on April 14. On that day Tarleton with Major Patrick Ferguson and his American Volunteers—also Tory with the exception of their commander—had annihilated the combined commands of General Huger and Colonel William Washington, destroying the American cavalry on the Ashley and Cooper rivers and leaving Lincoln no route of retreat from Charleston. Washington and Huger had escaped "by swimming the river," says Clinton; "by their knowledge of the country," says Lee; "by fleeing into Hell Hole Swamp," says another authority.[7] At any rate, blessedly, they escaped, to the later great glory and good fortune of American arms.

Buford and his Virginians, having advanced to within 40 miles of Charleston before that city's surrender, were ordered by Huger to retire to Hillsboro. They set about this with speed. Tarleton followed hard. After a march of 105 miles in 54 hours,[8] while the legionnaires killed several horses under them, Tarleton overtook Buford's little column at the Waxhaws a few miles from the Carolina border.

The British commander sent forward a flag representing himself as having 700 men instead of the less than 300 he actually had.[9] He stated that Cornwallis was close behind with nine battalions. This last statement was true enough, but Cornwallis was headed for Camden, not for Buford and his men. Tarleton demanded that Buford surrender on the same terms which had been granted the Charleston garrison. The American, after a brief consultation with his officers, refused the terms and prepared to march.

Tarleton had employed the time in which the flag was passing in preparations for attack. Upon receiving the rejection of the terms the British trumpeters blew the charge. The British horse struck, and Buford's rear guard was cut down to a man. The American colonel attempted to dispose his remaining force for defense, but his ranks were in confusion. Some of the men fired on their assailants; others threw down their arms and begged for quarter. No quarter was given. Although Buford hoisted a white flag and ordered his men to ground their arms, Tarleton did not attempt to stay his corps. They put the unarmed men to the saber, bayoneted the wounded, and pulled bodies off one another to get at the life that might lie beneath.

In all 113 were killed, 150 wounded so badly that they were left on the ground. Fifty-three capable of walking were herded into Camden to be presented as prisoners of war to Cornwallis, who had now arrived at that village.[10]

While the atmosphere of comparative good feelings in South Carolina was dissipating under the impact of this slaughter, Clinton on June 3 issued a proclamation which abolished the status of surrendered rebels as prisoners on parole in all cases except that of the actual Charleston garrison. All others who had borne arms, unless they returned to British allegiance by June 20, would be considered as enemies and rebels. This meant that those submitting by June 20 would be required, as British subjects, to bear arms against the Continental army in case of invasion and against their still rebellious friends and neighbors if need arose. Sir Henry had the fullest intention of embodying them in a loyal militia and in some instances had already done so. He remarked of those who had come in:

Their hearts, poor fellows, are British, though their language is not the most correct.... All the rebel grandees are come in. They put on a good face. They own honestly they have always been in arms against us. They confess their dread of the back country people, who, they say, are all up to join us, as well in North Carolina as in South. Their jealousy of their late government, their hopes of a better under us, and conviction that the rebels can never recover this country have induced them to surrender themselves. They seem to boggle at the idea of arming against Congress, but with respect to the French and Spaniards ... are willing to join most heartily against them.... They found argument themselves to reconcile their disaffection (as they call it) to Congress by saying it could no longer protect them.[11] As I had nothing material to lay to their charge but *rebellion at large,* I have received them and embodied them—under loyal officers, however....[12]

Having thus, as he happily thought, prepared for the pacification of South Carolina, Sir Henry Clinton with Admiral Arbuthnot sailed away for New York. Somewhat uneasily, Clinton left the "noble earl," Lord Cornwallis, with a considerable body of troops in command in South Carolina. Clinton did not entirely trust Cornwallis' loyalty to himself, nor his discretion. In Sir Henry's opinion, his Lordship was overly given to large plans and impetuosity. Yet leave Cornwallis he must, for pressing matters took Clinton north. Intelligence arrived from Lord George Germain on May 10, the day Lincoln petitioned for the surrender of Charleston, that made it imperative that Clinton and the navy move north. A French squadron of twelve ships of the line was preparing at Brest to convoy a large body of French land forces to North America—specific destination unknown.[13]

Actually what Clinton left behind him was a state of incipient civil war, which almost at once broke out in bitter fury. For one thing, he had made a grievous error. "All the rebel grandees" had not come in.

Cornwallis had been left with *"the safety of Charleston and the tranquility of South Carolina as the principal and indispensable objects of his attention."* This accomplished, he was at liberty *"to make a solid move into North Carolina upon condition it could at the time be made without risking the safety of the posts committed to his charge."*[14]

Cornwallis, after Clinton's departure, set about establishing tranquility and safety. In pursuing the subjection of the interior of South Carolina he continued Clinton's policy of using detachments for the purpose composed almost entirely of Tories. It must have seemed the natural thing to do: to use the well-affected of a conquered people to police the disaffected. Why waste regulars on such a mission when there was other work for them to the north, into the other Carolina, even on to Virginia? The policy has been used before and since to good effect. Why should it not have worked in South Carolina? The fact is that it did not work. Perhaps it did not work because the Whigs and Tories were too evenly divided. They were split geographically into too many small groups, divisions within counties, within parishes, within villages, even within households, brother against brother and father against son. Perhaps in the end it was that, although Whigs and Tories undoubtedly had an antipathy for or a

bias in favor of one side or the other—British or American—
their true, their passionate, enmity was reserved for one
another.[15]

Late in May Banastre Tarleton, that indefatigable brewer
of hatred for the British, burned Thomas Sumter's home
near Statesburgh. Sumter had resigned a Continental lieutenant colonel's commission in 1778. Since then he had lived
quietly on his plantation and seen some service in the state
legislature. He could hear the siege guns of Charleston from
his house, but they moved him to no action. However, when
his own home was burned, this was another matter.[16] "In a
trice," as his habit went, "he was all sweat and fury."[17] By
June 15 he was east of the Catawba at Tuckaseggee Ford with
a few followers who had elected him their general (Governor
Rutledge did not formally appoint him brigadier general of
militia until October, 1780[18]) and agreed to follow him to
the end. June 20, the expiration date for accepting British
allegiance, brought the Carolina Gamecock more recruits.
On July 12 he and his men attacked and destroyed a detachment of Tarleton's Green Horse under Captain Huck, and
fame swelled Sumter's ranks.

At this time in his forties, Thomas Sumter was a made
man, made by himself. Born of poor parents in Virginia, he
had come to South Carolina in 1762 in charge of a group
of Cherokee Indians returning much awed from a visit to the
Court of St. James. Aspiring to set himself up as a store-
keeper or small merchant, Sumter had been so fortunate as
to marry a rich widow older than himself and had become
one of the landed gentry.[19] "He was," said Henry Lee, "not
overscrupulous as a soldier in his use of means, and was apt to
make considerable allowance for a state of war. Believing it
warranted by the necessity of the case, he did not occupy his
mind with critical examinations of the equity of his measures, or of their bearings on individuals. . . . Determined to
deserve success, he risked his own life and the lives of his

associates without reserve. Enchanted with the splendor of victory, he would wade through torrents of blood to achieve it. . . . He traversed the region between Camden and Ninety-Six."[20]

Francis Marion, forty-eight years old at this time, had been a lieutenant colonel of Continentals in 1780 when the siege of Charleston began, but by accident escaped the surrender. As the siege progressed, General Lincoln ordered all men so disabled as to be incapable of bearing arms to leave the city. Marion, crippled by a fractured ankle at the time, had been one of the evacuées. He remained in obscurity until late June when the army under de Kalb, which was to be Gates' later, was resting for a week at Hillsboro, North Carolina, on its march to Camden. De Kalb expected some reinforcements in the form of a sizeable group of militia under the command of General Richard Caswell, which was reported to be in the vicinity. Instead there appeared in the American camp a tatterdemalion crew of about twenty men and boys, some white and some black, all mounted and armed but most of them miserably equipped. They were led by a taciturn little man in a tight-fitting black leather cap with a silver crescent on the front, the only semblance of a uniform he or his men wore. "The arms and aspect of some were so ludicrous that the Continental officers found it hard to keep their men from laughing at them."[21] De Kalb, who had made a considerable study of men, and of Americans in particular, found something in the lame, aquiline-nosed little leader to inspire confidence and respect. Gates, when he succeeded de Kalb, shared this view. Just before the battle of Camden he sent Marion down to the vicinity of the Santee River, where Marion had been born and which he knew blindfolded, to watch the enemy and harry his supply lines.[22]

Thus Marion entered on his career as the Swamp Fox. One of his first exploits after the battle of Camden was to release, on August 25, 160 prisoners from the battle, who were being escorted to Charleston by a mixed company of British and Tories. He accomplished this with a force of sixteen men.[23] Most of the prisoners unfortunately hastened straight for their homes rather than rejoining the army.

Lee said of Marion, "Calumny itself never charged him with violating the rights of person, property or humanity."[24] Then Lee added a very curious summing-up: "In stature he was of the smallest size, thin as well as low. His visage was not pleasing and his manners not captivating, and yet. . . . He was virtuous all over."[25]

A third partisan leader was Andrew Pickens. A few years younger than Sumter and Marion, Pickens, as a colonel of militia, had been at Ninety Six when Charleston fell. He had been one of those who asked for and accepted the status of a prisoner on parole, "not to be disturbed in his property so long as he observed his parole." However, Pickens' plantation was plundered by British Major James Dunlap. To a man of Pickens' forthright turn of mind, this was a violation of Britain's pledged word. He considered himself no longer bound by his parole. It was signally characteristic of him that he went out of his way to find a British captain to inform him of his altered status and the reason for it.[26]

Pickens has been described as very guarded in his conversation: "He would take the words out of his mouth, between his fingers, and examine them before he uttered them."[27] Thus he can have been under no illusion as to what the words were. The British captain can have been under no illusion either. The British by their action against his plantation had released Pickens from his parole. He was taking the field. The fact that legally, from the British viewpoint, Pickens was violating his parole and was liable to hanging if taken made no difference to the dour Presbyterian's conviction of the moral rectitude of his action.

Thus in the blackest days of the Revolution, in the complete absence of civil government, beginning six weeks after

Charleston fell, Sumter, Marion and Pickens kept the flame of resistance from being totally extinguished in South Carolina. What Cornwallis needed was another victory to brighten the fading glories of the Charleston capitulation and raise the drooping spirits of "our friends." He got it at Camden.

General Horatio Gates was the American commander at Camden. George Washington had wanted Nathanael Greene appointed to the command of the southern army, but Congress overruled him and picked Gates.[28] The southern army immediately after the loss of Lincoln's garrison at Charleston consisted of some 1400 men of all ranks, composed of Delaware and Maryland regiments plus Armand's (once Pulaski's) cavalry and a contingent of artillery, all under the over-all command of Major General Baron Jean de Kalb.[29] Washington dispatched this force in mid-April for the relief of Charleston. De Kalb's progress southward was slow, for Congress had been unable to make provision for the march. The army was obliged to live off the country. When news of the fall of Charleston arrived, de Kalb was still in North Carolina. He had found, as Greene was to find later, that North Carolina was a lean and hungry place to be. What scant supplies that state had were reserved for its own militia.[30] That militia, as Greene also learned, was reluctant to join and fleet to leave. Nevertheless, de Kalb persevered as far as Buffalo Ford on Deep River, south of Hillsboro, and there ground to a halt for lack of supplies.

There on July 25 he was superseded by General Horatio Gates. Congress, spurning Washington's recommendation of Greene, had appointed the hero of Saratoga to the command. It was obvious to everybody that Baron de Kalb, as a foreigner, whatever his ackowledged merits, was ineligible for the command of the only Continental army left in the south. Apparently it was obvious to de Kalb also. He was a big man but a modest one. Also he had for many weeks been faced

with an almost impossible task, and it may have been a welcome relief to lay it in someone else's lap. He had come a
long way from the sixteen-year-old Bavarian peasant's son,
Hans Kalb, who had left home in 1737 to seek his fortune.[31]
A man cannot have everything; it may be that the hero's
death which awaited Hans Kalb at Camden three weeks later
was sufficient. At any rate, he received Gates in his stead with
cordiality, respect, and the proper ceremonies, including a
salute of thirteen guns.[32]

Gates had come out of six months retirement on his
Virginia plantation at "Traveller's Rest" to take command
of what he termed the "Grand Army of the Southern Department."[33] There is a tradition, impossible to pin down, which
says that before he left his home place his friend and neigh-
bor, General Charles Lee, also in retirement, warned him,
"Take care lest your northern laurels turn to southern
willows."[34] True or not, the remark is typical of Lee's irony;
General Lee of Monmouth was well aware of how laurels
can fade. Lee was the kind of man who, in view of the outcome, would willingly have accepted the paternity of the
witticism whether he had sired it or no. For Gates did lose
his laurels at Camden.

General Gates seems to have been from the outset of
taking command in a condition of haste which befogged his
judgment.[35] He had been in retirement for six months and
may have been out of touch. He had not been in combat since
Saratoga in 1777. He was unfamiliar with the country and
appears to have had, with the exception of Otho Williams,
the scantiest acquaintance, if any, with the officers under his
command. He had tried before leaving Virginia to persuade
Daniel Morgan, who had served with him at Saratoga, to return to the army. Morgan, resentful over his treatment in the
matter of promotion, had tendered Congress a letter of
resignation in 1779. That body had persuaded him to accept

an "honorable furlough" instead.[36] The rifleman refused Gates' request for the moment.

In person Horatio Gates was a flabby, bespectacled, grand-fatherly looking man, of unmilitary bearing, although like de Kalb he had spent most of his life in military service. He was also in the eyes of most Americans of 1780 a hero and a military genius. He was faced with one of the most awkward of tasks—topping a triumph. If some of the interpretations of the battle of Saratoga are true, he must have known in his secret heart that the original triumph was not truly his,[37] which may have been why he had sent for Morgan.[38] General Gates took over from a courteous six-foot giant who was perhaps ten years senior, but looked ten years younger[39] and every inch a soldier. The appearance of the two commanders must have made a sharp contrast in the eyes of the troops. It is wonderful how revealing the wooden expressions on the faces of ranked columns of men on parade can be.

De Kalb had intended to approach Camden by way of Salisbury and Charlotte. It was a circuitous route but one which led through the friendly counties of Rowan and Mecklenburg with their well-stocked farms and relatively good roads. Gates would have none of that. He did not know the country, but he studied the map. He saw that the most direct route to Camden was fifty miles shorter than that proposed by de Kalb. He paid no attention to the remon-strances of his officers who told him that the way led through infertile pine barrens in which deep sand alternated with swamps, and water courses given to swelling floods after a few hours' rain were everywhere. The army would take the route Gates had selected. They were to prepare to march im-mediately. They set out on July 27 "with only a half ration for today, and not even a half ration for tomorrow."[40]

On August 15 they were in the vicinity of Camden—half-starved, half-sick, reeling from dysentery and exhaustion. Gates planned a night march. At the briefing his appalled officers heard him estimate his force, with Caswell's militia and Armand's cavalry, at roughly 7000 men. Otho Williams, the deputy adjutant general, called for an instant return of strength from the regimental commanders[41] The returns showed the total to be no more than 3052 fit for duty. Gates ran his eye casually over Williams' report: "They are enough for our purpose," he said.[42] The orders for the night march still held.

By malevolent coincidence Cornwallis had also ordered a night march. About two-thirty in the morning the two armies collided in the blackness of a pine forest. There was an outburst of firing which soon ceased as neither army could discern the other's position in the dark. From a few prisoners taken on either side each learned who the other was. There was little more action that night save for occasional short, sharp skirmishes as the advanced guards felt each other out. In the pine wood the militia stood still where they had halted, hearing one another rustle and breathe.

At dawn Williams informed Gates at his post in the rear that the enemy were deploying. Stevens, with the Virginia militia was already in line; he might make a good impression by attacking briskly. Williams made the suggestion tentatively. Gates answered, "Sir, that is right, let it be done."[43] It was the last order he ever gave in that or any other battle.

Stevens tried to follow Gates' order, but when the enemy advanced huzzaing the Virginians broke without firing a shot. North Carolina in the center, seeing Virginia in flight, panicked. More than 2500 terrified Virginians and North Carolinians went raving northward, sweeping Generals Gates and Caswell with them. "The militia, the general saw were in the air; and the regulars, he feared, were no more."[44] Gates did not stop to verify this latter speculation. Most of the Virginians fled to Hillsboro. "The North Carolina militia fled different ways, as their hopes led or their fears drove them."[45]

Only de Kalb and the veteran regiments of Maryland and Delaware held their ground. De Kalb fell bleeding from eleven wounds. Yet the decimated ranks closed and repelled yet another charge, until Tarleton's cavalry swept in and broke them. Then it was all over.

Cornwallis came riding by and rescued the mortally hurt de Kalb from looters who were bent on stealing his gold-laced coat.[46] British surgeons and his great heart kept him alive three days longer. Then he died in Camden.[47]

3

"IT IS MY WISH TO

APPOINT YOU"[1]

On October 31, 1780, Samuel Huntington, President of the Continental Congress, addressed the following letter to Major General Nathanael Greene:

Sir:

You will receive herewith enclosed a copy of an act of Congress of the 30 inst. by which you will be informed that your appointment to the command of the Southern Army meets with their approbation; and that Major General the Baron de Steuben is directed to repair to that department under your command.

That the army for that department will consist of all the regular regiments and corps raised or to be raised from the States of Delaware to Georgia inclusive until the further Orders of Congress or the Commander-in-Chief.

That all the powers given to General Gates while in that command are now vested in you, and acts of Congress during that period be considered as instructions to you in that department.

You, sir, are also authorized to organize and employ the army under your command in the manner you shall judge most proper, subject to the control of the Commander-in-Chief; and it is earnestly recommended to the legislatures and executives respectively in that department to afford you every necessary assistance and support and you are authorized to call for the same.

The heads of the several staff departments are directed to furnish to your orders such articles as cannot be obtained in the southern department.

You will also observe that you are empowered to co-operate with our Ally or His Catholic Majesty if occasion shall offer in your department in such manner as may appear most effectual.

To prevent all doubts on the subject of exchanging prisoners you are expressly authorized to negotiate from time to time an exchange of prisoners with the commanding officer of the British army in that department, provided such exchanges be not contrary to any general directions of Congress or the Commander-in-Chief.

The necessary information on this subject will be forthwith communicated to the supreme executive in the respective States in the Southern Department.

Be assured, sir, that my best wishes accompany you, that your command may be attended with desired success to the satisfaction of your country and your personal honor.

I am with sincere Esteem and Respect your most obedient and most humble servant

Sam. Huntington, President[2]

This document is the more remarkable in that this was the same man of whom Congress less than three months before had: "*Resolved* that the Commander-in-Chief be directed to inform Major General Greene that the United States have no further occasion for his services."[3] This resolution was taken on Congress' receipt of Greene's letter of resignation as Quartermaster General. Greene had held this post since March, 1778. At Washington's pleading he agreed to take it on for a year. He held it for more than two and a half years.

The position of Quartermaster General is perhaps a thankless post at the best of times. As Greene himself said to Washington, "Who ever heard of a quartermaster in history as such?"[4] In the chaotic state of the finances in the Revolution, the position presented almost insurmountable difficulties. Nevertheless Greene performed his duties well. He was the kind of man who performed any task allotted to him to the best of his abilities. To him, as to Washington, this was the foregone conclusion, the inevitable thing to do. He drove himself hard, and he took it for granted that other men should do likewise, if they were worthy of respect. This is not a trait of character necessarily guaranteed to endear oneself to one's associates.[5]

Greene had, however, in common with most of us, at least until we grow so old and wise as to be past our usefulness, the naive notion that the worth of his efforts deserved some recognition.[6] Consequently when Congress, far from applauding, proceeded to carp and even to imply that his private purse had benefited from his purchasing activities, Greene, as the climax of a long correspondence and as the reaction to what he considered Congress' inefficient reorganization of the Quartermaster Department, tendered a letter of resignation to the legislative body. It was a letter couched in terms which even his friends in that assemblage considered less than diplomatic:

... Administration seem to think it far less important to the public interest to have this department well filled and arranged for than it really is, and as they will find it by future experience.

My best endeavors have not been wanting to give success to the business committed to my care, and I leave the merit of my services to be determined hereafter by the future management of it under the direction of another hand.

... the sacrifices I have made on this account, together with the fatigue and anxiety I have undergone, far overbalance all the emolument. . . . Nor would double the consideration induce me to tread the same path over again, unless I saw it necessary to preserve my country from utter ruin and disgraceful servitude.[7]

It was the use of the word "administraton" that set tempers aflame. To the members of Congress this was a "gross insult" because it carried connotations of the days when *administration* in Great Britain sought to fasten the yoke on colonial necks.[8] Not all the members of Congress, however, were in unanimous passion. The motion of August 5 to resolve that there was no further occasion for Greene's services did not carry. Instead Colonel Timothy Pickering was appointed Quartermaster General, and a committee of five, which had been set up on receipt of Green's letter, was directed to consider the resolution and bring it up at a later date. Joseph Jones, delegate from Virginia, and a member of this committee, wrote Washington that many Congressmen hoped that Greene's suspension from the Quartermaster Generalcy would result in his final discharge.[9]

Greene was not discharged. It may be that Washington rescued him. By 1780 Washington had had five years' schooling in dealing with Congress through various tribulations too numerous to mention. The sometimes indiscreet freedom of expression which he had permitted himself in the early days of 1775-1776 had been tempered by experience.[10] He knew that he could not appeal to Congress on the basis of his personal friendship for Greene or his belief, born of five years' association, in that officer's worth and accomplishments. This would only raise the old accusations of the Conway cabal period, in which it was asserted that Greene had undue influence with Washington.[11] So the Commander-in-Chief appealed to Congress' fears. His letter was addressed to Joseph Jones, but as a committee member and a Congressman, not as a private individual. Washington must have intended that its contents would reach a wider audience than Jones himself. He said in part:

The subject of this letter will be confined to a single point. I shall make it as short as possible, and write with frankness. If any sentiment, therefore, is delivered which might be displeasing to you as a member of Congress, ascribe it to the freedom which is taken with you by a friend who has nothing in view but the public good. In your letter . . . which came to hand yesterday, an idea is held up as if the acceptance of General Greene's resignation of the Quartermaster's department was not all that Congress meant to do with him. If by this is in contemplation to suspend him from his command in the line . . . let me beseech you to consider well what you are about before you resolve. I shall neither condemn nor acquit General Greene's conduct . . . because all the antecedent correspondence is necessary to form a right judgment. . . . My sole aim at present is to advertise you of what I think would be the consequences of suspending him from his command in the line without a proper trial. A procedure of this kind must touch the feelings of every officer. It will show . . . the uncertain tenure by which they hold their commissions. In a word, it will exhibit such a specimen of power, that I question much if there is an officer in the whole line that will hold a commission beyond the end of the campaign, if he does till then. Such an act in the most despotic of governments would be attended at least by loud complaints.

It does not require with you, I am sure . . . arguments to prove that there is no set of men in the United States, considered as a body, that have made the same sacrifices of their interest in support of the common cause, as the officers of the American army; that nothing but love of their country, of honor, and a desire of seeing their labors crowned with success, could possibly induce them to continue one moment in the service; and that no officer can live upon his pay. . . .

Can it be supposed that men under these circumstances, who can derive at best, if the contest ends happily, only the advantages which accrue in equal proportion to others, will sit patient under such a precedent? Surely they will not . . . each will ask himself . . . if Congress by its mere fiat, without inquiry and without trial, will suspend an officer to-day, and an officer of such high rank, may it not be my turn tomorrow, and ought I to put it in the power of any man or any body of men to sport with my commission and my character, and lay me under the necessity of tamely acquiescing, or by an appeal to the public, exposing matters which must be injurious. . . .

Suffer not, my friend . . . so disagreeable an event to take place. I do not mean to justify, to countenance or excuse, in the most distant degree, any expressions of disrespect which the gentleman in question . . . may have offered to Congress . . . my letter is to prevent his suspension, because I fear, because I feel it must lead to very . . . injurious consequences. . . .

These sentiments are the result of my own reflections . . .[12]

In brief, suspension of Greene in umbrage could cost the country the entire officer corps of the Continental army. Washington certainly did not say that he himself would resign; equally certainly he did not say that he would not. General Washington has been severely criticized at times for bad strategy, perhaps with justice. However that may be, the letter above would seem to indicate that on one occasion his strategy was excellent.

What Jones and the committee did with the Washington letter is not clear, but they must have digested it slowly. There is no record in the Congressional journals from August 15 or 16, when the letter must have been received, to August 31 of any report by the committee to Congress on the matter of the resolution against Greene.

Meanwhile bad news was beating its slow way up from the south. On August 31 a letter from Horatio Gates was read to the assembled house. The letter was dated August 20 at Hillsboro, North Carolina, nearly 200 miles from Camden, South Carolina. The hero of Saratoga, the quondam potential Commander-in-Chief, the darling of Congress, was obliged to report that he had experienced a considerable defeat at the hands of Lords Cornwallis and Rawdon in a piney wood near Camden on August 16 last.[13] That letter in turn was referred to a committee of five, with a different membership than that of the committee on Greene.[14] In the weeks that followed there was no more mention of suspending general officers out of hand. Too many general officers had been lost already.

On September 17, 1780, General Washington went to Hartford to confer with the French General Rochambeau. The French fleet, intelligence of which had sent Clinton scudding north in June, had landed a French army at Newport. The Commander-in-Chief left General Greene as his acting commander with orders to march the army into camp at Tappan, New York. Greene made this move on the 19th. Near midnight of September 25 an express brought him a letter from Lieutenant Colonel Alexander Hamilton, who was stationed at Verplancks Point:

Sir:
There has just unfolded at this place a scene of the blackest treason, Arnold has fled to the Enemy. André, the British Adjutant General is in our possession as a spy. This capture unravelled the mystery. West Point was to have been the sacrifice, all the dispositions have been made for the purpose and 'tis possible, though not probable tonight may see the execution. The wind is fair, I came here in pursuit of Arnold but was too late. I advise your putting the Army under marching orders, and detaching a brigade immediately this way.   Alex Hamilton, Aid de camp.[15]

At a quarter past three in the morning of the 26th a second express brought a letter from Washington, who had stopped that day on his return trip from Hartford to inspect the fortifications at West Point. Greene, who had been very busy since midnight, was able to reply, "Before the receipt [of your letter] I had put the first Pennsylvania brigade in motion, and put the whole army under marching orders. . . ."[16]

Greene had taken Hamilton's letter seriously. The American army was in motion to cover West Point lest the British take advantage of the fair wind of that very night to launch their attack.

Major General Nathanael Greene was president of the Board of General Officers which sat to decide the fate of Major John André. He had written his wife on September 28, "I expect it will fall my lot to sit as president. . . . It will be a disagreeable business, but must be done."[17] Unlike young Alexander Hamilton, Greene did not censure Washington for refusing to accede to André's request that he be shot instead of hanged.[18] Like others who came in contact with him, including Washington, Greene was impressed by the grace and fortitude with which André bore himself in his evil circumstances. But hanging was the accepted punishment for spies. Any other mode of execution would throw doubt upon the Americans' conviction of his guilt.

In this affair of André we have perhaps the essence of Greene. Seeing what he conceived to be his duty, he did it, invariably, his humanity touched by some aspects of the necessity, but always in the serene conviction that his action was right. It does not matter that at times his self-justification was almost childishly naive. He rationalized his abandonment of Quakerism, for example, on the premise that all animals, man included, are equipped with weapons of defense—teeth, claws, talons, fists, and so on. Therefore, to his simple logic, wars were inevitable.[19] "The great principles which have governed my conduct through life have been justice and moderation . . . if they don't always lead in paths most pleasing, you are always certain of being right."[20] Such a man is infinitely more dangerous than half a hundred "lean and hungry" Cassius's. He is untroubled by the indecisions, the sense of sin and the need for atonement which plague the commonalty. If, coupled with this inner trust in his own

integrity, he is, as Greene was, alert, intelligent and resourceful with the tools at hand, he can be well nigh invincible.

Arnold's defection had left the command at West Point
vacant. Greene asked Washington for the post and received
it, although with some reservations on Washington's part.[21]
He took over his new duties on October 8 and found himself
at once much occupied. Arnold, by prearrangement,
had allowed the place to fall into decay, a circumstance
which Washington had noted with alarm the day of his
inspection when he had found Arnold unaccountably
absent.[22] Greene with his usual dispatch set to work to repair
matters[23] while he jubilantly anticipated the arrival of his
wife, Catherine Littlefield Greene, whom he had not seen
since she returned to their children in Rhode Island after
spending the bitterly cold season of 1779-1780 with him at
Morristown where the army lay in winter quarters.

However, events were already in train which were to post-
pone this joyful reunion for nearly two years.[24] As noted
above, Gates' letter to Congress announcing his defeat was
dated August 20 at Hillsboro, 180 miles from Camden. "Was
there ever so precipitate a flight?" Alexander Hamilton ex-
ploded. "One hundred and eighty miles in three days and a
half. It does admirable credit to the activity of a man of his
time of life."[25] Apparently to Hamilton's then twenty-three
or twenty-five years Gates' fifty-two winters approached
dotage. Gates himself denied that his long ride was a flight.
He was, he explained in his letter to Congress, writing from
Hillsboro because he felt that Hillsboro was best situated as a
base for building up a new army of Virginia and North
Carolina recruits.[26]

It is entirely probable that Gates was sincere when he
said this. Obviously he did not have to gallop all the way to
Hillsboro to escape from Cornwallis. He would personally
have been perfectly secure, at least for the time being, at
Charlotte, sixty miles from Camden, where he slept the night

after the battle.[27] Furthermore there were at least two alter-natives open to him other than Hillsboro. With such a head start he could simply have continued on to Berkeley County, Virginia, and withdrawn his shame into his plantation at "Traveller's Rest." Or, in other ages or other armies, he could have fallen upon his sword or blown his brains out. Gates did neither of these things, He wrote his report to Congress without delay after a grueling ride and set up his headquarters in a camp near Hillsboro. There he was joined by a few hundred half-starved men—"all but the militia who held straight on their homeward way"[28]—and officers. Among the latter were Colonel Otho Williams and Lieutenant Colonel John Eager Howard of the Maryland line and Daniel Morgan of Virginia. Morgan, hearing of the disaster at Cam-den, had put aside personal considerations and set out for Hillsboro before he had even received notification of his promotion to brigadier general.[29]

Gates resumed command over the remnants of an army which had received no pay, no clothes and scarcely enough food to sustain life, and which he had led to disaster in battle. Despite a flurry of resolves by Congress from September 7 onwards,[30] government was rarely able to provide Gates with the barest necessities. Yet within a few weeks he had re-organized the decimated battalions and established order and a semblance of discipline and regular duties.[31] To do this in the circumstances must have required considerable ad-ministrative ability and address, and, be it added, consider-able courage.

Nevertheless, after the first shock of the news, as the magnitude of the defeat trickled home to Congress and the northern army, Gates' reputation neared eclipse. On October 5, before Greene had even taken command at West Point, Congress:

Resolved, That the Commander-in-Chief be and hereby is directed to order a court of inquiry to be held on the con-

duct [of] Major General Gates, as commander of the southern
army.

Resolved, That the Commander-in-Chief be and is hereby
directed to appoint an officer to command the southern army,
in the room of Major General Gates until such inquiry be
made.[32]

Having then, and perhaps thankfully, put the responsibility into other hands than their own, the members
adjourned "to ten o'clock tomorrow."[33] Up to that time the
Continental Congress had selected the commanders of the
southern department with unfortunate results. Robert Howe
had lost Savannah and all of Georgia; Benjamin Lincoln had
lost Charleston and all of South Carolina; Horatio Gates had
lost an army and left the British poised to gobble up North
Carolina.[34] Congress' faith in its judgment may well have
been shaken.

The Congressional resolution concerning Gates reached
Washington at his headquarters near Passaic Falls on October 13, that on the appointment of a new commander for
the southern army on the 14th. He immediately wrote
Greene: "It is my wish to appoint You. . . ."[35] He added that
this concurred with the wishes of the delegates of Georgia,
South Carolina and North Carolina, who had informed him
on the 6th that they also wanted Greene in command.[36] On
October 15 he wrote Congress: "Major General Greene is
the Officer I shall nominate." At this point in the letter he
added, "I very sensibly feel this fresh mark of the confidence
of Congress in leaving to me the appointment of a General
Officer to so important a command." Then the Father of His
Country meditated a few moments, decided against this
courtesy and ordered his military secretary to strike out the
last sentence.[37]

Greene received Washington's letter on October 16. He
answered at once expressing his appreciation of the honor
and asked for leave to go home to settle his business affairs,

pointing out that he had been out of touch with his Quaker brother partners for five years. If he could not go home, might he at least wait until Mrs. Greene, now en route, arrived at West Point.[38] Washington replied with a letter that would brook no delay.[39] On October 21 Greene was on his way south, missing Caty by a matter of hours.

The physician-historian David Ramsay wrote:

Though Congress was unable to forward either men or money for the relief of the southern states, they did what was equivalent. They sent them a general whose head was a council, and whose military talents were equal to a reinforcement.[40]

To live up to such a eulogy would be a difficult task for any man. Greene endeavored.

4

"OF POOR MAJOR FERGUSON'S MISFORTUNE"[1]

Camden had been a complete victory for the British. On August 16, 1780, there appeared to be only one American force of any size left in the South—Sumter's partisans. Cornwallis took immediate steps for its destruction.[2]

On the very day of Gates' defeat Sumter had waylaid a British supply train on its way to the garrison at Camden. He took prisoner 100 British soldiers, 50 Tory militia, and 42 wagons loaded with ammunition, clothing, food, and other stores.[3] Sumter was able to do this partly through misplaced generosity on the part of Gates. The partisan general had, on August 14, asked Gates for reinforcements so that he could intercept the supply train at the Wateree Ferry. He pointed out the obvious fact that the famished American army could make good use of the stores. Gates, confident of victory, and of his overestimate of his own numbers, had obligingly detached 100 Maryland regulars and 300 North Carolina militia for Sumter's use.[4]

With Gates' 400 men and his own force of 300, plus two of Gates' eight field pieces, Sumter overwhelmed the British convoy.[5] Unlike Marion, Thomas Sumter seems customarily to have attacked only when he had an equality or superiority of numbers.[6] This habit does not seem to have been occasioned by any lack of personal courage; on the contrary, Marion was the more cautious and prudent of the two.[7] It was rather a function of different objectives. Needless to say, the bands of all the southern partisans were paid in plunder. With the collapse of state government and complete isolation from Congressional aid, it was the only way in which they could be paid. But where Marion and Pickens plundered only to the extent that was necessary to arm and provision their troops,[8] Sumter, at times at least, seems to have had pillage as his chief object.[9]

But for a timely warning from Major William R. Davie, Sumter might have marched the convoy he had captured into the arms of Cornwallis. Davie commanded a small partisan legion in North Carolina, which had at times operated in conjunction with Sumter. On August 16 Davie was hastening to join Gates at Camden. Four miles from the field of battle he was met, and very nearly engulfed, by the madly fleeing militia of Virginia and North Carolina.[10] He extricated himself from the terrified mob and pushed forward toward the battle "with an expectation of being useful in saving soldiers, baggage and stores."[11] Near the front he met General Isaac Huger of the South Carolina line fleeing slowly on a foundering horse. Huger told the young major of the hopeless situation of Gates' army and of the probability that Sumter on the Wateree might be ignorant of what had happened at Camden that morning. Davie immediately dispatched a courier to Sumter. That general at once decamped with his prisoners and booty up the west side of the Wateree.

Thanks thus to Davie, Sumter probably escaped capture by Lieutenant Colonel Turnbull and his New York Volunteers, whom Cornwallis—furious at this impudent stain on his victory—had sent to destroy the Gamecock. However, laden as he was, Sumter's progress was necessarily slow. On August 18 at high noon he was at Fishing Creek, a tributary of the Wateree, about thirty-eight miles from Camden. There he encamped on a ridge on the north side of the creek, secure in the knowledge that he had avoided Turnbull and his men, and apparently quite unaware that Tarleton, killing men and horses under him, was galloping up the west bank of the river in hot pursuit. "Tarleton was a strong believer in the old military adage that the only satisfactory way to destroy an enemy is to destroy him."[12]

Of Sumter's force of seven hundred, men and officers alike had had little rest for four days. Measures for the security of the camp had been neglected. Two drowsy videttes were posted in front of the ridge. The arms of the rest of the party were stacked in the center of the camp. Many of the men were asleep; others were bathing in the creek; still others "were more obedient to the calls of nature than attentive to her first law, self-preservation."[13] Sumter himself—bootless, hatless, and coatless in the heat of a Carolina August—slept under a wagon.[14]

Before anyone in the American camp knew what was happening, the noon quiet was broken by a hideous huzzaing and the thunder of hooves. Tarleton, with 100 dragoons and 60 infantry of the Legion, had maneuvered into Sumter's rear, where there were no videttes, drowsy or otherwise. Now he was upon the encampment. There were a few isolated pockets of resistance, which the dragoons soon liquidated. Neither the dripping bathers from the creek, nor the men sprawled about the camp could reach the neatly stacked arms. Tarleton killed 150, took 300 prisoners, released the 150 British and Tory captives, and retook all 42 wagons with their stores. Excepted were a few food parcels and a puncheon or two of rum.

General Sumter contrived to leap on an unsaddled horse on the picket line and escape. He rode into Charlotte two days later to rendezvous with Davie and the slowly assembling remnants of Gates' army. Somewhere he had acquired boots and a coat, but he was still bareback and lacking his hat and all of his men.[15]

"The victory of Camden and the entire dispersion of

Sumter's corps ... had certainly greatly humbled the dis-affected in South Carolina and seemed to promise a restora-tion of tranquility in every part of that province."[16] The disaffected were certainly humbled. Even Marion had fled the state.[17] The jubilant Loyalists joined up in droves in Colonel Turnbull's New York Volunteers, Major Ferguson's Amer-ican Volunteers, and Tarleton's British Legion.[18] Others, of the lone wolf persuasion, fell to murdering and pillaging their friends and neighbors with more than customary gusto. Marion, when he returned to the Santee, wrote to Gates, "I have never had more than seventy men to act with me, and sometimes they leave me to twenty or thirty. Many who had fought with me I am now obliged to fight against."[19]

Cornwallis wrote to Clinton on August 23: "It appears to me that I should endeavor to get as soon as possible to Hills-borough; and there assemble, and try to arrange the friends who are inclined to arm in our favor...."[20] In accordance with this plan, Cornwallis at once sent "persons well instruct-ed" in his intentions into North Carolina to incite the Loyalists to rise. He was prevented, however, from setting the army immediately in motion by the evils in that day attendant on the summer season in the Carolinas. "Our sick-ness is great and truly alarming. The Officers are particularly affected."[21] In the overcrowded village of Camden malaria, yellow jack, and smallpox raged through the British ranks. The American surgeons among the captives begged to be permitted to inoculate their troops for smallpox, but Corn-wallis categorically refused the request.[22] The contagion spread from the British to the Americans, doubtless relieving the overcrowding to an extent.

While thus immobilized by the illness of his army, Corn-wallis decided to employ the time in stamping out what he conceived to be the last remnants of disaffection in South Carolina. "Major Wemyss is going ... to disarm in the most rigid manner the Country between the Santee and the

Pedee. . . . I have myself ordered several Militia Men to be executed who had enrolled themselves and borne Arms with us, and afterwards revolted to the Enemy."[23] Somehow these measures did not have the salutary effect expected of them. "His Lordship," wrote Clinton, "very soon after tells me the indefatigable Sumter is again in the field. And the disaffection east of the Santee is so great that the account of our victory could not penetrate it, any person daring to speak of it being threatened with instant death."[24]

Cornwallis' answer to "provincial" impudence was simply to redouble the severity of his punishments. Rebel lands and property were sequestered throughout the state and rebel necks stretched without mercy.[25] Then, having with the best of good intentions stirred up a veritable hornets' nest, the "noble earl" in mid-September set his face for Hillsboro with those of his troops who were well enough to march. His march was not without incident. For one thing sickness still dogged his footsteps. At Fishing Creek the flamboyant Tarleton, weak as a starveling seven-day kitten, took to his bed with yellow fever. He could not be moved, and the army went on without him. At the Waxhaws Cornwallis encamped his main body, while the bereft Legion was billeted at Wahab's plantation some distance away.[26]

The British were now on the North Carolina border in a country that did not love them. "The counties of Mecklenburg and Rohan were more hostile to England than any in America."[27] The army was also in William R. Davie's territory. It will be recalled that Sumter had ridden to Charlotte to rendezvous with Davie and the fugitives from Camden. Gates' skeleton army lay now at Hillsboro, and Sumter had returned southward, but Davie, now colonel commandant of North Carolina's state cavalry, ranged active in the Charlotte area, twenty miles from the Waxhaws. Davie, who had been born in England and reared in the Carolinas, was just twenty-four years old and a very resourceful young man. On the morning of September 21 with about eighty dragoons, and two small companies of riflemen under Major George Davidson, Davie struck Tarleton's Legion hard. The British dragoons had just saddled up and mounted in front of the plantation house when Davie and his cavalry charged yelling down the lane leading to the yard. The surprised Green Horse, lacking the inspiration of their proper leader, broke and trotted to the rear of the house. There they were met by a withering fire from Davidson's riflemen, whom Davie had thoughtfully stationed in a cornfield cultivated almost to the back door. Sixty saddles emptied and the rest of the dragoons fled. Davie collected 120 stand of arms and 96 horses, fully equipped, before he hastily retreated to his camp at Providence, safely ahead of Cornwallis' alerted troops.[28]

Cornwallis broke camp at the Waxhaws on September 25 and marched on Charlotte, leaving word that the convalescent Tarleton should follow on a litter. The men of Tarleton's Legion, still somewhat shaken and reduced by sixty killed and wounded, led the van. Davie, with twenty horsemen, hovered on their flanks during the day and rode ahead of them into Charlotte that night. There he was met by a small body of militia. Charlotte at that time was a hamlet of twenty houses with two streets intersecting at right angles. At the intersection stood the court house; in front of it was a substantial wall. Davie dismounted his men and posted them behind the wall. From this shelter they poured such a steady fire into the advancing cavalry of the Legion that the dragoons twice retreated before it. Cornwallis himself was forced to ride among them and shame them into returning a third time to the charge. Davie's troopers, now mounted, gave them one more well-aimed volley and galloped away, with the satisfaction of knowing that for a few minutes a handful of men had held at bay a British army. "Indeed," Cornwallis wrote afterwards of the Legion, "the whole of them are very different when Tarleton is present or absent."[29]

Although possessed of Charlotte, Cornwallis was now forced to wait until the hundreds of convalescents at Camden could join him, when he proposed to push on to Salisbury and Hillsboro. He also expected to be joined shortly by Major Patrick Ferguson and his corps. Ferguson in June had been detached to cover the back country between the Catawba and Saluda rivers.[30] Ferguson had been instructed to organize the South Carolina Tories and rally all he could to the King's standard. He had been remarkably successful and had embodied seven militia regiments, some 4000 men all told, in addition to his own provincial regiment of rangers. He had taken "infinite pains" with the training of these men, most of whom were intended for the defense of the Ninety Six district. The regiments served in rotation, about 1000 men being on active service at a time.

While Cornwallis' army was immobilized by sickness at Camden in the last days of August, Ferguson had asked for permission to make an incursion into Tryon (now Polk) County, North Carolina. Cornwallis granted the request. "As he had only the Militia and the small remains of his own Corps, without baggage or Artillery, and as he promised to come back if He heard of any Superior force, I thought he could do no harm, and might help to keep alive the Spirits of our Friends. . . ."[31] When Cornwallis finally marched from Camden in September, he instructed Ferguson to move along the foothills to cover the army's left flank and then to join it at Charlotte.

Patrick Ferguson was a cooler and more humane man than Tarleton—less given to bloodshed. Nevertheless he was a bitter enemy of the rebels, whose homes and belongings he plundered and destroyed. As the son of a Scottish judge, he had an ingrained respect for the law and scant sympathy for those who broke it. In North Carolina he pursued Cornwallis' policy of severity. By proclamations and threats he induced some Loyalists to join him. However, he made one threat which was his undoing. Over the mountains in what is now Tennessee lay the Watauga settlements. The inhabitants were Scotch-Irish Presbyterians, some of them members of the hundreds of families who had left North Carolina in disgust after the Regulators had broken at the Battle of the Alamance. In the fertile valleys back of the mountains they had set up "a state independent of the authority of the British King,"[32] or, indeed, of much of any authority but their own. Most of these people favored the Patriot cause— not from any deep principles of political philosophy, however. They were simply men to whom the words "Tyranny" and "Government" were, for most practical purposes, synonymous.

Some of the Whigs who had suffered under Ferguson's plunderings and burnings had fled over the mountains spreading lively tales of terror.[33] Some of the "backwater men," as Ferguson insisted on calling them, had already had brief brushes with him, mere raiding expeditions from which they returned at once to their mountain valleys. The war had touched their home ground not at all, and they had acquired the firm conviction that this was as it should be.

Colonel Isaac Shelby of North Carolina had "become obnoxious to the British and Tories"[34] because of his part in an affair at a place called Musgrove's Mill. Ferguson, stationed at Gilbert Town a few miles from the Blue Ridge, was injudicious enough to send word to the Watauga area by a paroled rebel. If, said Ferguson's message, Colonel Shelby did not surrender, "he [Ferguson] would come over the mountains and put him to death and burn his whole country."[35]

This was challenge enough for the over-mountain men: "They would raise all the force they could and attack Ferguson; and if this was not practicable they would co-operate with any corps of the army of the United States with which they might meet."[36] If they should prove unfortunate and their country was invaded, the mountaineers planned to desert the Watauga area. They would "take water and go down to the Spaniards in Louisiana." In short they were motivated less by loyalty to the United States than by a determination to protect their own group.

"A numerous Army," wrote Lord Rawdon, "now appeared on the Frontiers drawn from Nolachucki and other Settlements beyond the mountains *whose very names had been unknown to us. . . ."*[37] There is a note of almost superstitious awe in Rawdon's words—the mysterious terror of the unknown back of beyond.

The buckskin-clad frontiersmen marched over the mountains on horseback, armed with their rifles and hunting knives. Each man had a blanket; his commissariat consisted of a bag of parched corn and a flask of maple syrup or honey for sweetening. They gathered in detachments as they marched until they numbered between 1400 and 1600 rifles under Isaac Shelby, John Sevier, William Campbell, Benjamin Cleveland, Charles McDowell, and others—all of them colonels and no one in over-all command. They solved this organizational dilemma on October 5 by having a board of officers meet each night to decide the operations of the next day. One of their number was selected as officer of the day to see that the plans were carried out. Choice of this officer fell on William Campbell of Virginia.[38]

Ferguson, meanwhile, had been informed by deserters of the approach of the enemy.[39] He sent word to Cornwallis asking for reinforcements, preferably dragoons, and telling the British commander that he was retreating with his 1100 men obedient to his Lordship's instruction. Cornwallis dispatched the Green Horse on October 10, but there was a lapse of possibly two or three days between Cornwallis' receipt of Ferguson's message and the departure of Tarleton and the Legion.[40]

On the evening of October 5 the mountain men learned

of Ferguson's retreat and learned also that he had with him only about 100 of his Provincial Rangers and 1000 militia. The Americans determined to overtake him before he could reach a British post or receive reinforcement. The men who rode the best horses, 910 in all, started next morning "as soon as they could see."[41] At sunset on October 6, after marching twenty-one miles, they reached a tree-dotted meadow, roughly five miles wide and five miles deep, known throughout the local area as Hannah's Cowpens. There they grazed their horses, and killed and ate a number of beeves belonging to an unfortunate Tory named Saunders, who penned his cattle at this place.[42] It may be hazarded as an assumption that they used the rails of the cattle pens to make their fires, for there is no mention by Daniel Morgan, or anyone else, of the existence of pens at the Cowpens on January 17, 1781, which was the next time the meadow witnessed the gathering of a large body of men.

After eating, and resting a few hours, the men marched all night "amidst an excessively hard rain." The rain continued all morning and by noon some of the mountaineers wished to halt. Shelby would not consider it, so on they went for another mile, when they learned that Ferguson was only seven miles distant from them at King's Mountain.[43]

Ferguson had discovered that he could not travel fast enough to elude his mounted pursuers. Therefore he decided to make a stand on what he considered an impregnable post. "He declared the Almighty could not drive him from it."[44] King's Mountain was a flat-topped hill five hundred yards long and varying in width from seventy to one hundred and twenty yards at its northeast end. It rose steeply sixty feet above the surrounding plain. The prospect of an attack upon such a natural fortress might have dismayed a force of regulars. The mountain men were forest-wise and crack shots with their long rifles. Moreover, they had kept their powder dry despite the downpour, which was more than Continental

troops were always able to do in similar circumstances.[45]
Dismounting, they formed into four columns and marched
on foot to the base of the mountain. Here they deployed to
right and left.

Thus surrounding the mountain they marched up, com-
mencing action on all sides.

Ferguson did all that an officer could do under the circumstances. His men, too, fought bravely. But his position,
which he thought impregnable against any force the Patriots
could raise, was really a disadvantage to him. The summit
was bare, whilst the sides of the mountain were covered with
trees. Ferguson's men were drawn up in close column on the
summit and thus presented fair marks for the mountaineers,
who approached them under cover of the trees. As either
column would approach the summit, Ferguson would order
out a charge with fixed bayonet, which was always successful,
for the riflemen retreated before the charging column slowly,
still firing as they retired. When Ferguson's men returned
again to their position on the mountain, the patriots would
again rally and pursue them. In one of these charges Shelby's
column was considerably broken; he rode back and rallied
his men and reached the summit whilst Ferguson was directing a charge against Cleveland.

Col. Sevier reached the summit about the same time with
Shelby. They united and drove back the enemy to one end of
the ridge. Cleveland's and Campbell's columns were still
pressing forward and firing as they came up. The slaughter
of the enemy was great, and it was evident that further
resistance would be unavailing. Still Ferguson's proud heart
could not think of surrender. He swore "he would never
yield to such a d---d banditti," and rushed from his men,
sword in hand, and cut away until his sword was broken and
he was shot down. His men, seeing their leader fall, immediately surrendered. The British loss, in killed and prisoners,
was eleven hundred and twenty-five. A more total defeat was
not practicable. Our loss was forty killed. Amongst them we
had to mourn the death of Col. Williams, a most gallant and
efficient officer. The battled lasted one hour.[46]

Many of the militia Ferguson had under him at King's Mountain were riflemen like their cousins from over the mountain, for they had enlisted mainly from the back country. As the bayonet charges were "always successful," since, by Shelby's own account, his men repeatedly retreated before them, the rifles accounted for most of the casualties among the Americans. "An unusual number of the killed were found to have been shot in the head. Riflemen took off riflemen with such exactness, that they killed each other when they were taking sight, so effectually that their eyes remained after they were dead, one shut and the other open, in the usual manner of marksmen when levelling at their objects."[47]

The immediate aftermath of the King's Mountain battle was not pretty. "We proceeded to bury the dead, but it was badly done. They were thrown into convenient piles and covered with old logs, the bark of old trees and rocks . . . [later] wolves became so plenty that it was dangerous for anyone to go out at night . . . also . . . hogs gathered."[48]

In extenuation here, it may be said that the mountain men had marched, with only one pause of any length—that at the Cowpens—from dawn on October 6 to three o'clock in the afternoon of October 7. They had then fought a strenuous battle and slept on the field with the dead and dying and 698 prisoners. On Sunday morning, October 8, they were in haste to be off to their homes, not only because they were in hourly expectation of the appearance of reinforcements sent by Cornwallis, but because they also knew from long experience that the Creeks and Cherokees on the frontier felt an insatiable curiosity toward unguarded settlements of women, children and old men. Their homes on the frontier were dangerously open to Indian attack. This accounts to an extent for the hasty and careless burial of the King's Mountain dead.

Less excusable was the treatment of the prisoners. At

Gilbert Town, to which the captives were marched on
October 8, Colonel Campbell was forced to issue an order
requesting that officers of all ranks "restrain the disorderly
manner of slaughtering and disturbing the prisoners."[49] A
species of court composed of a committee of colonels tried
between thirty and forty Tories known to have assisted the
British in raiding and looting. Twelve of these men were
condemned to execution, and nine were hanged.[50] The trial,
as Shelby later recalled, was held late at night.[51] Execution
was as summary as the trial.[52] These acts after King's Mountain gave Cornwallis excuse for many later barbarities.

Tarleton received the news of Ferguson's defeat when he
reached Smith's Ford below the forks of the Catawba: "Individuals with expresses were frequently murdered. . . . Very
few out of a great number of messengers could reach Charlotte town . . . to give intelligence of Ferguson's situation."[53]
When the intelligence did reach Cornwallis on October 14,
it was much swelled by rumor. It was reported that the force
of the mountain men was three thousand and that Ninety
Six and Camden were threatened.[54] Consequently Cornwallis
abandoned for the moment the subjugation of North Carolina and hurried south, harassed by pouring rains. What with
the wretched red clay roads and the bad weather, nearly
twenty wagons loaded with army supplies were destroyed or
left behind, giving the withdrawal an air of precipitancy
which had a dampening effect upon "our friends" in North
Carolina. A few of them had shown their true colors pre-
maturely and suffered for it in consequence after the British
left them to the mercies of their countrymen. The British
army after a miserable march of two weeks arrived in Winnsboro in the South Carolina Piedmont and there encamped.
Cornwallis himself arrived in a jolting wagon, so sick with a
bilious fever that he was obliged to turn the command over
to Lord Rawdon until he recovered.[55]

Sir Henry Clinton wrote later: "The instant I heard of

Major Ferguson's defeat, I foresaw most of the consequences likely to result from it.... The check so encouraged the spirit of rebellion in both Carolinas that it could never afterward be humbled.... [It] unhappily proved the first link in a chain of evils that followed in regular succession until they ended at last in the total loss of America."[56] Writing long after the event, Sir Henry is very likely crediting himself with a prescience he probably did not have at the time. Nevertheless, in the long run he was right. That short hour on King's Mountain, where Americans fought Americans and the son of a Scottish judge was the only British officer present, marked the turning of the tide in the south.

News of King's Mountain did not reach Washington until October 26. Then it was garbled in much the same manner that it had been when Cornwallis received it.[57] Congress did not receive a full account until November 7.[58] All that Washington, Congress, and Greene knew when Greene started south on October 21 was that a discredited Gates with a totally inadequate force was at Hillsboro and that Cornwallis had left Camden and marched to Charlotte with the entire British army of the southern department.[59] As the crow flies, Charlotte is one hundred miles from Hillsboro, and Hillsboro is forty miles from the Virginia border. Washington's intelligence had informed him that Major General Leslie had sailed with a British force from New York for Virginia to cooperate with Cornwallis. That was why Washington could not permit Greene leave to go to Newport or to wait at West Point for the arrival of his wife.

As for Gates, he was in no position to take much advantage of the battle at King's Mountain. But he made the proper military gesture. After Cornwallis withdrew, the hero of Saratoga marched his army of scarecrows to Charlotte and assumed what he could only hope was a posture of menace.

"TO EQUIP A FLYING

ARMY"[1]

Major Generals Nathanael Greene and George Washington notably shared at least one character trait, namely a tendency to view life from the gloomy side and to regard the future with foreboding.[2] Admittedly both of them frequently had much to be gloomy about. Nevertheless, there is a striking similarity between the manner in which Washington expressed himself with respect to his appointment to the newly created post of Commander-in-Chief in 1775 and the words Greene used concerning his own appointment to the command of the southern department in 1780. Washington said to his fellow delegate in Congress from Virginia, "Remember, Mr. Henry, from the day I enter upon the command of the American armies, I date my fall and the ruin of my reputation."[3]

Greene wrote Congress that whether he was to consider his appointment a misfortune or otherwise would depend on future events. He "was not altogether without hopes of proscribing some bounds to the ravages of the enemy."[4] He promised nothing closer to success. To Washington he wrote privately, "How I shall be able to support myself under all these embarrassments, God only knows. . . . My family is what hangs most heavy on my mind. . . . Misfourtune or disgrace to me must be ruin to them."[5]

However, there was also a curious similarity about the

pessimism of both Washington and Greene: the blacker the outlook became, the more indefatigable became their efforts.

It was Greene's misfortune that his assignment to the southern army not only coincided with a very low ebb in the new nation's military affairs but with the most dire financial straits the country had yet experienced.[6] The public treasury was empty and the public credit exhausted.

Greene's first stop on his way south was Philadelphia. There he hoped to obtain supplies and there he laid before Congress a letter from Washington naming him as successor to General Horatio Gates. Congress, without hesitation, and with no reference to the acrimonies of the preceding August, responded on October 30 with his appointment as commander "with all the powers heretofore given by Congress to Major General Gates."[7] In addition Congress gave him power to cooperate with "our great ally [France] and his Catholic Majesty [Spain]."[8] Furthermore, Greene's commission was free of the crippling injunction which Congress had placed on Washington when he was named Commander-in-Chief, namely that he be required to call a council of war of his officers to decide all important questions.[9] Greene simply was authorized "to employ the army in the Manner you shall judge most proper, subject only to the control of the commander-in-chief."[10]

Beyond this Congress could not go. The public chest was empty. The members of Congress could only recommend— they were powerless to order—that the legislators and executives of the southern department afford "every necessary Assistance and Support" to General Greene. They specifically authorized Greene "to call for the same." The heads of the staff departments of supply of the main army were also requested to provide what could not be obtained to the southward.[11]

Greene was under no illusions about the abilities of the ravaged southern states to furnish supplies, however earnestly

they might desire to do so. The stopovers on his trip south
were occasioned by a strenuous effort to procure the arms,
clothing, and transportation he knew he could not operate
without. Henry Knox of the artillery had promised him a
company of artificers. Joseph Reed, Governor of Pennsylvania, could provide only 1500 stand of arms of the 5000
requested of him. Congress had no clothing to give the army.
Greene tried to persuade the Philadelphia merchants to
furnish 5000 suits of clothes and take bills on France in pay-
ment. The merchants declined. There was promise of wagons
from Pennsylvania, but it was so hedged about with reservations as to be nearly valueless. Indeed, in almost all cases, the
reservations outweighed the promises.[12]

In Maryland Greene took instant advantage of the legislature being in session to plead his needs before it. They
promised all the assistance in their power, but told him
frankly to place but little dependence on them, "as they had
neither money nor credit."[13] Furthermore, Maryland was rife
with wildly optimistic rumors. Gates, perhaps with a human
desire to put the best face on a bad situation, or because he
himself was deceived by faulty intelligence, had somewhat
magnified the results of King's Mountain and the facts of his
own position.[14] He had been writing letters holding out
promise of speedy renewal of offensive operations and talking
sanguinely of "recovering all our losses."[15] Some of the
Marylanders, hoping for the good fortune of their regiments
in the south, were anticipating a swift capture of Cornwallis
and his army. Unable to convince them of the falseness of
their enthusiasm, Greene left General Mordecai Gist of the
Maryland line in that state to act as his agent to forward
promptly what supplies might ultimately be forthcoming.
"Make all your applications in writing," he told Gist, "that it
may appear hereafter for our justification that we left
nothing unessayed to promote the public service."[16]

Then Greene and the Baron de Steuben hastened on to

Virginia. At Richmond, for the first and only time in their respective careers, Greene and Governor Thomas Jefferson had a personal meeting. Jefferson had been trying for more than three weeks to collect one hundred wagons for the southern army. He was sorry to report that, although vested with full powers of impressment (which he was reluctant to use), he had collected only eighteen. As to the clothing situation, it was desperate. Greene seems to have acquired in this period of six days, from November 16 to November 21, 1780, a modicum of distrust for Jefferson's perspicacity in military matters,[17] as well he might. Thomas Jefferson, neither in the immediate nor more distant future, ever showed that he had the slightest conception of military exigency.[18] Nor, indeed, did he ever show any disposition to expose his own person to the discomforts of a military operation, although he was of military age all through the Revolution,[19] and his constitution may be assumed to have been of a rugged sort inasmuch as it served him well until the eighty-third year of his age.

While Greene was in Richmond there was a general alarm caused by the landing of a strong force of British under General Leslie at Portsmouth. The militia were called out by the governor and hasty and ineffectual preparations made for defense. Then, unaccountably, Leslie embarked his troops and fell down to Hampton Roads. Greene wrote Washington on November 19 that there must be some foreign cause for the withdrawal which time and further information would doubtless explain.[20] As time did explain, Cornwallis, as a result of the upset at King's Mountain, had diverted Leslie from the Chesapeake, first to Cape Fear and then to Charleston, to join forces with him for a new offensive into North Carolina.[21]

After securing such assurances of cooperation and supplies from Governor Jefferson as he could, Greene left Steuben in Virginia to forward men and materiel. If the enemy should return, Steuben was to take charge of the army's

defense of the state. Then Greene set out for Hillsboro,
where he still supposed Gates and the southern army to be.
His forebodings about the future had hardly been lessened
by his experiences with regard to obtaining assistance for that
army, but his spirit of doggedness had been considerably
enhanced. A habit acquired during his quartermaster days
was now firmly rooted. From here on, whenever he was in
need of anything, he asked for the whole of it from every possible source, believing that in this way he might get a grudg-
ing bit here and another scanty slice there until at least he
had a fairly adequate supply—or, at any rate, something.

He took full advantage of the clause in his appointment
which authorized him to call on the legislatures and staff
departments for aid:

> Be instant in supplication. . . . Abundance [of this] can do
> no evil. . . . Public bodies should not be permitted to forget
> you, and will often yield to importunity what they refuse to
> justice; because some would get rid of the trouble of it;
> others are forced into reflection by it; and to others it affords
> a sufficient excuse for doing that which without your im-
> portunity, they might themselves be thought importunate in
> pressing.[22]

General Greene's own importunities embarrassed him not at
all. He believed that he must do what he did to promote the
public service.

The Rhode Islander had never been farther south than
Maryland, but he had since mid-October corresponded with
Washington on, among other matters, the subject of southern
topography.[23] Greene proposed "to equip a flying army of
about eight hundred horse and one thousand infantry." He
saw little prospect of contending with the enemy on equal
grounds and planned a kind of partisan war.[24] Washington
endorsed Greene's plan and pointed out the problem of the
great number of rivers in the south and the need for water
transport. "Pray," wrote Washington, perhaps with recollec-

tions of Brooklyn, Manhattan and the Delaware, "direct particular attention to the Boats."[25]

As events turned out this was sage advice. Greene, who idolized the Commander-in-Chief and modeled his conduct after Washington's so far as he was able, scrupulously followed it. In Richmond the American commander had encountered Lieutenant Colonel Edward Carrington, a young artillerist of the Virginia line, who had been out of employment since the Charleston debacle.[26] Gates had previously used Carrington as his agent to examine the Roanoke River as a means of transport or retreat. Greene immediately assigned the young officer to explore the Dan River for similar purposes. Shortly thereafter he sent another party to examine the Yadkin and Catawba rivers with like object. The river parties were also to determine the distances from town to town in the areas and the condition of the roads. They were further to investigate the practicability of constructing flat-bottomed boats that would carry loads of forty or fifty barrels yet draw little more water than a lightly loaded canoe.[27] Thus, thanks to the exertions of his deputies and to the minute observations Greene himself made along his route, General William Davidson of North Carolina observed weeks later that although General Greene had never seen the Catawba, he knew more about it than men who been raised on its banks.[28] Nathanael Greene's military abilities were not of the romantic kind in which the dashing leader gallops up on a white charger or a black stallion and cries, "Follow me!" or "Come on, you sons of bitches, do you want to live forever?" His genius lay rather in an infinite capacity for taking pains in advance.

General Greene arrived in Hillsboro on November 27 to find Gates gone. The little town was the seat of government in North Carolina, but the legislature was not then in session. Greene spent some time therefore in writing letters to Governor Abner Nash presenting the needs of the army.[29] As

usual he asked for everything and received the customary assurances of good will and little more. From Hillsboro he
pushed on to Salisbury where he learned that Gates was encamped just outside of Charlotte.

The new commander arrived in the army camp on
December 2. This time the respectfully wooden expressions
on the faces of men and officers endeavored to conceal a lively
curiosity, for it was known that the past relations of Greene
and Gates had not always been friendly. If the onlookers
expected a display of overbearing triumph on Greene's part
or of offended pride on Gates', they were disappointed.
Greene met Gates "with respectful sympathy and Gates,
whose manners were those of a man of the world, returned
his greeting with dignified politeness," wrote Otho Williams
later. "Their conduct was an elegant lesson of propriety ex-
hibited on a most delicate and interesting occasion."[30]

Greene, whose own distant family was always nearest his
heart, was much distressed that Gates, in addition to losing
his command, had only recently been informed of the death
of his only son.[31] Therefore, it was probably with relief that
he discovered that it would be impossible to convene the
court of inquiry which Congress had resolved should be held
on Gates' conduct at Camden.[32] There were not enough
senior officers present at Charlotte for the purpose. Steuben
would have had to be called from his command in Virginia
to make up the requisite number. All of the officers under
Greene's command advised against such a step.[33] Gates accordingly departed shortly after Greene took over the command on December 3 and made a slow progress to Richmond
where the Virginia Assembly, far from censuring him, voted
a resolution of gratitude for his services.[34]

Back in Charlotte Greene's first concern was to ascertain
the strength of his army. The returns were not encouraging.
The total force consisted of 90 cavalrymen, 60 artillerists
(both groups short of horses and guns); and 2307 infantry

"on paper." Of these 1482 were present and fit for duty. Only 949 of them were Continentals and less than 800 of the whole were properly clothed and equipped.[35] The clothing situation was so bad, said Greene, "that there is a great number that have not a rag of clothes on them except a little piece of blanket, in the Indian form, around their waists."[36]

Small as the army was, it was too large for the exhausted country around Charlotte. In spite of all Gates' efforts, there were not three days rations on hand when Greene arrived. The general spent his first evening with Colonel Polk of Gates' Commissariat studying the resources of the area. The following morning Polk declared that Greene understood the situation better than Gates had done in the whole period of his command.[37]

The condition of the Quartermaster Department was even worse than that of the Commissariat. All of the public wagons and horses had been lost at Camden, along with all the vehicles that had been obtained by hire or impressment from private individuals. Without hard money the difficulty of obtaining new wagons or animals in a countryside that had been desolated by the armies of both sides for the past six months seemed all but insurmountable. Greene considered the problem with outward calm, seeking remedies. He found one in the form of the energetic Lieutenant Colonel Carrington. Greene knew, none better, what qualities were necessary in a Quartermaster General. He felt that Carrington possessed them. Accordingly he wrote to Carrington on December 4 asking the young artilleryman to accept the appointment of Deputy Quartermaster General. With his usual thoroughness he also wrote the governors of the southern states, informing them of the appointment and desiring them to furnish Carrington with every assistance.[38] Carrington accepted the post and entered on his duties with zeal and alacrity.

The Quartermaster Department being so happily cared

for, Greene returned to the matter of a Commissary General. Colonel Polk, who had held the office under Gates, begged to be excused. He pled advanced years and fatigue. He was a local man of the Charlotte area. If Greene planned to move, Polk would be forced to resign because his family circumstances were such that he could not leave. Greene was planning to move and had already alerted General Daniel Morgan to that effect. The general found his new Commissary General in Morgan's outfit in the person of Colonel William R. Davie whose partisan cavalry had been disbanded about the end of November. When Greene approached him, Davie was already eagerly engaged in raising a new body of troops to serve on detached duty under the famous rifleman who had acquitted himself so notably at Quebec and Saratoga. To the fiery twenty-four-year-old the prospect of the Commissary Generalship was not alluring. He thanked General Greene for the honor done Colonel Davie, but respectfully pointed out that since Davie had left Princeton College in 1776 he had spent nearly his whole time in the field. Thus he knew something of the management of troops, but—and the young man who saw his cherished hope of serving under Morgan go glimmering must have advanced this with triumph—Colonel Davie knew absolutely nothing of *money* or *accounts,* and was therefore unfit for the position.

Greene, who had made it his business to learn much about Davie's activities from Colonel Polk and others, was undismayed. He assured the young officer that as to money and accounts, he would be troubled by neither, as there was not a single dollar in the war chest, nor any prospect of any to come. Davie would subsist the army exactly as he had subsisted his own dragoons and Gates' for the past six months, namely off the country. Greene knew, as Davie now realized he knew, that the short rations in camp were the direct result of the recent disbandment of the Colonel's time-expired cavalry. Prior to this, the dragoons had pushed their foraging parties from the advanced post at Lansford clear down to the fat Loyalist districts in front of Camden to obtain food for themselves and the southern army. If Davie could not raise a new force to pursue the same method in those or other areas, the southern army must fall back on Virginia, or disperse, leaving the enemy in peaceful possession of the two Carolinas. Colonel William R. Davie left the commander's presence a Commissary General in spite of himself and an ever loyal admirer of Nathanael Greene.[39]

What intelligence Gates had been receiving from the southward had come chiefly from Francis Marion, who continued to act as a gadfly to the British army, picking off foraging parties, harassing "Torrys" and making an ubiquitous nuisance of himself. The little man was forever short of ammunition, clothes for his troops, tents, rum, and even "quit [*sic*] out of paper."[40] Nonetheless he reported his men "remarkable healthy, notwithstanding." Greene on his arrival in the south took measures to step up the transmission of intelligence. "I have not the honor of your acquaintance," he wrote Marion on December 4, "but I am no stranger to your character and merit." He wished Marion to send him the earliest information of any reinforcements which might arrive at Charleston or join Cornwallis.[41] All through December and January, Marion kept Greene informed.[42] He was to lose track of Greene for a time during the race to the Dan.

Greene now turned to the question of future operations. When Gates marched to Charlotte upon Cornwallis' withdrawal to Winnsboro, the American general had no real intent of further renewing active hostilities. He briefly assumed his menacing posture; then he prepared to go into winter quarters. The Polish general, Thaddeus Kosciuszko, who had served Gates so brilliantly building fortifications at Ticonderoga and Saratoga[43] was put to work supervising the construction of huts for shelter against the cold. As the days idled by officers and men fell into habits of negligence and

disorder. The food shortage encouraged a dangerous practice Steuben had earlier found prevalent at Valley Forge.
The men simply took leaves without permission and returned
at will. One of Greene's first acts was to seize one of these
vacationers when he came back over the hill, try him, convict
him, and hang him before the whole army. The effect was
salutary. "We must not do as we have been used," said the
men as they huddled about the fires that night. "It is new
lords new laws."[44] It was a firm hand, but it was good. A man
at least knows where he is under a taut command.

However, with the whole force now present and accounted for, the situation at Charlotte became untenable.
Patriotic as the counties of Rowan and Mecklenburg were,
they were becoming restive at the presence of hungry, ragged,
and idle soldiers. Greene must move. He wished to establish
a "camp of repose" for the purpose of repairing the wagons,
recruiting fresh horses, and disciplining the troops.[45] The
country on the banks of the Pee Dee River, which in its
upper reaches becomes the Yadkin, had been little ravaged
by either army. Greene relieved Kosciuszko of his hut-build-
ing chores and sent him on an exploring trip. The Polish
officer reported that at Hick's Creek, on the east bank of the
Pee Dee nearly across from the Cheraws, there was a suitable
site for a camp. The country was well supplied with food,
and abundant canebrakes afforded excellent forage for horses.
Greene could establish his camp of repose here and await the
arrival from the north of increased cavalry support in the
shape of Lieutenant Colonel Henry Lee and his Legion. This
was a mixed force of cavalry and infantry which Congress
had authorized and Washington had detached for duty with
the southern army.[46]

There was one difficulty, however; on Hick's Creek the
army would be farther from Winnsboro and Cornwallis than
if it remained at Charlotte. Thus Greene's first movement
would appear to be retrograde. In that country of divided

loyalties, it was quite as incumbent on Greene as on Cornwallis to do nothing that might lower the spirits of "our friends." Yet in the wretched condition of his little force Greene could not afford to offer battle to Cornwallis. "In this command I am obliged to put everything to the hazard . . . to make detachments that nothing but absolute necessity could authorize. . . ."[47] Therefore, Greene, in the face of Cornwallis' much superior force, divided his army. He did it himself, on his own responsibility. He called no council of war. He simply issued the orders, knowing full well that he was violating all the classic rules of warfare. The erstwhile Quaker ironmonger had studied diligently every military treatise he could lay his hands on.[48] What he was doing appeared to be suicidal, and did not need classical examples to tell him so. Washington had split his army at New York and Long Island in 1776 and met disaster. Howe had scattered his Hessians in New Jersey in December of that year, and Washington had trounced Rall at Trenton. Burgoyne had sent another detachment of Hessians to Bennington in August of 1777 to meet defeat at the hands of Stark and his militia. Cornwallis had allowed Ferguson to march to his death at King's Mountain only three months before.[49]

Greene knew the rules and the penalties for breaking them, but he was also a realist. "When I am obliged to speak of men and things, I must speak of them as I find them."[50] In 1780 Napoleon Bonaparte was a downy-faced cadet at the Brienne Military Academy. He had yet to make his famous remark about an army traveling on its stomach. Few armies, fortunately, have been so relentlessly committed to this form of transport as the Grand Army of the Southern Department. It was no accident that so many of the engagements of the southern theatre occurred at places with such names as Ramsour's Mills, Wahab Plantation, Oliphant's Mills, Wetzell's Mills, Hogg's Mill and the like. At mills there was apt to be corn meal, and the meal was always an object.[51] The southern army was hungry. It never really stopped being hungry, even in the relatively fat days outside of Charleston in 1782. Greene, in December of 1780, saw that by separating his army into two parts, he made it easier for both divisions to live off the country.[52] This, of course, was not grand strategy; it was simply necessity.

Nevertheless, there was strategy also. Greene marched for the Cheraws with the Continental brigade under Colonel Otho Williams, the Virginia militia under General Stevens, and the artillery. Of these latter there were 60 men, very few guns, and very few horses to draw the guns.[53] General Isaac Huger of South Carolina was in over-all command of the combined militia and Continentals, with which force Greene remained in his capacity as commandant of the entire southern theatre of operations. Brigadier Daniel Morgan with the light infantry, composed of 320 Maryland and Delaware Continentals, 200 Virginia riflemen, and about 80 dragoons under Colonel William Washington, was detached to cross the Catawba River to its western side and operate between the Broad and Pacolet rivers, roughly in Major Ferguson's old territory. Both divisions of the army were put under marching orders on December 16, but several successive days of incessant rain so inundated the country that it was December 20 before Greene's corps could set out and December 21 before Morgan marched for the Catawba.[54]

Cornwallis at Winnsboro, with an army now perfectly healthy and in good order, was astounded when he received intelligence of Greene's division of his army. The British commander had reported to Clinton that the opposite army always kept at a considerable distance and retired upon being approached. His troubles were not occasioned by it but by the "constant Incursions of Refugees, Back Mountain Men and the perpetual Risings in the different parts of the Province."[55] Now he was faced with a temerity he could not understand. Cornwallis knew that Greene had relieved Gates.

He was perfectly informed as to the size and composition of Greene's force.[56] How then could the man have the audacity to divide it? Tarleton assured his commander that Greene could only have done it out of ignorance of the addition to Cornwallis' army of General Leslie's corps of 1500 men.[57] When Greene issued his marching orders on December 16, it is highly unlikely that he knew of Leslie's arrival at Charleston on December 14.[58] But he knew, thanks to Marion,[59] very shortly thereafter, and it did not alter his resolve to keep his force divided.[60]

More astute—certainly more experienced—than Banastre Tarleton, Cornwallis sat down and mulled the puzzle of the enemy's movements. Presently, map spread before him, he saw what Greene had seen. At Winnsboro Cornwallis was between Greene on Hick's Creek and Morgan west of the Catawba. If the British army turned back toward Charleston, it would have a fighting force on either flank. If it turned against Morgan, the route to Charleston lay open to Greene. If it turned against Greene, Morgan could advance on Ninety Six or Augusta. If Cornwallis sat still, both his flanks were in constant danger of harassment, and the experience of the past few months with Marion and Sumter had proved how annoying that harassment could be.[61] Furthermore, although Cornwallis was aware that the present American army was weak and inconsiderable, there was one thing that the British were always unsure of. The constant comings and goings of the militia, which were such a trial to Washington, to Greene and all other American commanders, were an equal source of bafflement to the British. Because of them they could never be entirely sure what strength they faced. Cornwallis knew he had for the moment neutralized the back mountain men. According to Colonel Thomas Brown of the King's Rangers, the chiefs of 2500 Cherokees had promised to march immediately against the settlements of the "Watoga, Holstein, Caintuck, Nolachuckie, Cumberland and Green Rivers."[62]

This diversion should effectively keep the settlers back of the mountains busy with their own concerns and make up for the evaporation of those seven fine regiments of Tory militia which Ferguson had organized before his defeat. Blessedly Sumter had been put out of action for a time when he was severely wounded in the right shoulder in a drawn skirmish between his people and Tarleton at Blackstock's plantation in mid-December. There remained, of course, Marion and the "perpetual Risings." Yet, with his army reinforced by Leslie's corps, it appeared to Cornwallis that the time for action had come.

The British commander sent for Tarleton on December 27. On December 28, from his position twenty miles away, the cavalryman rode in to confer with Cornwallis in the general's tent.[63] If one account of the conference be true, both officers were unaware that as they talked a small boy with large ears had one of those ears glued attentively to the outside of the tent canvas.[64]

Cornwallis had decided to divide his own army, not into two parts, but into three. Lord Rawdon would be left to hold Camden against attack by General Huger. Tarleton would proceed immediately to crush Morgan. Cornwallis himself would move up into North Carolina to intercept and destroy any remnants of Morgan's force that might escape Tarleton. Then it would be a simple matter to defeat Greene and Huger and proceed with the invasion of North Carolina.[65] That is to say, Cornwallis thought it would be a simple matter.

"HEAVEN ONLY KNOWS HOW WE SHALL EMPLOY OUR TEETH"[1]

Greene's army reached the camp site at the mouth of Hick's Creek, a tributary of the Pee Dee, on December 26, 1780. The country, Green wrote, was no Egypt, but food and forage were abundant.[2] While the general settled to the task of bringing his troops under much needed drill and discipline, he continued to dispatch letters to all possible sources that might supply the necessary clothing without which the troops could not march. "Our men are naked for want of overhauls." The plaint in one form or another occurs again and again throughout Greene's correspondence.[3]

These "overhauls," fashioned of wool in winter and unbleached linen in summer, consisted of close-fitting trousers or leggings, the bottoms of which extended over the instep. They had a strap which passed under the arch of the foot to hold them in place snugly.[4] Worn with a fringed hunting shirt of matching material, the garments made a serviceable, if easily soiled, uniform for field duty. Moreover, unlike the breeches of the earlier American army, the "overhauls" could be worn without stockings, since the instep flap extended over an ordinary low shoe. Since stockings for officers a few weeks later cost $46,450 in Continental paper for 101 pair, "Not all of quality as might be wished,"[5] the advantage of dispensing with stockings for the men is obvious.

During the march from Charlotte, Greene made his

customary astute observations of the countryside. He determined then that he must do his fighting above the fall lines
of the rivers. Below the falls, he wrote to Washington, the
country was "all champaign," open plain with no natural
barriers that could be held by an inferior force against a
superior enemy. Moreover, below the falls the rivers were
deep, their approaches beset by swamps and morasses. Such
roads as existed occurred only at long intervals, offering
hazardous avenues of retreat at best, subject to flooding with
each heavy rain. "I cannot," said Greene, "afford to get entangled among the difficulties they present, until I can turn
upon my adversary and fight him when I please."[6]

Nevertheless, to guard against the contingency of being
unable to choose his line of retreat, Greene employed the
versatile Kosciuszko in building flat-bottomed boats which
could be fitted on wheels and transported with the army.
That is to say, they could be so transported if ever Greene
could procure the horses to transport them.[7]

Within a fortnight of the arrival at the camp on the Pee
Dee a distinct improvement showed in the American army.
To be sure, the entire Virginia militia remained shoeless, and
body clothing of all units had altered but little. Yet, thanks
to ample provisions, the bones of the men had fleshed over
and their bellies were comfortably full. Their improved
physical condition, combined with unceasing drill, made
their steps brisker and their whole appearance smarter.

On January 6, 1781, or possibly a day or so earlier, the
camp personnel were treated to a sight many of them had
never seen before and which the remainder had not observed
for many months. There trotted into camp a splendid body of
horse and foot, fully equipped and fully uniformed, at their
head a magnificently mounted officer who rode like the very
epitome of a cavalryman. To the gaping, raggamuffin battalions the newcomers, in their white leather breeches, tight-
fitting green jackets and shining helmets adorned with

plumes, must have appeared something to dream on. This was the Legion of Lieutenant Cólonel Henry Lee, 280 strong, 140 horse and 140 foot, which had been handpicked by Washington for service in the southern department.[8]

Henry Lee, Jr., was at this time twenty-six years of age. He had been promoted from major to lieutenant colonel upon his assignment to the Southern Department. Like his opposite number in the British army, the twenty-seven-year-old Banastre Tarleton, Lee had studied for the law. Tarleton entered the army from Oxford in 1775; Lee from Princeton in 1776. Both men were magnificent horsemen, and both had the instinct for showmanship that the layman, at least, expects of a cavalry leader. Here the resemblance seems to end, unless it be added that both Lee and Tarleton were tender of their own failings, jealous of their own worth, and hypercritical of the failings and accomplishments of others—a common weakness of ambitious men.

Physically, Lee was a good head taller than the stocky Tarleton. Looking down on his fellows from an easy height above most of them, Lieutenant Colonel Lee could afford to be magnanimous and gracious where Lieutenant Colonel Tarleton was belligerent and brutal. Socially, the gap between the two was greater than a mere matter of inches. The wealth Tarleton's family had amassed in business had enabled the young man's mother to buy him a comission in the British army.[9] This made him socially acceptable in the company of gentlemen, but somehow suspect nonetheless by the British standards of the time. Lee, on the other hand, was a Lee of Virginia. Whatever can be, and has been, said of the origins of Virginia's first families does not alter the fact that a Lee of Virginia in the 1780's was not a member of the commonalty. He was the child of an aristocracy whose members had been trained from birth to regard their group as superior to all assemblages of lesser folk. Individuals in such a group frequently come to transfer the belief in group or class supe-

riority specifically to themselves as individuals. It is a naiveté
on the whole quite charming, especially when accompanied
by a handsome physical presence, gentle manners, and a
schooled and active mind—all of which Lee possessed in full
measure.

Lee had good reason to think well of himself. He had
performed with distinction at Paulus Hook, Stony Point, and
under Greene at Springfield.[10] As light cavalry, Lee's Legion
was employed primarily in reconnaissance and intelligence
capacity. Lee's services in the area of intelligence with respect
to enemy movements were so valuable to Washington that
Lee was instructed to mark all of his communications to the
Commander-in-Chief "private." This meant that they could
not be examined by even members of the general's official
family, but were for Washington's eyes alone.[11] Perhaps the
service which most endeared him to Washington was one
which failed. Arnold's treason had outraged Washington's
sense of integrity. He was determined to recapture the traitor
alive and make a public example of him.[12] The resourceful
Lee with the help of John Champe, his sergeant major, very
nearly accomplished Arnold's seizure in New York, failure
being due only to a happenstance beyond their control. The
day of the night Arnold was to be taken, Clinton unwittingly
foiled the plot by ordering Arnold to Virginia.[13]

This, then, was Lee in 1781—young, romantic, and hardy,
already crowned with laurels and eager for more. He was of
course mercifully unaware of his own future and of the fact
that he would, in his middle age, sire a son who would do his
dedicated utmost to destroy the union which his father strove
so hard to bring to birth.

It is a measure of Washington's regard for Nathanael
Greene that he sent him as reinforcement an officer in whose
attributes he had so much confidence,[14] one indeed whom he
may have regarded as the son he might have had. Tradition

has it that Lee's mother, Lucy Grymes, inspired Washington to limping sonnets the summer he was sixteen.[15]

Lee, in his turn, had much admiration for Greene, whom he referred to in his correspondence and in his memoirs as "this illustrious man."[16] Coming from Lee with his knowledge of Latin, this was a compliment of no mean order. Nonetheless, Greene's illustrious qualities did not save him from receiving much gratuitous advice from his young subordinate.[17] It was advice which Greene took always in good part, acting upon it or not as his own judgment served him. As has already been noted, Greene seldom resorted to councils of war, but relied on his own decisions. Yet he was singularly ungiven to hauteur or personal vanity and willingly accepted other men's ideas, regardless of origin, if they appeared to him sound. Equally, he would reject guidance and assume responsibility for the consequences of his personal judgment if the advice did not seem to him to fit the circumstances or the end he wished to accomplish.[18]

With Lee's arrival, Greene had a corps equipped and battle-ready. But 280 men could do little against the main body of the British army. Nevertheless, Greene did not propose that they sit idle. He had sent Morgan west of the Catawba to harass Cornwallis' left flank. He immediately put Lee under marching orders to join Marion in the Santee country and aid in the embarrassment of Cornwallis' right. But Lee did not march the day after his arrival as has frequently been stated, and even implied by Lee himself. The error seems to have originated with William Gordon in his history and to have been compounded by subsequent writers.[19]

On January 7 Lee wrote General Anthony Wayne a letter headed "Camp on Pedee River, South Carolina." In the letter he mentioned the shoeless condition of the Virginia militia, the strength of Greene's army—which he considerably over-estimated—and the skirmishings of Sumter and Marion.

Evidence that Lee had arrived in camp by at least January
6 appears in a remark in the letter, "I heard General Greene
say yesterday" that most of the six hundred prisoners taken at
King's Mountain had been permitted to escape. This was circumstance that caused Greene considerable chagrin, for he
had counted on exchanging them for a like number of
Americans taken in the fall of Charleston. Lee's letter to
Wayne of January 7 also reports on the plentiful provisions
for men and animals available at the moment in the camp,
but speculates that once the army leaves this lush area,
"Heaven only knows how we shall employ our teeth."[20]

Lee left the Pee Dee to join Marion on January 13 or
16.[21] The delay of approximately a week between his arrival
and his departure has several possible explanations. First, it
was necessary for Greene to brief Lee on how he was to cooperate with Marion. Greene, as we have seen, was using
Marion as an intelligence source and an instrument of harassment to the enemy, which was exactly the way in which Lee
had been employed by Washington. Lee with his Legion
would be an invaluable addition to Marion's ragged and
fluctuating bands. Secondly, it was necessary to locate
Marion, inform him that Lee was joining him, and determine when and where the units of Lee and Marion would
meet. Marion on his own advisement, and with Greene's
full concurrence, was constantly shifting position. Even as
late as April, 1781, when Lee again joined Marion at
Greene's orders, the Virginian had the greatest difficulty in
finding the little Huguenot in his swampy hideout, despite
the fact that an advance party had been sent out some days
ahead to determine the position of the southern partisan.[22]
Location of Marion in January of 1781 in a country with
which Lee was as yet unfamiliar would have been still more
difficult. Thirdly, with Kosciuszko's advice, Greene had
chosen the camp on the Pee Dee not only because of the
availability of food for the men, but because of the existence

of plentiful forage for the horses. Lee's mounts had come many miles, and it was only reasonable to allow them to graze for a few days. The swamp where they were going was not prolific in horse fodder.

By January 23 Lee had joined forces with Marion.[23] How Lee and his Legion employed their teeth after this juncture is not recorded, but on Marion's customary diet of sweet potatoes, swamp water, and vinegar, it seems unlikely that they fared luxuriously. Nevertheless, Marion and Lee, disparately matched as they were, became instant allies. Their status could hardly have been more dissimilar, but their roles, and their understanding of them, were much alike. Said Lee: "Marion and Lee were singularly tender of the lives of their soldiers; and preferred moderate success with little loss, to the most brilliant enterprise, with the destruction of many troops."[24]

Lee also found that, although he was technically Marion's junior in rank, he could, in view of his past experience and associations and his equipped and uniformed Legion, in large measure dictate planning. He wrote Greene that Marion had not the necessary information for the design proposed. Therefore Lee had proposed another "too long to explain which I have great hopes in the accomplishment of."[25] This was the expedition against Georgetown, which proved interesting but abortive. They captured the commander, but were unable to take the fortress for want of artillery and retired without having accomplished much more than a diversion, although Greene in his official reports made as much of the affair as possible.[26]

As for Marion, he wrote Greene that "Colonel Lee's Interprising Genius promises much."[27]

"BY SOUND JUDGMENT AND GOOD REASONING"[1]

Meanwhile, in the country on the west side of the Catawba, General Daniel Morgan was unhappy. He, as he informed Greene, reached the banks of Pacolet Creek on Christmas Day [1780].[2] There he encamped and proceeded to the business of carrying out Greene's orders, which were explicit enough up to a point. Morgan had under his immediate command a corps of light infantry, a detachment of militia, and Lieutenant Colonel William Washington's regiment of light dragoons. This force, after it crossed the Catawba, was expected to be joined by a body of North Carolina men under Brigadier General William Davidson, plus the militia lately under the command of General Thomas Sumter. Sumter, as noted previously, had been wounded at Blackstock's in a skirmish with Tarleton and was still out of action.

"This force," read Greene's orders to Morgan, "you will employ against the enemy . . . either offensively or defensively, as your own prudence and discretion may direct, acting with caution and avoiding surprises by every possible precaution."[3] In addition Morgan was to protect and "spirit up" the people of the western area, as well as to collect provision and forage and store such collections in small magazines in the rear of his selected position. Above all, he was to spare no pains to get good intelligence of the enemy movements and to keep Greene advised of Cornwallis' situation.

In the last days of December Morgan was able to protect and "spirit up" the local Patriots by dispatching William Washington and his dragoons to attack a party of Tories who were ravaging the country along Fair Forest Creek. Washington's 80 dragoons with 200 local mounted militia rode 40 miles in one day to succor the good people of Fair Forest. With a savagery characteristic of southern Patriot and Tory encounters, the men of Washington's command killed or wounded 150 of the Georgia Tories and took 40 prisoners without any loss to themselves. Sixty of the more agile Tories escaped.[4] On their way back to the Pacolet, Washington's corps, for good measure, seized and destroyed a stockaded log house known as Fort William. The British occupants of the fort, alerted by the slaughter at Fair Forest, had already evacuated the house before Washington attacked, but the fact that the post was only 15 miles north of Ninety Six was sufficient cause for alarm to Cornwallis when he heard of the incident.[5]

Meanwhile, the militia were coming in so fast that Morgan could not supply them. The plan of forming a number of small magazines of provisions failed because of the monumental pique of Thomas Sumter. Although he was incapacitated with an infected right arm as a result of the wound received at Blackstock's, Sumter seems to have regarded Morgan's appearance in the Catawba country much as a bull regards an alien intrusion into his private pasture. He made it clear that Morgan's appointment to command in an area which Sumter regarded as his particular preserve "embarrassed" the Gamecock.[6] He made it equally clear to Morgan that that general could expect no help from him in the matter of supplies. Morgan's commissary of purchases, Captain Chitty, returned empty-handed from a foraging expedition with the information that Colonel Hill, Sumter's deputy, had been instructed to obey no orders from Morgan unless they came through Sumter.[7]

Greene was astonished at Morgan's report of this difficulty. There must, Greene wrote, be some misunderstanding by Colonel Hill of Sumter's order, "unless personal glory [to Sumter] is more than public good, which I cannot suppose is the case with him, or any other man who fights the cause of liberty."[8] This sentiment, of course, afforded Morgan no immediate practical service and merely proves that Greene did not yet know Sumter.

Morgan did what he could with the plethora of militia for whom he had no immediate employment. Some of the North Carolina men who had come in under Andrew Pickens were sent off to secure their effects. The others were disposed as best could be. The fact that the southern militia nearly all came in mounted added to the problem. The horses they rode were a means of transport only, or of escape. The men normally fought on foot, except in the instance at Cowpens when Morgan ingeniously turned them into cavalry. Consequently the horses, once arrived, were mere encumbrances of empty guts on four feet, which unfortunately consumed quite as much forage as any blooded stallion drilled to battle. Thus Morgan could not keep all the militia together in the camp on the Pacolet. He was compelled to disperse some with the horses to places where there was forage. Furthermore, he wrote Greene that it was beyond the art of man to keep militia from straggling.[9]

With a view of future action he asked Greene to forward pack saddles. The wagons were an impediment. In Morgan's opinion it was incompatible with the nature of light troops to be encumbered with baggage.[10] Having made this request, Morgan sat in his camp on the Pacolet, listening to an almost incessant rain and awaiting a reply to his proposal to Greene that he march into Georgia once the militia were fully collected. It was either advance or retreat, he told Greene. Food and forage would soon be exhausted where Morgan was. If he retreated, the militia would either desert or go over to the enemy. If he advanced and became entangled with a superior force in Georgia, Pickens and Davidson, who knew the back country well, had assured him that he could safely get away up the Savannah River and over the heads of tributary rivers along the Indian line.[11]

Morgan was a fighter and a man of action. He had been one for all of his forty-eight years. The enforced waiting with no sure knowledge of what was to come was galling to his characteristic impatience with inactivity. Moreover, orders to employ a force of uncertain numbers either offensively or defensively at one's own prudence or discretion leave a man with much leeway for possible grief. The unspecific quality of the orders was no fault of Greene's as Morgan must have known. The situation was such that the Americans could not attack. They could only await developments and seize whatever advantage they could from such developments or escape whatever disasters as presented themselves therein. It was not a situation in which anyone could feel relaxed or confident, least of all a man of Morgan's temperament.

His depression was deepened by the fact that he was becoming ill with an old misery with which he was all too familiar. The exactions he had made over the years on his magnificent body were beginning to take their toll. Of late Morgan had been wracked by bouts of rheumatism or sciatica, which, in their increasing severity, all but crippled him.[12] The damp ground of the camp and the frequent soakings from the incessant rains brought on so great an aching in his bones and a stiffening in his joints that already he found it all but impossible to crawl aboard a horse. Experience had taught him that this was but a prelude to worse to come. So he sat in the rain and the cold in a profound and typical Celtic gloom, while a black dog ate at his heart.

Daniel Morgan was the son of Welsh parents, who had settled in New Jersey. He had left home at the age of seventeen after a quarrel with his father. Like many young men

before and after him he headed for the frontier, in this case
western Virginia. He worked at odd jobs of manual labor,
including that of wagoner. At the age of twenty he had prospered sufficiently to be able to drive his own wagon and
horses over the mountains carrying stores for Braddock's
army. He fought as a ranker in the French and Indian War.
In the process he lost all the teeth in his left lower jaw to an
Indian bullet and acquired the scars of 499 British lashes on
his back for striking a British lieutenant.[13] The story has it
that Morgan's provocation for striking the lieutenant was
great, but it is also well known that in his young days he
needed little excuse for fisticuffs and became very adept at
taking on all comers whether he or they were in liquor or
out. After the French war the young wagoner's physical
prowess and love of brawling made him the acknowledged
king of Battletown (now Berryville), a tavern center ten
miles east of Winchester, Virginia.[14]

When the Revolution broke out, Daniel Morgan, now
somewhat gentled by marriage and the birth of two daugh-
ters,[15] raised a regiment of 96 riflemen and marched them
from Winchester to Boston, a distance of 600 miles in three
weeks without losing a man. In September of 1775 he set out
for Quebec with the little army under Benedict Arnold
which proposed to make Canada a fourteenth embattled
colony against Britain. Eleven hundred men marched from
Boston on that expedition on September 13, 1775. On
November 9 the wondering French habitants on the banks of
the St. Lawrence saw 600 starving scarecrows emerge from the
forest and prepare to attack a fortress. This tattered band
had fought its way through 350 miles of winter wilderness,
portaging 400-pound bateaux over the terrible Height of
Land, only to lose them in the rapids of Seven Mile Stream
and the Chaudiere River. After their food ran out their diet
consisted of such things as boiled moccasins, roasted shot
pouches, the captain's Newfoundland dog, soap, and hair

grease, but not, to their eternal credit, one another. In their forefront all the way was Daniel Morgan, six feet tall, broad in the shoulder and deep in the chest, with a mule skinner's voice and a temper to match, but quick to cool as he was to explode, incapable of bearing a grudge for long, and capable of enduring hardships that would have killed ten ordinary men.[16]

Furthermore, after General Montgomery and Colonel Arnold were put out of action in the first phases of the night assault on Quebec, Captain Morgan all but succeeded in taking the fortress citadel. He probably never really had a chance of holding it, save in his own estimation, but for a brief period of glory the city's capture was a tangible possibility. The affair happened in this manner: after Arnold was wounded, three field officers with the advance attacking force refused to take over Arnold's command and asked Morgan to accept it instead since he had seen previous combat and they had not. Morgan considered that their argument reflected "great credit on their judgment." He promptly took charge and attacked a two-gun battery. The snow-clogged guns missed fire. Morgan's troops rushed forward with ladders to scale the battlement. Morgan was first up the ladder and over the wall, his men following fast behind him. The gun crews fled. Morgan pursued, bellowing at them to throw down their arms if they expected quarter. The terrified soldiers obeyed. The noise and confusion created by Morgan and his handful of men in the snow and the darkness caused the townspeople to believe that the entire American army was upon them. People ran from the upper town and surrendered in "whole platoons." Commandeering a priest to act as interpreter, Morgan went in to the upper town in a state he described as *"incog."* He found no persons in arms at all. Returning to his men he called a council of the few officers he had with him, but here he was overruled by what he termed *"sound judgment and good reasoning."* The field officers who had refused to act earlier now assumed the prerogatives of rank. They pointed out that Morgan had more prisoners than he had men, that if he went on without waiting for General Montgomery and the main body to catch up with him he would be breaking orders, that *prudence* and *caution* demanded that he wait for the general. They did not know of course that Montgomery was already dead. *"To these good reasons,"* said Morgan, *"I gave up my own opinion and lost the town. . . . It was still in our power to have taken the garrison."*[17]

Now this is important, for it is the very essence of Morgan. He knew perfectly well when, in later years, he wrote his own account of his military career, from which the above is extracted, that sound judgment and good reasoning were quite correct when they told him that he could not hold Quebec. But he also knew, or the foolhardy and antic Celt in him knew, that there are times when sound judgment and good reasoning are not quite enough, not quite what is needed for the purpose—times when the fantastic, the unorthodox win out over the conventional and proper. It may be added that the frontiersman in Morgan also knew, from hard schooling, that the right tools are not always at hand. On such occasions a man makes do with those that are available—retooling or realigning them to suit the necessity. Imagination to conceive the untried and ability to make use of what one has were crucial to the battle of Cowpens.

Morgan's proposal of a diversion into Georgia was checked effectively by receipt from Greene of news of General Alexander Leslie's arrival with 2000 reinforcements for Cornwallis.[18] Morgan had also learned through his own intelligence that Tarleton was probably on the march. Early in January, 1781, a lad of nine, accompanied by his father, sought out Morgan in the camp at Grindall's Shoals on the Pacolet. The boy said that he had been in Cornwallis' camp a few days earlier. "I drove the old bull and some potatoes down to the British camp and Daddy told me not to forget anything I heard." His youth and innocent mien had effectively disguised from the British the size and sensitivity of the lad's ears. He had managed to loiter close to Cornwallis' tent upon the heels of a booted young officer in a green jacket, plumes, and a hurry.

"Colonel Tarleton," the boy told Morgan, "was ordered to take a thousand men and follow you up and fight you wherever you could be found." The Old Wagoner was sufficiently impressed by this information to offer the boy a guinea as reward. The lad asked instead to be enrolled as drummer with Morgan's army. With his father's consent Morgan accepted him. Two weeks later the boy beat his first charge at Cowpens.[19]

The Dummer Boy of Cowpens may be as apocryphal as the Drummer Boy of Shiloh or the geese that alerted Rome. That the father came may indicate that the father was the agent and the boy the instrument; the boy could enter the British camp without much suspicion being aroused, where the father could not. That both man and boy are nameless is no discredit to the story. Persons who deliver intelligence are, by their own and the recipient's discretion, frequently nameless. A guinea offered to a boy of nine seems excessive in view of the known lack of specie in the southern war chest. However, it is also known that two categories of personnel in the American Revolution, both British and American, could, and did, demand specie for their services. These were intelligence agents and express riders. For both categories the wages of failure were violent, sudden, and often ignominious death; consequently the wages of success were high.[20]

In any case, there appears to have been an interval of a week or more without anything happening to bear out the boy's information. On January 15, 1781, General Daniel Morgan wrote a letter to General Nathanael Greene. Just

how much knowledge he had of Tarleton's whereabouts
when he began the letter, it is impossible to determine. His
later battle report states that on the 14th he "received certain
intelligence that Lord Cornwallis and Lt. Col. Tarleton were
both in motion, and that their movements clearly indicated
their intentions of dislodging me . . ."[21]

However, in the opening of his letter on the 15th to
Greene, Morgan merely mentions that he has changed position from Grindall's Shoals on the Pacolet to Burr's Mills on
Thicketty Creek. The implication could well be that the
move was occasioned, as was so often the case, simply by the
fact that there was corn meal available at Burr's Mills while
the supply on the Pacolet was exhausted, for Morgan goes on
to say: "I find it impracticable to procure more provisions in
this quarter than is absolutely necessary; indeed it has been
with the greatest difficulty that I have been able to effect
this."[22]

Then Morgan's aching body and his discouragement got
the best of him:

I request that I may be recalled with my detachment and
that General Davidson and Colonel Pickens may be left with
the militia of North and South Carolina and Georgia. They
will not be so much an object of the enemy's attention and
will be capable of being a check on the disaffected, which is
all that I can effect. Colonel Pickens is a valuable, discreet,
and attentive officer, and has the confidence of the militia.[23]

In brief, Morgan asked that he and his 290 Marylanders,
his Virginia militia, and Washington's cavalry be permitted to
return to the main Continental army, leaving Pickens and
Davidson with what Morgan estimated as 340 militia[24] to
continue the job of harassing Tories and "spiriting up"
Patriots in the back country. This certainly does not sound as
though Morgan, at this writing, knew of any large enemy
force in his vicinity, but merely, as he stated in the later

battle report, that he had learned that Tarleton and Cornwallis were on the move and that he considered it highly
probable that their intent was to seek him out. Lest Morgan
be accused of contemplating outright desertion of Pickens'
and Davidson's men, it should be remembered that these
militia, if they found themselves hard pressed, could do as
they had done many times before in the seesaw of southern
fortunes—simply melt in un-uniformed, homespun anony-
mity into the swamps and forests, to come out and fight again
another day. Morgan's Maryland regulars were a much more
obvious target that could not so easily disappear into the
countryside.

Morgan's letter to Greene must have been written over a
period of time and interruptions. Before its conclusion one,
or more probably two, expresses arrived with news that
radically altered the course of events. Morgan was in the
process of assuring Greene that, while wishing to be recalled,
he would cheerfully acquiesce in Greene's determination
when he heard: "Colonel Tarleton has crossed the Tyger at
Musgroves's Mill; his force we cannot learn."[25] But learn it
he did in the course of the next few hours or minutes: "We
have just heard that Tarleton's force is eleven to twelve
hundred British."[26] The 1100 to 1200 British when they
crossed the Tyger were some ten miles from Morgan. The
Old Wagoner sent off his letter to Greene and prepared to
march.

Cornwallis had not been idle. At his interview with Tarleton on December 28, he had told his trusted subordinate that
he planned to resume his campaign in North Carolina.[27] The
addition to his command of 2000 British regulars made the
earl sanguine of success and of an early juncture with Benedict Arnold in what Cornwallis had long considered the
crucial state of Virginia.[28] First, however, the menace to
Ninety Six which Morgan's presence in the back country

offered must be destroyed. Tarleton was to seek out Morgan and "push him to the utmost."[29]

Tarleton set off with his usual celerity. On January 4 he wrote Cornwallis that Morgan was on the west side of the Broad River with 1200 men. Tarleton proposed to advance and either destroy this force or push it before him over the Broad towards King's Mountain. In the latter case, if Cornwallis on his march into North Carolina would proceed up the east bank of the Broad toward the mountain, Morgan, presuming he escaped destruction by Tarleton before he forded the river, would certainly be caught between two British corps after he crossed it and be crushed completely.[30]

Cornwallis replied to Tarleton's letter on January 5 saying that Tarleton had understood him perfectly, that Tarleton's baggage had been forwarded under the escort of the British regular reinforcements requested. Cornwallis and the van would march on January 6 for Bullock Creek with General Leslie to follow next day.[31]

By January 9 Cornwallis was at McAlister's plantation and somewhat behind schedule. The rains that plagued Morgan fell equally from heaven on the British. Leslie, striving to join Cornwallis, bogged down in sudden swamps, which a few days previously had been dry ground. Cornwallis stopped to wait for him, supposing that the rising waters had also slowed Tarleton. Tarleton, informed of this, shortened his own marches until Cornwallis wrote him on January 14 that "Leslie is at last got out of the swamps."[32] At that Tarleton again put spurs to his horses, reflecting sourly that he "had had many more difficulties with swamps on the Tyger and the Enoree rivers than Leslie could possibly have found between the Catawba and the Broad."[33]

Nevertheless, the young dragoon was now confident that Cornwallis would attack Morgan's rear when the Old Wagoner crossed the Broad River. At eight in the morning of January 16, Tarleton wrote Cornwallis:

My Lord

I have been most cruelly retarded by the waters. Morgan is in force and gone for Cherokee Ford. I am now on my march. I wish he could be stopped.

> I have the Honor to be Your most
> Devoted Serv't
> Ban. Tarleton.[34]

"THE TROOPS I HAVE THE HONOR TO COMMAND"[1]

Roughly twenty-four hours elapsed between the time that Morgan at Burr's Mills on Thicketty Creek heard of Tarleton's advance in force and the time the American commander took position at the Cowpens on the evening of January 16, 1781. Just what Morgan's plans were, or how they developed during those hours, will probably never be accurately known. Certain it is that he was putting distance between himself and Tarleton. But whether his object was to elude his pursuer by retreat or to withdraw only until he could make a stand on ground of his own choosing is by no means clear. Morgan's own letters of this period are no great source of information on this point. He says that he left Grindall's Ford (or Shoals) on the 14th. By his own account he was at the mills at an unspecified time on January 15 and left that place "in the morning" of January 16. "In the evening" of January 16 he was at the Cowpens, distant from Burr's Mills about twelve miles, and about seven miles from Cherokee Ford on Broad River, where Tarleton believed him headed.

Morgan knew that Tarleton was hard on his heels. "On the evening of the 16th inst., they [the British] took possession of the ground I had removed from in the morning....."[2] Tarleton bears this out: "Tarleton's Legion occupied some log houses (built before by Ferguson) from which Morgan had retreated so recently as to leave a meal half cooked, which the Legion promptly ate."[3] The British were hungry after their march. For many of them it was their last meal. Morgan's troops were more fortunate. All these ate supper on January 16 and breakfast on January 17.

There has been much after-the-fact criticism of Morgan for making a stand at Cowpens. Morgan, in his later years had his own explanation,[4] but this also was much after the fact. The sober truth appears to be that he had no great choice in the matter.[5] On January 15 his troops, as already noted, were scattered. There were small detachments of them all along the Pacolet guarding the numerous fords, as Tarleton found when he attempted to cross the swollen stream.[6] This he succeeded in doing only by the strategem of doubling back on his tracks and going into a darkened camp on the night of the 15th. Before dawn of the 16th Morgan's scattered troops were on the march to join their commander, and Tarleton managed to ford the Pacolet at Easterwood Shoals six miles below Morgan's rear guard.[7]

Morgan, meanwhile, was pointed toward Cherokee Ford, moving through byways. He was encumbered by those wagons which he had already told Greene were an impediment,[8] and had only part of his force collected. Besides those from the fords on the Pacolet now on their way to join him, he expected hourly to be reinforced by Colonel Pickens with 150 newly embodied militia.[9] All of these people must make junction with Morgan somewhere. The meeting place in this wooded, wilderness country without even a village worthy of the name, must be specific, well-known, large enough to accommodate several hundred men, and if possible it must provide forage for horses and food for men. Cherokee Ford did not fit this description. With the Broad in flood, or any river in flood, a ford may be wiped out by rising waters. The waters had been rising all over this misbegotten country for the past five weeks. To have gathered hundreds of men, horses, and accompanying baggage at a crossing which might prove impassable was to invite disaster, especially when most of the men were raw recruits and Morgan had no boats.

However, seven miles from the ford was a spot that met all of the necessary qualifications. Hannah's Cowpens was an open meadow with a scattering of trees and burned tree stumps. The area contained a few fine springs where horses and cattle might be watered. Between the trees grew a coarse wild grass that throve hardily both summer and winter.[10] Here, then, was room for the troops to gather, and forage for the horses. Without forage Morgan could not march. There might even be food at the Cowpens for the men. It was customary in the Carolinas for the farmers to mark the young cattle by clipping their ears and then turn them loose in the woods to fend for themselves until roundup time in the fall. Quite possibly some of these lean, semiwild steers had sought the lush grass of the Cowpens for winter feed. Best of all, everyone for miles around knew the Cowpens. It made an ideal meeting place. Here it was that the King's Mountain men had gathered the previous October to march to Ferguson's destruction.

Perhaps Morgan meant merely to collect his men at the Cowpens, allow them and the horses to feed, and then march them in some sort of order to the ford on Broad River. "My situation at the Cowpens," he wrote, "enabled me to improve any advantage I might gain, and to provide better for my own security should I be unfortunate. These reasons induced me to take this post at the risk of its wearing the face of a retreat."[11]

Henry Lee, in his criticism of Morgan's choice of position, is quick to seize on the word "retreat." Morgan, Lee says, was a fighter who did not relish the thought of running from his enemy. "This decision [to fight] grew out of irritation of temper which . . . overruled the suggestions of his sound and discriminating judgment."[12]

We have already heard Morgan on the matter of sound

judgment and good reasoning. But let us consider the situation more closely. For one thing, there is no evidence that when he halted at the Cowpens at dusk, Morgan was in any kind of temper or excitement. Since dawn he had come twelve miles over very rough country, hauling wagons with him, on roads that were at best mere cattle trails of red clay mud. Twelve miles is no great distance, but in the circumstances it was probably the best that could be managed. The season was January when the hours of daylight are brief. At dusk Morgan was still seven miles from Cherokee Ford, and Pickens and his militia had not yet joined the main body. Morgan sent scouts ahead to determine the present condition of the ford; he dispatched others to the rear to feel out Tarleton's whereabouts. While his men had an evening meal, Morgan and his officers examined the terrain.

It was an open wood, some five hundred yards long and nearly as wide, entirely free from underbrush. From the edge of the forest through which the American troops had come, the ground rose gradually to a small hill about three hundred yards from the forest edge. This hill dipped behind to a grassy swale about eighty yards in length to rise again to a second slightly higher hill almost parallel with the first. Behind this hill was more open wood with Broad River in the rear. "Certainly as good a place for action as Lt. Col. Tarleton could desire," wrote Tarleton later. "America does not produce any more suitable for the nature of the troops under his command."[13] In short, it was an ideal field for cavalry, and Tarleton had at least three times as many cavalry as Morgan had. Furthermore, Morgan's flanks were "in the air." There was nothing in that open plain in the way of cover either to the right or left, no wood or swamp close by for protection.

If it came to fighting, Morgan considered this absence of morasses an advantage. He knew from past experience all about militiamen and swamps. If there was a swamp within view, militia immediately became seized with an all but uncontrollable desire to make for it. "Nothing could have detained them from it."[14] When his scouts reported the Broad River still dangerously high and difficult to cross, Morgan considered this good also. "As for the fighting part of the matter, men fight as much as they find necessary and no more,"[15] he said. "When men are forced to fight, they will sell their lives dearly."[16]

All through the bitter night parties of militia rode into camp. Pickens, dour and rock-steady as usual, brought 150 with him. Others followed in bands of fifteen, twenty, and thirty. They were all in good spirits, full of the ignorant courage of puppies, calling for ammunition after the manner of all militia and thirsting, so they said, for Tarleton's blood.[17] Whatever his earlier plan may have been, Morgan in the course of the evening determined to fight, to the loud cheers of his troops.[18] It is hard to see this as a decision of pique; rather it was a function of necessity. Without boats he dare not attempt the passage of the river in the dark. If he waited until dawn, it would almost certainly be too late. His patrols reported in at intervals until well past midnight. As they came out of the dark forest their reports were always the same. Tarleton was getting closer and closer, putting ever fewer miles and fewer swollen rivulets between himself and his adversary.[19]

Morgan was quite aware that, however judicious and in accordance with Greene's orders his withdrawal had been, to the men under him the day's march represented a shameful lack of courage. "Many a hearty curse had been vented against General Morgan . . . for retreating, as we thought, to avoid a fight."[20] If this was the temper of the men who knew him, to the eager and green would-be warriors who had just joined him, further withdrawal would look like a rout; they would undoubtedly melt away to their homes as fast as they had left them.

Most important of all, Morgan knew Tarleton's manner of fighting. There was no question of Tarleton's courage, but "it seems to have borne a stronger affinity to the ferocity of a bloodhound than to the bravery of a bull-dog, and to have been more thoroughly aroused by the flight of the enemy than by his opposition."[21] "These dragoons never fought well; they had repeatedly hacked to pieces a flying, unarmed, or supplicating enemy."[22] But, as we have seen, when faced by the determined opposition of Davie's handful of men at Charlotte, and also by the more numerous force at Blackstock's where Sumter was so severely wounded, the Green Horse had displayed considerable circumspection, if not timidity. In short, their *forte* was never to stand and fight but to pursue, to overhaul and to destroy. Since Morgan knew from the reports he had that there were eleven hundred British on his tail, he knew that Tarleton's Legion made up but a portion of them. The fighting attributes of the other units were an unknown quantity. Yet this was a chance Morgan had to take. The one thing he was perfectly sure of was that he could not let Tarleton catch him in the act of running. Even if by some miracle he crossed the Broad with the militia still collected, the nearest place beyond the river where he could make a stand was King's Mountain, and that was twenty miles away. Tarleton, at the rate he was pushing his men, would surely close with him before he had covered half that distance.[23] The time for running was past.

Once Morgan determined to fight he was indefatigable in his preparations. He had made no miraculous recovery from his ailments. The sciatica still gnawed at his hip. All day long it had been agony to trot a horse. But his spirits rose above the pain. He seemed to be everywhere in the firelit camp. Bawling at the wagon masters, he directed them with the baggage wagons safely five miles to the rear, close to the river. The transport infantry horses were picketed well back also, secured to the boughs of young pine trees in a small grove that provided some cover. They were saddled and bridled to be ready for immediate use should the need arise, but they were also closely guarded to protect them against the chance that some faint hearts might leap aboard them and be off when the going became rough.[24] Forward of these animals Washington's eighty cavalry horses and fifty selected infantry horses formed a picket line behind the second little hillock that broke the rolling meadow. Morgan's first care was to strengthen Washington's dragoons by the addition of volunteer mounted infantry, thus equalizing somewhat the discrepancy in numbers between the horse of the Americans and those of Tarleton. There was no lack of volunteer horsemen. The best qualified of them drew swords from the quartermaster and were premitted to impress any horse they chose, exclusive of the cavalry mounts, for their own use.[25]

These arrangements completed, Morgan explained to his officers his proposed disposition of the troops. On the first of the two hillocks in the Cowpens, the one closest to the wood from which Tarleton must emerge, Morgan placed the main line under the command of Colonel John Eager Howard of the Maryland contingent. Howard's light infantry and the Maryland and Delaware Continentals held the center. Virginia and Georgia militia were on the left and a body of Virginia militia on the right. One hundred and fifty yards in advance Morgan placed three hundred militia of North and South Carolina under Andrew Pickens in a thin line three hundred yards broad. In front of them and at about the same distance from Pickens as Pickens was from the main line, one hundred and fifty picked riflemen from Georgia and North Carolina under Majors John Cunningham and Joseph McDowell were thrown out as sharpshooters. Back of all these, just behind the crest of the rear hillock, Washington's cavalry and Georgia's mounted infantry under Lieutenant Colonel James McCall were posted as reserve,[26] "so

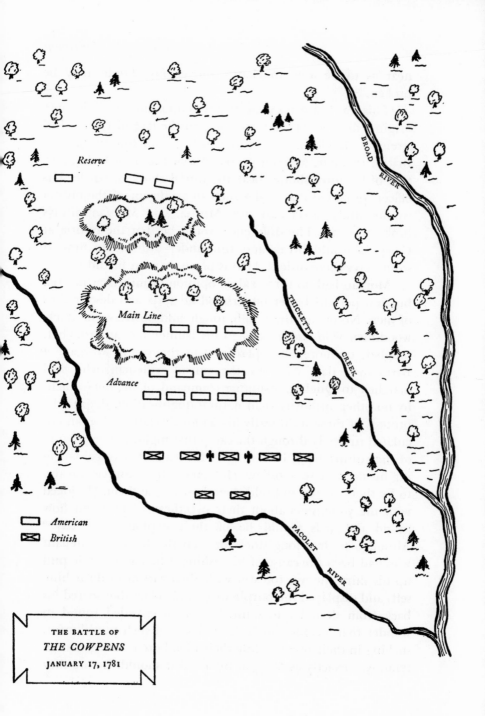

Reserve

Main Line

Advance

American
British

THICKETTY CREEK

BROAD RIVER

PACOLET RIVER

THE BATTLE OF
THE COWPENS
JANUARY 17, 1781

near as to be able to charge the enemy should they be broken."[27]

This was Morgan's plan. It was as unorthodox as Greene's original division of his weak army in the face of Cornwallis' strength. By placing his militia in the front line to face the British regulars, Morgan proposed that the most feeble portion of his force should bear the initial shock of battle. His officers protested that under such an arrangement the militia would surely break and run. Militia, said Morgan, always broke and ran. The difference would be that the militia at Cowpens would break and run under orders. He himself would give those orders. That is precisely what he did.[28]

Morgan had no very exalted opinion of militia as militia, but few persons better understood all sorts and descriptions of men. No one of the rough, tough, and obstreperous backwoodsmen who had flocked to his banner was any rougher, tougher, or more obstreperous than the young Morgan of Battletown days or than the unruly rifleman who had marched to Quebec, assuming command of his detachment by no other authority than natural qualification, despite the protests of those technically his seniors.[29] Daniel Morgan circulated tirelessly through the camp that night, the very figure of the culture hero, bellowing in his teamster's voice, laughing his deep-chested guffaw. He helped the volunteer cavalry to fix their swords and told them how to use them. He joked with the youngsters about their sweethearts and about how proud the girls would be of their exploits next day.[30] Although he had long since forgiven the British lieutenant who had been the cause of his lashing,[31] he had his aide pull up his shirt (he was too stiff with rheumatism to do it himself) and displayed the purple weals and ridges that scored his back from shoulder to waist. The men crowded round in wonder that anyone should have survived such punishment, sucking in their breath while their blood grew hot against all tyranny,[32] exactly as Morgan intended it should. Before they wound themselves into their blankets that night, not only the officers, but every man in the command knew what was expected of him in the morning and was determined to do it or die trying. After all, what was asked of the militia was not impossible:

"Just hold up your heads, boys, three fires, and you are free, and then when you return to your homes, how the old folks will bless you, and the girls kiss you for your gallant conduct!" I don't believe he slept a wink that night.[33]

Probably Morgan did not. Quite possibly he had not slept much for many nights before. A man in his physical condition dozes briefly and wakes to pain. But now he had something more pressing to think on than his own misery. It acted as a kind of tonic for a while.

The next morning, January 17, 1781, between six and six-thirty, an hour before daylight, Morgan's videttes were driven in. Captain Inman of the Georgia militia, who had been in charge of the videttes, reported that Tarleton was five miles away, marching light and fast. Morgan filled his lungs and shouted, "Boys, get up! Benny is coming!"[34] Men spilled out of blankets into the cold. The horses on the picket line whickered and rolled white eyes in the leaping fire-shine. Five miles. Before Tarleton could make that five miles the men could have a hot breakfast. Morgan saw to it that they did.

Banastre Tarleton when he crossed the Pacolet had with him his own Legion of 550 horse and foot. In addition he had a contingent of Royal Artillery armed with two three-pounders—light field guns mounted on legs and therefore referred to as grasshoppers. He had also three battalions from British regular regiments—the 7th Foot, the 17th Light Dragoons, and the 71st Highlanders. The men of these battalions were trained troops, veterans of many campaigns, well equipped and beautifully uniformed. They were officered by men who had made a profession of the army; some of them had seen service before Tarleton was born. They had battle-scarred colors, trumpeters, drummers and bagpipers, and proud regimental traditions that went back for generations. By contrast the legionnaires, American Tories all of them, had no tradition but that of allegiance to their young commander and pride in their reputation for prowess and ferocity. Moreover, the Legion had seen hard service since the fall of Charleston. The ranks had been thinned by attrition. Some of those recruited to take the place of the fallen had previously seen service on both sides of the conflict. Some may have served under Gates at Camden. They were hired sabers of dubious worth, capable but not entirely reliable. Their first loyalty was to their own skins.[35]

When Tarleton reached Morgan's old camp on Thicketty Creek on the evening of January 16 to find that his quarry had fled, he immediately dispatched "patroles and spies" to reconnoitre. Early in the night "a party of determined loyalists made an American colonel prisoner, who had casually left the line of march and conducted him to the British camp."[36] Tarleton examined the militia colonel, rather thoroughly it may be assumed, and determined to hang on Morgan's rear with the double object of cutting off reinforcements said to be approaching and preventing Morgan from passing Broad River. The identity of the moonlit colonel remains unestablished, but it is not impossible that his casual wandering had a purpose. Certainly somebody during the night gave Tarleton a good deal of misinformation as to the enemy's strength. Tarleton believed, or professed to believe, that his opponent had a force of 1920 men.[37]

Nevertheless, at two o'clock in the morning of January 17, the buglers sounded reveille in the British camp. By three o'clock, traveling light, the army was on the march over the route the Americans had taken the previous day. The baggage and wagons remained behind with orders to move up at day-break. As Tarleton described it:

Three companies of light infantry, supported by the legion infantry, formed the advance: the 7th regiment and the guns, and the 1st battalion of the 71st, composed the center; and the cavalry and the mounted infantry brought up the rear. The ground which the Americans had passed being broken and much intersected by creeks and ravines, the march of the British troops during the darkness was exceedingly slow, on account of the time employed in examining the front and flanks as they proceeded. Before dawn, Thinkelle [Thicketty] creek was passed, when an advanced guard of cavalry was ordered to the front. The enemy's patrole was approaching, was pursued and overtaken: two troops of dragoons, under Captain Ogilvie, of the legion, were then ordered to reinforce the advanced guard, and to harass the rear of the enemy. The march had not continued long in this manner, before the commanding officer in front reported that the American troops were halted and forming.[38]

This would seem to indicate that Tarleton had not been sure up to this point that he was not pursuing a fleeing foe. It had been a long eight miles in the dark and the cold with men stumbling over tree trunks, in and out of creeks, and over one another, cursing softly. The dragoon horses, following close, purposefully nudged the rear of any stragglers. The pace of the march was broken periodically by little alarums and excursions as the "patroles and spies" came in to report, tersely making themselves known and shoving past the troops to get to the officers they were concerned with, then pelting off again as mysteriously as they had come, into the swallowing dark. The guides who led the army were Loyalist backwoodsmen. At least one hoped they were loyal. This was one of the minor horrors of this war. One never knew for sure, on British side or American, just how true was the allegiance of guides or spies.

Marching at night in weariness in unfamiliar country can cause a man's courage to run out of him like sawdust out of a rag doll. It is to the credit of British discipline that when, toward eight in the morning, after five hours of footing it up hill and down dale, Tarleton proposed immediate battle "the animation of the officers and the alacrity of the soldiers afforded the most promising assurance of success."[39]

Meanwhile, Morgan's men, having breakfasted comfortably, formed in line of battle according to plan. Morgan rode up and down the lines telling them to "ease their joints," that is, to sit or stand at ease in place, while they waited for "Benny" to appear. The general told the sharpshooters in the front to take advantage of any cover the trees or grass afforded and to hold their fire until the enemy was within shooting distance. He put them on their mettle by exciting the Georgians and Carolinians in the line to prove which state could outshoot the other. Riding back to the militia line under Pickens, he reminded them that they were to fire two well directed volleys and then retire in good order, firing by regiments as they fell back to take position on the left of the main line in the rear. To the main line of Continentals and Virginians he repeated his warning not to be alarmed at the apparent retreat of the front line; it was all part of the plan. He dispatched orders to Washington and the cavalry reserve to assist in rallying the militia should they fly, and to protect them should they be pursued. Then, confidently and with an air of the greatest assurance, he took post in the rear of the main line and awaited the approach of the enemy.[40]

He had not long to wait. The morning was bitter cold. The men were slapping their hands together and stamping their feet against the chill. As the sky yellowed in the east with the sunrise, the troops saw movement in the shadow of the forest at the lower end of the long, frost-covered meadow. Horsemen in green jackets and plumed brass helmets moved out from the trees and stood briefly looking, their horses' breaths steaming in the still air. Then they went back into the wood to emerge again, accompained by long lines of men in scarlet and white, by Highlanders in kilts, and horsemen in green and horsemen in scarlet. The lines deployed, their members shedding excess gear as they did so. The now risen sun winked off the muzzles of two three-pounders, manned by soldiers in the blue uniform of the Royal Artillery.

Tarleton placed his light infantry on the right with the Legion infantry to the left of it, forming the center, and the 7th Regiment on the left. The two guns on their grasshopper legs were placed midway of the left and right. Fifty dragoons protected each British flank and stood alert to threaten the flanks of the enemy. The kilted Highlanders of the 71st and two hundred dragoons composed a reserve one hundred and fifty yards in the rear.[41]

While his lines were forming, Tarleton moved forward with a small party to investigate the disposition of Morgan's troops. A sharp fire from the nearly concealed skirmish line decided him that it would be prudent to withdraw, which he did with some alacrity. He then directed fifty cavalry to charge the sharpshooters. The horsemen galloped forward with a shout. Cunningham with his Georgians on the left and McDowell with his Carolinians on the right held the riflemen steady. They retired slowly according to orders, firing as they did so to such effect as to empty fifteen saddles. The remaining cavalrymen recoiled on the British front and the American riflemen withdrew upslope into the line of Pickens' militia.[42]

The sudden check displeased the impetuous Tarleton. His lines were not yet completely formed. Major Newmarsh of the 7th on the left was still posting his officers, and the Highlanders of the reserve had not yet assumed their positions. Nevertheless, Tarleton ordered the grasshopper on the right to open fire. The light and Legion infantry advanced under cover of the gun to within three hundred yards of the enemy.[43] Shortly thereafter the second three-pounder joined in the fire, and the 7th Regiment moved into position. Tarleton, taking post in the rear, ordered the whole line forward. The 7th Regiment had a proportion of recruits. Some of these nervously opened fire as they moved out. This, says Tarleton, "was suppressed and the troops moved in as good a line as troops could move at open files."[44]

Apparently Tarleton's British-drilled eyes found the advance a little ragged. It was otherwise with Thomas Young. Young had volunteered as a mounted infantryman to support Washington's cavalry. The British artillery made it so hot for this reserve posted on the hill where Morgan believed it to be out of the line of fire[45] that Washington felt compelled to shift to the rear of the American right wing.[46] Young, however, forgot any personal fears he may have entertained of the cannon shot in sheer delight at the glory of the scene: "The British line advanced at a sort of trot with a loud halloo. It was the most beautiful line I ever saw. . . . I heard Morgan say, 'They gave us the British halloo, boys. Give them the Indian halloo, by G--!' "[47]

As the British advance came on, the Americans showed signs of being about to emulate the 7th Regiment recruits by firing too soon. Morgan galloped along the lines shouting, "Don't fire!" Then when the British line was one hundred yards from the American front, the order came to fire. Pickens' militia held steady and poured in a withering volley at killing distance, aiming for the epaulets. The resultant toll in officers was disproportionately high, and disorder immediately prevailed in the British line. The militia calmly reloaded and fired again with telling effect. The British sagged, then rallied and prepared to charge with the bayonet. Pickens ordered the planned retreat to the American left.[48]

At first the withdrawal was orderly, but those militia on the right had to make a long traverse of the American main line to reach the left. The fifty cavalry posted on the British right saw their opportunity and charged, sabers aloft and yelling like the baying of all the hounds of hell.[49] James Collins, a veteran of King's Mountain, who by his own admission usually became sick at the sight of blood, was so unfortunate as to be posted on the militia right. With lively visions of his own imminent destruction, he took to his heels, accompanied helter-skelter by many of his companions. "Now," thought he, "my hide is in the loft."[50]

The commander of the militia company on the right was Lieutenant Joseph Hughes. Hughes was also a veteran of King's Mountain, a tall young man of twenty years, remarkable for his fleetness of foot. The sight of his men scampering off in panic before the Green Horse struck him as undignified and disgraceful. He proceeded to outrun them, pass them, face about to strike at them with the flat of his sword, and, no whit winded by his exertions, shout, "You damned cowards, halt and fight!" The men, however, were at first too demoralized to hear anything but the thunder of hooves behind them. They eluded Hughes and scampered on unheeding, whereupon Hughes again put wings on his heels, outdistanced them and repeated his tactics, still to no avail.[51]

Meanwhile, the British, taking the flight of the militia as indication of early victory, added their shouts to those of the dragoons and moved forward rapidly, if unevenly, (they were in some confusion through the loss of so many of their officers) toward the American main line. The latter let them come until the last of the militia crossed the front. Then Howard's Continentals and Tate's and Triplett's Virginians opened fire with deadly accuracy.[52] The British, who had been coming on at a run intending to bayonet what they believed to be the demoralized Americans, were brought to a sudden, disillusioned halt. They returned the American fire with a volley from their muskets. Here, however, they were at a great disadvantage. The Americans on the hillock were in good order. While a part of them reloaded their muskets, others protected their comrades with a volley. A musket can only be reloaded by a man on his feet and standing still. In the ragged formation in which the British now found themselves the unfortunate individual engaged in loading made an excellent target, as he quickly discovered. However, these were veteran regiments. Although checked briefly they came on again courageously, and a bitter struggle ensued for nearly half an hour. Then Tarleton, watching from the rear, saw the British advance slacken: "Indications of a disposition to retire making themselves manifest, Tarleton ordered the reserve infantry and cavalry into action."[53]

The Highlanders of the 71st, bagpipes skirling, stepped smartly forward under Major McArthur to the support of the sagging British line, which immediately showed signs of reanimation. Tarleton at the head of the cavalry reserve commenced a wide sweep preparatory to attacking the American flank.[54]

At this moment that body of British horse which had pursued the militia behind the hill flew past the American left in the wildest disorder, wearing expressions of pained astonishment. They had scattered out in careless abandon as they approached the hill expecting to saber defenseless militia when Colonel Washington's dragoons, who had been watching them all the while, were suddenly among them like a whirlwind. Taken completely by surprise they turned and fled with Washington's cavalry hot on their heels. The pleased James Collins, whose hide had been saved from the loft, for that day at least, noted that the British troopers "appeared to be as hard to stop as a drove of wild Choctaw steers going to a Pennsylvania market."[55]

Washington pursued them almost into the British lines and then turned and trotted back to his position in the rear, his observant eyes noting as he did so the disorder in the

British advanced line which had never wholly recovered from its loss of officers in the first volley.[56]

The repulse of the British cavalry had relieved the militia of their greatest terror. In the swale behind the second hill Pickens, Morgan, and the redoubtable Hughes—oblivious of the blood oozing from a bandaged saber cut on his hand—[57] were able to rally most of the Georgians and Carolinians, although some few of them succeeded in mounting their horses and quitting the field for that day.[58] Reforming under Pickens, the militiamen prepared to advance to the support of the American right. They had made a complete circuit of the field during the half hour that the stubborn Continentals held off the British advance.

By now the American right faced serious trouble. Tarleton had extended his Highlanders so far to his left that their line stretched beyond the American right. Howard, in command of both Continentals and Virginians, saw that he was in danger of being outflanked. It was obvious also that the reserve cavalry was about to charge his flank. Howard hastily ordered the Virginia company on the extreme right to face about so as to make a right angle with the others for the purpose of repelling the flankers. The order as given required the Virginians to turn completely around, facing the rear, and then to wheel in a quarter circle, which would leave them facing left.[59] In the confusion of the moment the order was misunderstood. "First a part and then the whole of the company commenced a retreat. The officers along the line seeing this and supposing that order had been given for retreat, faced their men about and moved off."[60]

Thus when Morgan galloped up to inform Howard of the rallying of the militia, he found the whole second line moving to the rear. He immediately sought out Howard, who explained but pointed out the steadiness with which the men marched and said "that men were not beaten who retreated in that order."[61] Morgan observed them and agreed. The men were now descending the slope behind the first eminence on which they had originally been posted. Morgan ordered Howard to keep them moving until they came to the rising ground of the second hill near Washington's horse. He then galloped back to explain the maneuver to Pickens and Washington and to fix a proper place for Howard's men to halt and face about.[62]

Tarleton, seeing this withdrawal of the second line, was now sure of his victory. He ordered up the Legion cavalry and threw his entire reserve against the Americans. The men broke ranks and surged forward in jubilant disorder, each anxious to receive his share of glory. They reached the eminence the Americans had lately vacated and rushed madly down the rear slope. The watchful Washington from his post on the right could see more of the field than Morgan behind the hill. He sent word to Morgan, "They're coming on like a mob. Give them one fire and I'll charge them."[63]

Morgan's stentorian voice rang out along the line ordering the men to halt and face about. "Give them one fire and the day is ours!"[64] The oncoming British were within fifty yards of Howard's line when it turned like clockwork. "An unexpected fire at this instant from the Americans, who came about when they were retreating, stopped the British and threw them into confusion."[65] Most of Howard's men did not even raise their muskets; they fired from the hip. Thus when Howard ordered a bayonet charge they instantly poured down the slope on the broken British ranks.[66]

At the same period of time the militia, whom the British had last seen fleeing madly around the American left, and whom no Britisher expected to see again, turned up quite unexpectedly on the American right and opened a most galling fire on McArthur and his Highlanders, halting them in their tracks. At the same moment the British cavalry, who were in the act of charging the American flank, felt the full weight of Washington's horse. This tall, heavy, moon-faced young man, who had once been destined for the ministry,[67] appears to have combined on the battlefield the mobility of a centaur with the ferocity of a tiger. He led his dragoons completely through the charging British column at the first onslaught. Then he succeeded in checking the galloping horses and wheeling them—a most difficult maneuver—and charging the British again "with terrible effect."[68] The Green Horse had been hit twice in a matter of minutes, and this was quite enough for them. They took no further part in the action. Said Tarleton, "Above 200 dragoons forsook the field of battle."[69]

In the center, while the British were reeling under Howard's bayonet charge, Washington, now in their rear, bore down on them with his cavalry at full gallop. The greater part of the 7th Regiment threw down their arms and "fell upon their faces."[70] The light and Legion infantry likewise threw down their arms but attempted to seek safety in flight, scattering cartouche boxes on the way and doing "the prettiest sort of running."[71] They were soon overtaken by the volunteer mounted infantry, and all but a few of the fleetest surrendered about two hundred yards from the battle line. "An unaccountable panic," said Tarleton, "extended itself along the whole line."[72] Considering the overwhelming reversal they had all met within the period of a few minutes, the panic seems on the whole accountable.

The only part of the field on which resistance continued was on the American right. Pickens' militia and the stubborn Highlanders were there still engaged, the Highlanders falling back but fighting fiercely. Howard wheeled upon them with his regulars, throwing them off balance, whereupon the militia rushed in for hand-to-hand combat. Colonel James Jackson of Georgia seized the regimental colors, lost them at great risk of life and limb, and pushed on to seize the person of Major McArthur.[73] Their commander taken, and themselves surrounded by enemies and deserted by the cavalry, the 71st at last responded to Colonel Howard's summons to ground their arms. Colonel Pickens as commander of the militia, whose fight it had actually been, received McArthur's sword.[74]

The mortified Tarleton, meanwhile, had vainly been trying to induce the Legion cavalry to return to the field. Most of them refused to budge, but "fourteen officers and forty horsemen were not unmindful of their reputations, or the situation of their commanding officer."[75] With this loyal handful, Tarleton advanced with the object of bearing off the two grasshoppers, which comprised the only artillery he had. Even this solace was denied him. The blue-coated gunners had fiercely defended their pieces. Now all were either killed or wounded.[76] Colonel Howard noticed one of the untended guns and ordered Captain Ewing to take it. Captain Anderson, hearing the order, was seized with a desire for the prize. Both young officers raced for the piece neck and neck, until Anderson conceived the ingenious notion of using his spontoon (a kind of short pike with which junior infantry officers were armed) as a pole vault. This enabled him to make a long leap upon the gun and so claim the honor of capture.[77]

Balked of any chance to retrieve the guns, Tarleton was about to leave the field. Washington, busy securing prisoners, saw the small group of green-jacketed horsemen and surmised that Tarleton was among them. He instantly commanded a pursuit, but in the confusion that was going on over the surrender, few of his people heard him. Washington far outdistanced those who did. Tarleton, perceiving over his shoulder that Washington was virtually alone, wheeled his horse and, with two of his officers, advanced to meet him. One of the officers parried a blow aimed at him by Washington. Washington's sword, meeting the other's, broke midway. The British officer rose in his stirrups to cut Washington down when Washington's orderly, a fourteen-year-old boy named Collin, rode up and discharged his pistol into the officer's shoulder. The second officer with Tarleton now raised his sword, but Sergeant Major Perry, now come up, parried the blow and wounded this officer in the sword arm. Tarleton at last took advantage of his opportunity and thrust at Washington, who parried the blow with the remnants of his sword. As the American cavalry were now approaching in force the three British officers understandably galloped away but not before Tarleton discharged his pistol at Washington. He missed the man and wounded his horse. Thus Tarleton had the dubious honor of firing the last shot of the Battle of Cowpens at a disarmed adversary.[78]

While the above incident was taking place, Colonel Howard was busily engaged in receiving the swords of the officers of the 71st. One Captain Duncanson, having surrendered, remained very close to Howard's side. When Howard mounted and was about to ride off, Duncanson pulled at his saddle so vigorously as nearly to unhorse him. Howard turned on him angrily and demanded of him what he was about. Duncanson explained that the British had orders to give no quarter and so expected none. He feared what might happen when Howard's men, who were now coming toward him, got within reach of him.[79]

As a matter of record, the American officers were for a while hard put to it to restrain the men from giving the vanquished what they called "Tarleton's quarters."[80] Thanks, however, to the officers' swift efforts, Morgan wrote later, "Not a man was killed, wounded, or even insulted, after he surrendered. Had not the Britons during this contest received so many lessons in humanity, I should flatter myself that this might teach them a little, but I fear they are incorrigible."[81]

Tarleton, with his fourteen officers and forty horsemen, continued his retreat through the wood. In an open space they came upon what Tarleton later described as "a body of

Americans who had preceded the flight of the British and taken possession of their baggage."[82] Just how such a body had managed to penetrate unmolested quite through the British army to the back of the lines, Tarleton did not attempt to explain. The party was American in a sense, but it happened to consist of some fifty Loyalists who had been employed by the British in guiding and spying during the advance on the American camp. These worthies had prudently moved off when the battle was joined. Finding the British baggage unprotected, they conceived the notion of saving the British officers' equipment from the enemy by putting it to their own uses. When they heard the clatter of Tarleton's horses, they retreated to the bushes, expecting enemy cavalry. They were not quick enough for the dragoons, however, and since their homespun clothing and accoutrements differed in no way from that worn by many militiamen, the frustrated legionnaires vented their spleen on them, sabering them without mercy with their booty in their hands.[83]

Having disposed of the unfortunate Loyalists, Tarleton directed his column toward Broad River, intending to cross at one of the fords below Cherokee Ford. He still supposed that Cornwallis, from whom he had not heard since the letter of January 14, had proceeded as indicated to a post near King's Mountain on the east side of the Broad. Morgan could have informed him otherwise; he had had news about Cornwallis the night before.[84] Tarleton did not receive any account of the British army's movement until after the battle on January 17. "On route Tarleton heard with infinite grief and astonishment that the main army had not progressed beyond Turkey Creek."[85] Turkey Creek was twenty-five miles short of where Tarleton confidently expected his superior to be. From Winnsboro, Lord Cornwallis had taken ten full days to march forty miles. He had then sat down to wait for

Leslie without informing the commander of his light troops of his change in plan.

With heavy heart, Tarleton turned his column toward Hamilton's Ford. It is probably because of this change in course that Washington's dragoons, now pounding in pursuit, lost his trail.[86]

Morgan was left in command of the field after about an hour of very strenuous fighting. Despite the heat of the contest, the American loss proved surprisingly small: 12 killed and 60 wounded; no officer of rank was among either. The British lost 100 killed, 39 of them officers. Prisoners amounted to 229 wounded and more than 400 unhurt, nearly nine-tenths of the entire British force. Much of the British baggage was burned by the retreating British cavalry. Nevertheless, Morgan captured 800 stand of arms, two three-pound cannon, 60 Negro servants, 100 horses, 35 wagons, the colors of the 7th Regiment, a traveling forge, and "all the enemy's music."[87] Howard expressed to the captured Major McArthur his surprise at the precipitate manner in which the British troops had been brought into action. "And what can ye expect," replied the greying Scot dourly, "when troops are commanded by a rash, foolish boy?"[88]

"The troops I have the honor to command," wrote Morgan to Greene, "have been so fortunate as to obtain a complete victory over a detachment of the British army, commanded by Lt. Col. Tarleton. . . . We fought only eight hundred men, of which two-thirds were militia. The British . . . officers confess that they fought one thousand and thirty-seven, and these veteran troops."[89]

Morgan must have contemplated that statement and liked it, must have savored the wonder of it and rolled it round under his tongue, for in the appendix at the end of his report, he said it again: "Although our success was complete, we fought only eight hundred men, and were opposed by upwards of one thousand British troops."[90]

9

RETREAT FROM COWPENS

Cornwallis led a country dance
The like was never seen, sir,
Much retrograde and much advance,
And all with General Greene sir.[1]

(To the tune of "Yankee Doodle")

Morgan's victory at the Cowpens was complete, but he was well aware that his position there was untenable. He had to move out and move out fast. Cornwallis' camp was only twenty-five miles away. The flying British cavalry could reach it by late afternoon. "Reasoning what his adversary would do from a knowledge of what he ought to do,"[2] Morgan fully expected Cornwallis to be in motion to cut off his retreat before nightfall. The American general resolved to make an immediate dash for the fords of the Catawba. Cornwallis, unfortunately, was closer to those fords in his position at Turkey Creek than the Americans were at the Cowpens. Consequently, while hurrying preparations for retreat, Morgan was careful to keep his actual objective secret from all but his principal officers, while allowing the impression to arise that he intended to hold the country north of Broad River.[3]

The "valuable and discreet"[4] Pickens, possibly in double capacity as a chivalrous soldier and elder of the Presbyterian

Church, was, with a body of mounted militia, directed to remain on the field to cope with the sorry aftermath of battle—to bury the dead, console the dying, and succor the wounded of both armies. The captured baggage of the enemy was a Godsend to this purpose, for it provided tools, tents, bedding, and other useful and even luxurious things entirely lacking in the rebel supply train.[5]

Morgan paused on the ground only long enough to refresh his troops and collect the prisoners. The wagons were loaded with the arms and cannon and other military supplies of the British. The troops were formed in marching order. Washington with his dragoons was still absent in pursuit of the enemy. Orders were left for him to follow after the main body upon his return. By noon the line was in motion, and by evening it had crossed Cherokee Ford and encamped for the night on the north bank of Broad River.[6]

Before daybreak of January 18 Morgan was again in motion. Pickens and the mounted militia, having left the wounded on the field in charge of Dr. Pindell, the American surgeon, and Robert Jackson, surgeon's mate of the 71st Regiment, joined Morgan during the day.[7] So also did Washington. Tarleton had eluded him, but he did not return empty-handed. Many more prisoners had been flushed out of the woods, chiefly dragoons and some redcoats.[8] This brought the tally of prisoners to nearly six hundred, two-thirds the size of Morgan' entire force.

Since Morgan expected hourly to hear that Cornwallis was at hand, the encumbrance of the prisoners was a major problem. Yet they were sorely needed as they would form a basis of exchange for the hundreds of Americans who had been rotting in the British hulks since the fall of Charleston. Morgan knew how chagrined Greene had been over the carelessness which had resulted in the loss of all but a handful of the six hundred prisoners taken at King's Mountain in October.[9] The Old Wagoner determined that such would not

be the fortune of his six hundred. Accordingly he placed
them in charge of Washington and Pickens with instructions
to move them higher up the country and cross the Catawba at
the Island Ford. Morgan and the main body struck into the
direct road for Ramsour's Mills on the Little Catawba. If,
Morgan grimly reflected, he and his weary troops were attacked by the full force of the enemy before they could ford
the river, there was now at least a chance of foiling Cornwallis' recapture of his light troops.[10]

Happily for Morgan, Cornwallis did not do what he ought
to have done, according to Morgan's reasoning.[11] As the
American general had anticipated, the news of Tarleton's
defeat reached the British camp late on January 17, spilled
from the tongues of a few fugitives from the field. Tarleton
himself did not appear until the morning of the 18th. He had
gone into bivouac after crossing Hamilton's Ford and spent
a sleepless night collecting the remnants of his dragoons.[12]
Consequently, contrary to Morgan's expectations, Cornwallis
did nothing the night of January 17 but wait for Tarleton's
confirmation of the evil news, hoping doubtless that it was
not as evil as it sounded.

Next morning Tarleton arrived with about two hundred
chapfallen dragoons to report the loss of the light infantry,
the Legion infantry, McArthur's battalion of Frasier's Highlanders with its bagpipes, the detachment of Royal Artillery
with its guns, and the entire 7th Regiment with its colors.[13]
The day of January 18 in the British camp was spent in
explanations, exculpations, and not a few recriminations.[14]
Cornwallis may have hitherto regarded Tarleton as a father
does a favored son, but there were older officers over whose
heads the young man had been promoted who shared the
captured Major McArthur's opinion of the "rash, foolish
boy." Tarleton could not fail to sense the covert animosity
that appeared now that the golden youth had met misfortune.[15]

Leslie and his force, which had presumably "got out of the swamps"[16] on the 14th, still had not joined, but was expected momentarily. As Tarleton persisted, in his own extenuation, in estimating Morgan's little force at nearly two thousand, Cornwallis deemed it prudent not to move until the junction with Leslie had been effected. This was accomplished during the course of the day,[17] but not until the day was too far spent to permit of any further effort.

That evening Cornwallis penned to Clinton the second (King's Mountain had been the first) of what was to be a sad series of accounts of reversal. He put the best face he could on the matter:

Everything now bore the most promising Aspect; the Enemy were drawn up in an open Wood...no room to doubt of the most Brilliant Success.... Tarleton...charged and repulsed Washington's Horse, retook the Baggage of the Corps, and cut to pieces the Detachment of the Enemy who had taken Possession of it.... The loss of our cavalry is inconsiderable.... Your Excellency may be assured that Nothing...shall induce me to give up...the Winter's Campaign.[18]

However, try as he might, he could not gloss over the fact that in the course of a short winter morning he had lost nearly all the light troops of the British southern army. As luck and slow communications would have it, Sir Henry Clinton in New York, on February 16, 1781, received by H. M. S. *Halifax* the following dispatches from his southern commander: (1) the news of General Leslie's arrival in Charleston[19] ("The species of Troops which compose the Reinforcements are, exclusive of the Guards and the Regiment of Bose, exceedingly bad"); (2) news of Ferguson's defeat at King's Mountain;[20] (3) news of Tarleton's defeat at the Cowpens.[21] All of this in one day would be enough to upset the most placid of men. The state of the always apoplectic British commander's blood pressure can only be imagined.

Cornwallis' movements in the next few days after Leslie joined him on January 18 were characterized by that ponderous slowness which seems to have been typical of the motion of all British army commanders in America from Howe on down. On the 19th the army moved toward King's Creek in the general direction of the Cowpens. There it paused and waited for intelligence of Morgan's movements. No intelligence was forthcoming. It is possible to surmise that the extinction by Tarleton's dragoons of the Tory guides and spies who were rifling the baggage may have had some bearing on the dearth of information. Any Loyalists who escaped could hardly have been eager to approach the British encampment.

On the 20th Cornwallis dispatched Tarleton and the dragoons with some Hessian jägers across the Broad River to reconnoitre. Tarleton returned in the evening to report that Morgan, soon after the battle, had passed the Broad at Cherokee Ford, leaving the wounded on the field under the protection of a flag.[22]

Cornwallis now fancied that he understood Morgan's actions. Under the impression that Morgan had twice the force he actually did have, the British commander believed the American intended to hold the ground near Broad River in the vicinity of King's Mountain. Accordingly, on January 21 Cornwallis put his army in motion. Crossing Buffalo Creek, he pushed on to Broad River, which he passed on January 22. He continued toward King's Mountain only to discover that the enemy had eluded him.[23]

Meanwhile, Morgan, encumbered by the British muskets, artillery, and ammunition captured at the Cowpens, made slow but steady progress to Sherrald's Ford on the Catawba. He heard from his patrols on the night of January 18 that Cornwallis had not yet moved and did not propose doing so until the junction with Leslie was completed. However, Morgan had no thought that his enemy would long remain stationary, and he knew that if Cornwallis marched directly north with due speed he could still cut him off at the Catawba.[24] Yet while there was any chance of escape, the Old Wagoner dared not leave the captured muskets and ammunition, for they were the means of arming the militia he hoped to embody in North Carolina. The time of service of Triplett's Virginians was nearly up, and they would be going home with their arms. Furthermore, the South Carolinians and Georgians, being volunteers, would fall away, as was their habit, as the army moved north.[25]

With infinite labor, in heavy rains, Morgan's wagons toiled over the mountainous country of the Carolina Piedmont. On the 18th they crossed the Little Broad; on the 21st they forded the Little Catawba at Ramsour's Mills; and on the morning of the 23rd they sat down wearily at Sherrald's Ford on the east bank of the Catawba proper. Burdened as they were, they had come scarcely sixty miles, but they had outdistanced Cornwallis.

Morgan wrote to Greene. The prisoners, he told Greene, would be sent on to Salisbury under guard of Triplett's Virginians, whose time was up that day. "If they are to be send any further, Major Triplett wishes, and thinks it right, that the militia under Gen. Stevens should have the tureble of them as they have not underwent so much fatigue as his men."[26] Morgan intended to remain at Sherrald's Ford until he heard from Greene.[27] He knew by now that Cornwallis had made a false start in pursuit of him and was still some distance behind, with two swollen rivers—not to mention as well numerous, creeks, mountains, and gullies—to cross in order to reach him. Morgan could afford to give his men a chance to draw their breaths while he sought to recruit new militia to replace the time-expired Virginians.

This same day, January 23, Morgan's aide, Major Edward Giles, splashed with red clay mud to the hips, but wearing a broad smile, rode a tired horse into Greene's camp on the Pee

Dee. Giles brought the news of the victory at the Cowpens.[28]
Jubilation filled the camp. Colonel Otho Williams, with his
customary grace, wrote Morgan:

Next to the happiness which a man feels at his own good
fortune is that which attends his friend. I am much better
pleased that you have plucked the laurels from the brow
of the hitherto fortunate Tarleton, than if they had fallen by
the hands of Lucifer.

We have had a *feu-de-joie,* drunk all your healths, swore
you were the finest fellows on earth, and love you, if possible, more than ever. The General has, I think, made his
compliments in very handsome terms. Enclosed is a copy of
his orders. It was written immediately after we received the
news, and during the operation of some cherry bounce.
. . . . Compliments to Howard and all friends. Adieu.

Yrs. sincerely,

O. H. Williams[29]

The orders Greene wrote during the operation of the
cherry bounce do not seem to be extant. Perhaps sober re-
flection altered them. Greene was truly in an unenviable
position. The detachment under Morgan had won a great
victory. But Greene was completely without the means to
take advantage of it. His men were still half-clothed and
badly equipped. He had no money in his war chest and was
obliged to depend for provision upon what he could collect
day by day from the countryside.[30] Although Cornwallis had
suffered a severe loss of numbers and prestige by the affair at
the Cowpens, he was still formidable with Leslie's reinforcement and amply supplied with equipment and munitions.

On January 24 Greene sent Major Giles, possibly a bit
fuzzy-headed from the *feu-de-joie* of the previous evening,
but presumably on a fresh horse, galloping off to Congress,
bearing a copy of Morgan's battle report and Greene's letter
to Washington regarding the victory: "Major Edward Giles
will deliver these dispatches and have the honor to give

Congress such further information as they may request."[31]

Then, withdrawing from the rejoicings, Greene meditated. "I am of a Spanish disposition," he wrote his wife, "always the most serious when there is the greatest run of good fortune, for fear of some ill-fated stroke."[32] His first impulse seems to have been to adopt the plan—earlier suggested by Morgan—[33] of moving into the rear of the enemy in the direction of Georgia or Ninety Six. In this way he might distract Cornwallis' attention from Morgan's army and possibly even from the proposed campaign into North Carolina. Greene wrote Lee about this plan on January 26, enjoining him to the utmost secrecy: "Don't let no mortal have the least intimation of what I have in contemplation."[34] He had written Marion the day before, indicating that Lee was to continue to operate in the enemy's rear but saying nothing of the main army's intent to do so.[35]

However, the obstacles in the way of accomplishment of such a maneuver were simply too great. The enlistments of General Stevens' militia were expiring as those of Major Triplett's men had already done. The men were determined to march home, and Greene could do nothing to stop them, for coercion would inevitably result in future non-appearance of any new levies. The only thing he could do was to take advantage of the situation by sending them off as speedily as possible, before their time had quite expired, with instruction to intercept the prisoners Morgan had taken and move them into the interior counties of Virginia, thus securing them from Cornwallis.[36] This was in accordance with Morgan's suggestion made in his letter of the 23rd from Sherrald's Ford.[37]

The army on the Pee Dee had been put under marching orders upon receipt of the news of the Cowpens. All detachments but Lee's were called in.[38] It remained only to fix definitely upon the army's objective. Three letters from Morgan, received in quick succession, probably went far toward settling this question in Greene's mind. The exertions the Old Wagoner had made at the Cowpens and during the retreat had so aggravated his illness as to all but incapacitate him. On January 24 he wrote:

Dear Sir: After my late success and my sanguine expectations to do something clever this campaign, I must inform you that I shall be obliged to give over the pursuit by reason of an old pain returning upon me. . . . If I can procure a chaise, I will endeavor to get home. Gen. Davidson [and] Col. Pickens . . . can manage the militia better than I can, and will well supply my place.[39]

That Greene should be in imminent danger of losing his gallant commander of light troops was bad enough, but on January 25 Morgan sent off two hurried scrawls containing increasingly ominous news:

Sir: I am this minute informed by express, that Lord Cornwallis is at Ramsey's [Ramsour's Mills] on their march this way, destroying all before them. . . .[40]

The above note was written at sunrise. At two o'clock in the afternoon Morgan sent another:

Dear General: I receive intelligence every hour of the enemy's rapid approach, in consequence of which I am sending off my wagons. My numbers at this time are too weak to fight them. I intend to move towards Salisbury, in order to get near the main army. . . .
I expect you will move somewhere on the Yadkin to oppose their crossing. I think it would be advisable to join our forces and fight them before they join Phillips [in Virginia], which they most certainly will do if they are not stopped. . . . I sent to Davidson to join me, which I expect he will do tomorrow. His strength I do not know, as his men were collecting yesterday.[41]

That decided Greene. Orders had already gone out to the commissaries at Salisbury and Hillsboro to get ready to move their wagons and stores to Virginia. Carrington, the Quarter-master General, was already assembling boats on the Dan River, in south Virginia, against the necessity of retreat. General Isaac Huger was placed in command of the main army on the Pee Dee with Colonel Otho Williams as second-in-command. They were alerted to be ready to march up the east bank of the Pee Dee, which becomes in its upper reaches the Yadkin, to Salisbury, there to join forces with Morgan's complement, which Greene proposed to send to that place.[42]

These arrangements being made, Greene on January 28, escorted by a single aide and two mounted infantrymen, set out—with the almost insolent faith of a Galahad—to cross 125 miles of Tory-infested country and join Morgan on the Catawba.[43] Somewhere en route he received Morgan's third letter of the 25th or confirmation of its contents.[44]

What Morgan anticipated with regard to the militia of South Carolina had taken place. They had all dispersed. General Davidson was doing his best to gather the militia of North Carolina, but Morgan did not yet know with what success. The Old Wagoner had now learned that Cornwallis was encamped at Ramsour's Mills. At midnight of January 25, Morgan sent off his last message of the day: "I have at this moment received intelligence that the enemy is within a few miles of this place, moving on rapidly. My party is so weak that I think it must give way."[45]

On receipt of this information, Greene dispatched an express to Huger and Williams, directing them to march immediately for a possible junction with the light troops at Salisbury or Charlotte. Lee also was directed to join the main army. Greene and his little party pushed on. They arrived at the Catawba on January 30[46] in time to witness a miracle, or an extraordinary example of British inepitude, or both. It has been variously described.

Cornwallis, when he learned on January 22 that he had misjudged Morgan's movements, changed his line of march and headed for Ramsour's Mills on the Little Catawba with what speed he could. His pace was inconsiderable, for he dragged behind him the immense attirail of his own and Leslie's corps—all the gear or equipage for the entire winter's campaign and the proposed junction with Phillips in Virginia.[47] He reached the mills on January 25 only to find that the Americans had passed that point at least two days before and had now crossed the Catawba, putting two rivers between themselves and him.[48] Cornwallis later reported that after the "unfortunate affair of January 17,"[49] he had employed January 18 in forming a junction with General Leslie and Tarleton's corps. In the succeeding days, according to the British commander: "Great exertions were made by part of the army without baggage to retake our prisoners and to intercept General Morgan's corps on its retreat to the Catawba. But the celerity of their movements and the swelling of numberless creeks in our way rendered all our efforts fruitless."[50]

The part of the army without baggage consisted of Tarleton's cavalry and other British horse. What Cornwallis neglected to explain was that they were used only for reconnaissance forward and on the flanks of the main army during the day. As they had orders to return to the safety of the camp at night, they actually moved with no greater speed than the main body and thus were unable to overtake Morgan.[51]

From the 19th to the 22nd Cornwallis marched thirty-one miles. From the 22nd to the 25th he marched thirty-six miles, only five miles better than the previous days, despite the fact that he had lightened his train somewhat by the detachment of the women and heavy baggage under the escort of Brigadier General Howard with orders to follow after more slowly.[52] At his present rate the British would never catch up with the American army. This fact seems to have struck Cornwallis forcibly for the first time on January 25, when he went into bivouac at Ramsour's Mills. There he pondered the matter and came up with a solution that showed more imagination than had been common to British commanders in America. Fortunately for Morgan, this flash of originality came eight days too late to accomplish the immediate object. The enemy had deprived Cornwallis of nearly all of his light troops. He would retaliate by turning his entire force into light troops through relieving it of all cumbersome baggage.

Cornwallis spent the 26th and all of the 27th of January destroying his superfluous impedimenta. He had sent the cavalry across the Little Catawba on January 25 to scout the enemy. This was the detachment Morgan took for the whole army.[53] However, the horsemen, having ascertained that Morgan was on the east side of the ford, tamely turned round and returned to the shelter of the British camp.

Morgan took advantage of the respite to embody the militia under Davidson. The weather was abominable—cold, with frequent squalls of rain. Morgan had given up thought of looking for a chaise for the moment, but he was so ill that he dared not go out in the damp. He lay in a house outside the camp, fuming at being unable to see to things for himself and wondering what could be keeping Cornwallis so long immobile at Ramsour's Mills. Davidson set the slowly gathering militia to watching the fords. All the private fords they could reach they filled with dead trees and branches so as to make them impassable to foot or horse.[54]

Meanwhile Cornwallis continued systematically to destroy his baggage. He burned all the wagons except those indispensable for the transport of salt, ammunition and hospital stores; an additional four were allotted to the sick and wounded. All the provisions except what the men could carry in their haversacks went into the fire. The earl and his officers set a noble example by drastically reducing their personal gear.[55] Out of their portmanteaus poured hair powder and playing cards, sentimental novels and salacious plays. Flames crackled merrily on hair grease, and the scent of pomade perfumed the North Carolina woods.[56]

Last and most irretrievable of all, the rum kegs were stove in, the liquor poured out on the red earth. The hapless troops, perforce, looked on in silence while the great solace of the soldier sank before their horrified eyes into the muck, and the camp dogs came up and sniffed and lapped experimentally and trotted off, rather jauntily.[57] Perhaps the saddest of all the troops at the sight were the mustachioed Hessians of the Regiment von Bose, who thus saw vanish the one source of comfort and warmth they knew in a bewildering war for which they had never volunteered and which they did not understand.

Of this destruction of provisions and liquor Cornwallis wrote, "I must in justice to this army say that there was a most general and cheerful acquiescence."[58] Light Horse Harry Lee termed the reaction of the men "a memorable instance . . . of the immutable disposition of the British soldiers to endure every privation in support of their king and country."[59]

In the light of all this cheerful disposition to self-sacrifice, it is rather curious that in the month following the funeral pyre of equipment at Ramsour's Mills, the British returns show a reduction in the force with Cornwallis of 227 men, although no battle was fought and no epidemic occurred. In the same period there was a proportionate increase in the number of Hessian and English laborers at large in the interior of Carolina. There were more Hessians among these than English, but the gallant British Guards were reduced by one-eighth their strength.[60]

Incredibly, it does not seem to have occurred to Cornwallis that the task of destroying the baggage might have been left to a subordinate, and that the two days consumed in the operation might have been put by him to better advantage. He was less than twenty miles from Morgan. The

Catawba was fordable in many places. The cavalry which reconnoitred the American camp must have seen by its size that the number encamped was nothing like two thousand.

As we have seen, during this time Davidson's men were still collecting. Moreover, as Davidson despairingly wrote Greene, it was the season of the year when the Carolina farmers prepared their fields for sowing. The heads of families in particular were busy with this work. Davidson also pointed out that Cornwallis had marched this way before in the previous autumn. Experience had taught the people that if the British found the master of the house away, they, as a matter of course, assumed him to be in arms against themselves and treated his unhappy family accordingly. Hence, the character of the militia who answered Davidson's call left much to be desired. They represented the footloose and irresponsible—vagrant bondsmen; schoolboys with squirrel rifles and no flints; octogenarians, full of zeal but apt to be equally full of ague and rheumatics.[61]

If Cornwallis with a corps of light troops had advanced on January 26, he could in all probability have destroyed Morgan, for on that day the Catawba was still passable. However, apparently he preferred to set his men a good example by burning the contents of his portmanteau. Consequently it was not until the morning of January 28 that the British army resumed its march to the Catawba. The weather, as noted, had been wet for some days before, and the columns took the road in a slight drizzle. By mid-morning the drizzle had become a downpour. The rain fell without let or stay through the balance of the 28th and all of the 29th.[62] On the evening of the 29th, the Catawba began to swell. By morning of the 30th it was completely unfordable. Cornwallis' now tentless army sought what shelter it could find under trees and in the few log houses in the area and of necessity sat down to wait again.[63] "The rains had rendered . . . the Catawba impassable, and Gen'l Morgan's corps, the militia . . . under Gen'l Davidson, or the gang of plunderers usually under the command of Gen'l Sumter had occupied all the fords in the space of more than forty miles. . . ."[64]

News of Cornwallis' approach had routed Morgan from his sickbed early on the 29th. He inspected the eight hundred militia which Davidson had collected at Beattie's Ford and distributed them at the various fords to the best advantage he could on the basis of his interpretation of Cornwallis' intentions. The largest number remained at Beattie's, from which Cornwallis lay distant about ten miles. The regulars continued to guard Sherrald's Ford. As Morgan was about to return from Davidson's camp to his own, an express arrived with the information that the British had burned their wagons and loaded their men very heavily. Four prisoners taken declared that the enemy's objective was Salisbury. "I expect," Morgan wrote Greene, "they will attempt to cross in the morning. I will let you hear of every particular."[65]

In the night the Catawba foamed rapidly into flood stage, and Cornwallis did not cross next day. This fortuitous occurrence was made much of in the newspapers of the time as an action of Providence to save the American army, and the legend was incorporated in the early histories of the southern war.[66] Morgan, it was stated, crossed the Catawba only hours before Cornwallis' advance, and the swelling of the river saved him from destruction. As we have seen, this was not the case. Morgan was across the Catawba on the 23rd. Cornwallis, when he arrived at Ramsour's Mills, had four full days to march the twenty miles which separated him from Morgan. When the downpour began on January 28, any countryman could have told Cornwallis what effect it would have on all the mountain-born streams in the district. Yet the British general did not hurry his march. As Judge Johnson in his biography of Greene has correctly pointed out, *"The miracle that saved the Americans . . . was, that Corn-*

wallis should have halted his whole army two days at Ramsour's Mills for the purpose of destroying his baggage."[67]

While the frustrated earl waited for the waters to subside, he coped with another source of irritation. As long as he could, Tarleton had endured the thinly veiled sneers of his fellow officers and listened to them lament their fallen comrades-in-arms at the Cowpens.[68] "Colonel Tarleton acquired power without any extraordinary merit, and upon most occasions exercised it without discretion," said Cornwallis' civilian commissary, Charles Stedman.[69] Apparently this attitude fairly represented the consensus. Tarleton was accused of arrogance and impetuosity, of failing to consult with Majors Newmarsh and McArthur, much his superiors in age and experience if not in rank, before going into battle.[70] "Lt. Col. Tarleton, some days after the action, required Cornwallis' approbation of his proceedings, or his leave to retire till inquiry could be instituted to investigate his conduct. The noble earl's decided support is fully expressed in a letter. . . ."[71]

While the Catawba foamed muddy, turbulent, and uncontrollable on January 30, Cornwallis drew firm rein on his own temper and wrote:

You have forfeited no part of my esteem as an officer by the unfortunate event of the action of the 17th: The means you used to bring the enemy to action were able and masterly, and must ever do you honor. Your disposition was unexceptionable; the total misbehaviour of the troops could alone have deprived you of the glory which is so justly your due.[72]

It is difficult to see how Cornwallis could have written otherwise. In a howling wilderness, stripped, as it were, to his running shorts, His Lordship could not afford to lose his cavalry commander at this stage of the campaign. An investigation at any time might have raised the embarrassing question of how Cornwallis in ten days time had managed to progress only so far as Turkey Creek in spite of his assurances to Tarleton that he would be in a position to seize Morgan when Tarleton forced him over Broad River. Tarleton's action against his commander at this time was little short of blackmail.

This was the situation when Greene arrived at Sherrald's Ford on January 30. The British and American armies lay within a few miles of each other, but in perfect security as long as the Catawba remained in flood.

―――

FOX CHASE TO THE DAN

―――

> *They rambled up and rambled down,*
> *Joined hands and off they ran, sir;*
> *And General Greene was like to drown*
> *Cornwallis in the Dan, sir.*[1]
> (To the tune of "Yankee Doodle")

Greene was much relieved upon his arrival at Sherrald's
Ford to find that Morgan's situation was not quite as desperate as the letters of January 25 had led him to believe.
He heard with satisfaction that Cornwallis had destroyed his
baggage.[2] Although the British commander was more mobile
in his present state, Greene felt that Morgan's detachment
could keep ahead of him and tease him ever farther from his
supply base. Then when a junction with Huger was accomplished and a substantial force collected, it might be
possible to turn and meet the British in battle on ground of
Greene's own choosing to Cornwallis' disadvantage.

The American general spent January 30, 1781, writing
letters designed to help him put this plan into action. Huger
was directed to proceed to Salisbury, but to send the bulk
of the stores to Guilford Court House. Lee was to make a
forced march to join the army: "Here is a fine field and great
glory ahead."[3] Greene was well aware of Lee's eagerness for
laurels.

In the hope of providing himself with some reliable militia, Greene addressed the first of a series of urgent letters to William Campbell, the hero of King's Mountain, desiring him to join as quickly as possible with one thousand mountain men: "Such a force will add our splendor to your own glory and give the World another proof of the bravery of the Mountain Militia."[4]

In addition to the threat from Cornwallis, Nathanael Greene had another cause for concern. An intelligence report recently received indicated that a British force was en route to Wilmington, North Carolina. Actually this detachment consisted of a token force from Charleston under Major James H. Craig. It was designed to hold the port of Wilmington as a supply base and rallying area for North Carolina Loyalists, a move long recommended by Sir Henry Clinton, but one about which Cornwallis had procrastinated until this time.[5] Greene, however, did not know this on January 30. The scanty intelligence led him to believe that an invading force was about to land under the command of Benedict Arnold to cooperate with Cornwallis in his winter campaign. If this was true, the urgency of uniting the two parts of the southern Continental army was all the more pressing.[6]

In late December Sir Henry Clinton had dispatched Benedict Arnold to the Chesapeake area for the primary purpose of establishing a post at Portsmouth, Virginia, as a rallying point for Loyalists. A secondary objective was the destruction of American magazines in Virginia, if this should prove feasible and entail no great risk to the relatively small detachment.[7] Inasmuch as part of Arnold's purchase price had been a commission as brigadier general in the British army, he was nominally in command of the expedition.[8] However, since no man ever quite trusts a turncoat, Clinton was careful to see that the general was accompained by officers in whom he did have confidence. He made it quite clear to Arnold in his orders that the American was on probation.

Lieutenant Colonels Dundas and Simcoe went with him with the proviso written into the traitor's orders: "I am to desire that you will always consult these gentlemen previous to your undertaking any operation of consequence."[9] The lot of Judas entails its own humiliations.

General Washington had written several times to Governor Jefferson that his state was in danger of being invaded,[10] but the governor seems to have assumed—or hoped—that this expedition, like Leslie's earlier, was intended for South Carolina to reinforce Cornwallis.[11] On December 31, 1780, Jefferson reported to Baron Steuben that "27 sail of vessels, 18 of which were square-rigged," had been sighted on December 30 below Willoughby's Point.[12] Jefferson directed General Nelson to alert the low country militia, but he seems to have been quite uncertain whether the ships were friendly or "hostile," as he expressed it.[13] In any case, the day being Sunday, the Governor of Virginia deemed it unnecessary to disturb the Sabbath calm by calling the Virginia Council into session. When the body did meet on Monday, Jefferson merely informed the House of Delegates that the fleet in the Chesapeake was "suspected of being hostile" and that their destination was unknown.[14] Consequently nothing was really done in the way of organizing resistance until Tuesday, January 2, 1781, when, in mid-morning, Jefferson was informed that the enemy advance was at Warrasqueak Bay.[15] By then it was too late. As a result, Arnold debarked at Westover on James River and marched unopposed to Richmond, which he entered on January 5 with less than 1000 men. On his march he destroyed a cannon foundry, several warehouses full of tobacco, buildings public and private, state papers, military stores,[16] "and a great number of vessels richly laden . . . thereby spreading terror and alarm through the country and doing a most essential injury to the enemy and their allies."[17] The latter observation is Sir Henry Clinton's.

Having accomplished this without any whiff of grapeshot, General Arnold, heedful of his orders and the advice of Dundas and Simcoe, returned to Portsmouth and there encamped.[18] Clinton may well have reflected that the erstwhile rebel had repaid his purchase price several times over. "A perfidious Villain," wrote Otho Williams to his friend Dr. McHenry, "laid her [Virginia's] rich inhabitants under contribution, and her Honors in the dust. . . . The governor is said to boast he is no military man."[19]

Late in January Greene mulled over what little news he had of Arnold's movements. A Quaker general will ever be an anomaly, but in all other matters Greene was a very reasonable man. Like Morgan, Greene predicated that the enemy would do what it would be most efficient for him to do.[20] Therefore, Greene readily credited the idea that Arnold was for Wilmington. Since so much had been accomplished with so little effort in such a rich and populous state as Virginia by an inconsiderable force, it seemed entirely logical to Greene that the British would assume that the poor and thinly-populated state of North Carolina would be yet easier prey. He felt relief but some surprise when the rumor proved false.[21]

Meanwhile, whether by divine agency, as the newspapers termed it, or in natural response to the meteorological phenomena of the season, the Catawba boiled foaming out of its banks all through January 30 and the early part of January 31. Cornwallis, during the height of the flood, sought to confuse the enemy (and incidentally to keep the blood circulating in the veins of his cold and sodden troops) by approaching the river in short marches "so as to give the enemy equal apprehensions for several fords."[22]

Greene and Morgan had hoped that the river would continue high long enough to permit them to gather more militia or until Huger with the main army could join them. However, by afternoon of January 31, the stream began to fall so rapidly that it became evident the British could attempt a crossing on the morrow. As Huger was still some distance away and it was obvious that few, if any, more militia were forthcoming, there was nothing for Greene to do but send Morgan off in hasty retreat to the Yadkin.[23] Davidson's men to the number of two hundred were posted at the various fords. Davidson himself with a corps of mounted riflemen amounting to about three hundred acted as a roving force until they might determine which particular ford Cornwallis planned to cross.[24] When this was known they were to offer as much opposition as feasible to delay the British in order to give Morgan a head start. When Cornwallis had crossed the river, the militia and Davidson would join Greene at the house of David Carr sixteen miles distant on the road to Salisbury. These arrangements completed, the general repaired with a small mounted escort to Carr's house to await events.[25]

Meanwhile Cornwallis, having procured the best information he could about the various fords, resolved to attempt passage at a private ford known as Cowan's on the morning of February 1. From his intelligence reports he believed this ford to be lightly guarded.[26] In order to outwit his opponents, his Lordship had Lieutenant Colonel Webster with a small part of the army and all the remaining baggage make a feint at Beattie's Ford six miles above Cowan's. Webster was directed to open a noisy cannonade to attract Davidson's attention. Cornwallis with the Brigade of Guards, Regiment von Bose, 23rd Regiment, two hundred cavalry under Tarleton, and two three-pounders set out at one in the morning of February 1 for Cowan's Ford.[27]

The sky was dark at that hour, and a rain had begun to fall. While the army floundered in a wood through which there was no road, one of the guns in front of the 23rd Regiment overset in a swamp.[28] Horse and foot came to a halt. There was much low-voiced questioning, interspersed with a certain amount of profanity, and similar explanation. When it was discovered that the gun was badly stuck and would take some time to extricate, the 23rd Regiment and the cavalry marched around it. Some of the artillerymen with the other gun sent it on in charge of their mates. They themselves remained behind to help the cannoneers with the mired gun. This would have been admirably helpful had it not been for the fact that one of the gunners who remained behind held the only match with which to fire the advancing three-pounder.[29]

Thus it was that Cornwallis arrived at the river bank to find himself without artillery, for nobody had a match. By then dawn was near, and the rain was pelting down in such a manner as to presage a fresh rise in the Catawba. To have waited while someone went back for the thoughtless gunner with the match would have been to risk detection from the Americans on the opposite bank. Cornwallis could see from the number of fires on the other side that his opposition was likely to be greater than he had expected.[30] Moreover, although he did not yet know that Morgan had retreated, he had been informed the evening previous that Greene had joined Morgan and that Greene's army was marching after him with the greatest expedition.[31] Therefore, Cornwallis decided to ford the river without artillery cover. Brigadier General O'Hara and the Brigade of Guards, led by a Tory guide, a local man named Dick Beal, plunged into the stream. To prevent confusion Cornwallis ordered them not to fire until they reached the opposite bank. With cartridge boxes strapped high on their shoulders and muskets held over their heads, the Guards struggled in to thigh-deep water. Cornwallis and the van followed.

Cowan's Ford was five hundred yards across. About two hundred and fifty yards from the opposite bank the ford split in two, a circumstance with which the Tory guide alone was familiar. The straight course, normally utilized by wagons, was deeper and rougher than the course which diverged to the right downriver. The downriver route, the one usually taken by horsemen and travellers afoot, was longer and shallower with a smoother bottom. It emerged from the river about one-fourth of a mile below the wagon route.[32] The Guards had advanced almost to midstream when, as the water suddenly deepened, someone on the American shore fired a shot.

The feint toward Beattie's Ford had not deceived General William Davidson. Davidson was an alert and observant officer with considerable previous experience and his own local sources of information. Before Greene left for the rendezvous point arranged upon, he had told Davidson that he expected that Cornwallis would try to pass his cavalry at some private ford during the night in order that it might be in a position to harass the Americans from the rear when the infantry forced a passage by day.[33] Davidson considered the horse ford at Cowan's a likely spot for a crossing of cavalry. He posted about three hundred of his infantry there. At the emergence of the wagon ford he had only a small picket since he knew that this portion of the ford was deep and swift and in the ordinary way only used by heavy-laden wagons. To guard against surprise, Davidson had patrols well acquainted with the country pass up and down the river, alert to report any unusual movement from the British side of the stream.[34]

As noted in the preceding chapter, because it was the planting season, heads of families were reluctant to answer the call for militia. Consequently the men composing the picket at the wagon ford were a motley lot. Among them was young Robert Henry, a veteran of sixteen. Henry had recovered from a bayonet wound received at King's Mountain and was back in school when an urgent appeal from Davidson and Greene called out the last of the local militia. Mr. Beatty, the schoolmaster, had resisted earlier entreaties, but when word came that the Catawba had fallen and Cornwallis was on the march, the pedagogue closed his books and went home for his musket. Robert Henry and his brother Joseph shouldered their squirrel rifles and set out for Cowan's Ford. By way of preparation, they stopped on the road to spend $200 in Continental paper for half a pint of whiskey and half a bushel of potatoes. The whiskey they dispatched at once. Thus fortified, toting the potatoes and their rifles, the two boys arrived at the wagon exit of the ford. There they found about thirty men on guard. One was the lame schoolmaster, Mr. Beatty; another was a man named Joel Jetton, a sharp-eared impulsive type of character, as will appear presently.[35]

The officer of the guard made the lads welcome and directed each of them to choose a stand. All of the other men, he told them, had already chosen a particular spot from which to annoy the British. That way, when the alarm was given, there would be no crowding or confusion. Robert Henry selected a position low on the bank near the "getting-out place" of the wagon ford. He studied the water in the ford and noted a place where the ripples broke over a projecting rock. When the British reached that rock, Henry decided, "then it would be time to run."[36]

Not long after dark an owl's hoot, with human overtones, came from across the river. It was answered by a not entirely convincing hoot from the American side. Downstream a man slid a canoe into the river. He was back shortly with word that all was quiet in the British camp.[37] The guard at the wagon ford posted a sentry and lay down on their arms. At daybreak all were fast asleep when the quick-eared Joel Jetton awoke to the sound of horses in deep water. Dick Beal, the Tory guide, had become confused or frightened by the American camp fires. He missed the turn into the horse ford and led the men into the wagon route where the water was swimming deep.[38]

Jetton leaped to his feet and ran with his rifle to the water's edge. There he found the sentry sound asleep. Outraged by this impropriety, without making any attempt to waken the man, Jetton kicked him into the river. He then attempted to fire his rifle, but it was wet. Rushing back up the bank, he shouted "The British! The British!!" Then he seized someone else's gun and fired the shot heard by Cornwallis' troops as they floundered in midstream.

Robert Henry, fogged with sleep, was slow getting to his stand: "By the time I was ready to fire, the rest of the guard had fired. I then heard the British splashing and making a noise as if drowning."[39] Henry dashed water into his eyes to get the sleep out, leveled his squirrel rifle, fired, and continued to fire. He did not fail to remember, however, the rock in the ford with the ripples breaking over it. When "one on horseback" had passed the rock, the boy turned and fled up the bank. The American guns were suddenly silent as the men reloaded. Henry, scrambling and slipping in the mud, heard a gun fired at the water's edge, "which I thought Dick Beal had fired at me."[40]

This stimulation was sufficient to lend wings to Henry's heels. He catapulted into the light of the watch fires to find that General Davidson and his men had come up from the horse ford at the sound of the shooting. But Robert Henry had made his own decision about the rock the evening before; the reinforcement did not alter his determination. He was about to make good his personal retreat when he saw Mr. Beatty calmly loading his gun behind a tree. The schoolmaster was lame, and, in young Henry's eyes, old. The boy found himself a tree of comfortable girth near Beatty's and commenced reloading his rifle, keeping a weather eye on his mentor: "I thought I could stand it as long as he could." First Beatty, then Henry fired at the heads and shoulders of the advancing British, just visible now above the slope of the river bank.

The Guards, obedient to orders still held their fire. Beatty loaded again. Henry began ramming down another load. The schoolmaster fired. Then he called to his pupil, "It's time to run, Bob." The boy, just through loading, thrust his head out from behind his tree and looked into the lowered muzzles of the British guns. He withdrew his head with all possible speed and flattened himself against the rough trunk of his tree as bark spattered about him. When he looked again Beatty was down and wounded but still shouting to him to run in the tone he used when a caning was due. Obedient to the voice of authority, Henry ran.[41]

The British had had their problems fording the stream. Thanks to the happenstance that led them into the wrong ford, they did not suffer as severely as they might have done. The first volley of the Americans noticeably thinned the forward ranks. Cornwallis was well to the fore, however, on a spirited horse. His exhortations and those of the other officers moved the disciplined columns steadily ahead after the first check. The deep water swept some men and horses off their feet, but the main body advanced. Colonel Hall of the Guards had his horse shot from under him. His men pulled him out of the water and saved him from drowning only, as it developed, that he might keep his particular appointment in Samarra on the river bank minutes later. Cornwallis' horse was shot from under him, but the animal's great heart kept it going until it fell dead on the bank beside the mortally wounded Hall.[42] Cornwallis himself was unhurt.

"The light infantry," said Cornwallis, "landing first immediately formed, and in a few minutes killed or dispersed every thing that appeared before them, the rest of the troops forming and advancing in succession.... Their general [Davidson] and two or three other officers were among the killed ... a few were taken prisoner."[43]

The prisoners were few indeed. Davidson, seeing that he could not hold the river bank, withdrew his men from the river's edge to the cover of the undergrowth. His movement as he led them off silhouetted him against the light of the watch fires. A well directed ball struck him in the chest. He died instantly.[44] The loss of their leader was catastrophic for American resistance. Bereft of Davidson, the militia broke and ran so fast that they "made straight shirt tails."[45]

Cornwallis sent Tarleton after the flying militia. Most of these forest-wise countrymen made straight for their homes, unmindful of any rendezvous with Greene on the Salisbury Road. About one hundred, however, proceeded through byways to a point about ten miles from Cowan's Ford to a tavern called Tarrant's. Six miles beyond this was David Carr's house where Greene waited for Davidson and the militia. Greene expected to march them on to join Morgan. The militia, being mounted and without baggage, would have no difficulty catching up with Morgan's heavier body.[46]

Unfortunately, when the militia found themselves at Tarrant's, they also found that they were in great need of refreshment. Unaware that Tarleton was in pursuit, they decided to avail themselves of the hospitality of the tavern before joining Greene. The senior officer amongst them posted guards. When Tarleton's cavalry came clattering up, the more active of the militia had time to deliver a hasty fire, run to their horses, and disappear into the woods. Only a few aged men and boys on brokendown nags remained. With his usual facility for promoting the cause of British arms and loyalty to His Majesty's government, Tarleton cut them down without mercy, adjuring his men to "Remember the Cowpens!" Cornwallis estimated forty or fifty killed by Tarleton's report,[47] although a British officer who rode over the area shortly thereafter, counted only ten bodies on the ground.[48]

"This stroke," said Cornwallis, "with our passage of the ford so effectually dispirited the militia that we met with no further opposition on our march to the Yadkin through one of the most rebellious tracts in America."[49] Unhappily he was right. One great misfortune, however, was averted. Had Tarleton questioned his adversaries instead of slaying them, he might have learned what a prize lay ready to his hands just six miles up the road.

Greene waited, almost alone, at the place of rendezvous until mid-night when a weary messenger brought him the news that Davidson was dead, the militia dispersed, and Cornwallis over the Catawba.[50] There was nothing for Greene to do but to proceed on to Salisbury and make all haste to join Morgan. At Salisbury Greene breakfasted at Steele's Tavern. There, if tradition is to be credited, Mrs. Steele, the landlady, seeing his discouragement and overhearing him remark that he was penniless, contributed two little leather bags of hard money, which for Greene formed the entire contents of the military chest of the Grand Army of the Southern Department of the United States of America.[51]

An incessant rain fell all through the day and night of February 1. From the meticulous care he had taken to familiarize himself with every aspect of the southern country, Greene knew that a rise of the rivers could be expected about two days after such a downpour. He was therefore most anxious that Morgan should cross the Yadkin before February 3. As the general hastened on from Salisbury to the river, it became obvious that not only were the militia afraid to embody, but that the inhabitants of the district were so terrified at the approach of the British that they were prepared to abandon their homes and trust their possessions to the protection of the American army. The road became increasingly obstructed by the wagons of the fugitives.[52] Nevertheless, Morgan and Greene and the army succeeded in crossing the river. They were encamped on the opposite shore by the evening of February 3, thanks to the foresight with which Greene had ordered Kosciuszko's boats up to the Trading

Ford.[53] The Yadkin was now in full flood. A few of the wagons of the country people still remained on the western shore. The folk themselves had nearly all passed over.

Meanwhile, Cornwallis' choice of a private ford as a crossing place over the Catawba proved to have its disadvantages. Since the ford was private, the roading leading away from it was poorly developed. Cornwallis had much difficulty extricating his wagons and artillery from the mud. Viewing these objects while the struggling horses panted and slithered to extricate them, Cornwallis decided that a second conflagration of wagons was in order.[54] He sent O'Hara's mounted infantry and his own cavalry ahead to catch Greene and Morgan before they crossed the Yadkin while he disposed of baggage and doubled the teams of the remaining wagons.

When O'Hara's van reached the Yadkin on February 3, they had the pleasure of exchanging a few shots with some men who were guarding the loaded wagons of the country folk on the west bank. Then the men dispersed and O'Hara got the wagons, but that was all. Morgan and Greene and all the boats were on the far side of the river. O'Hara sent word back to Cornwallis who, with his doubled teams, had now reached Salisbury. The British commander sent forward some field pieces with which O'Hara attempted to bombard the American camp. The grasshoppers taken at the Cowpens, the only artillery Greene had save for that with the main army, had gone forward with the prisoners. Greene could not, therefore, reply to the bombardment, but neither could the British do him much damage. His camp lay behind a high, rocky ridge which paralleled the Yadkin.[55]

About the only thing visible of the camp to the British on the opposite shore was the roof of a small cabin in which Greene was busy with correspondence. Gradually the enemy fire concentrated on this roof. In a few minutes clapboards were flying about in all directions. Greene, however, took no notice but continued to push his pen evenly over the paper, pausing only when some official visitor required his attention. His replies to each visitor were calm and precise. Then he resumed his writing.[56]

The above is only one of the many instances of Greene's imperturbability to danger. It does not seem to have been bravado, nor the courage of the legendary valiant who never taste of death but once. Greene's domestic letters to his family reveal that he had his human share of anxieties. Rather, it was a kind of concentration. When he was doing what he conceived to be his duty, he was certainly not unaware of what was going on about him, but he did not consider it as particularly important as compared with what he felt was the main issue. In this case he had correspondence to deal with. The cannon balls, like the interruptions by messengers and so on, were merely ancillary nuisances to be dealt with in the measure of their priority; the priority of the cannon shot was on a lower level.

On February 3 he was writing to Governor Abner Nash of what had taken place since the battle at Cowpens, and he was mincing no words.[57] He informed Nash of the dispatch of the prisoners taken in the battle, of Cornwallis' advance, of Greene's juncture with Morgan, of the death of Davidson, of the retreat across the Yadkin, and the dispersal of the militia. Unless, he told Nash, decided measures were taken for the reinforcement of the Continental army, "doubtless the enemy will improve the present opportunity . . . to effect an entire reduction of your state."[58]

The fate of the southern states did indeed appear to be in hazard. But Greene still hoped, if he could collect twelve to fifteen hundred militia, to check Cornwallis somewhere between the Yadkin and the Dan.[59] After Cornwallis had crossed the Catawba, it was obviously impracticable for Greene to meet Huger at Salisbury. Therefore, Huger was directed to Guilford Court House, where the baggage had already been sent. Orders were forwarded to Lee requesting him to move up his horse with all dispatch to the same place; if necessary the Legion infantry could follow later[60]

Meanwhile, everything possible was done to keep Cornwallis from learning Greene's plans. He and Morgan remained in the camp on the Yadkin until the evening of February 4, when the stream began to fall so rapidly as to indicate that it might be passable next morning.[61] Then the army marched off in a northerly direction in order to induce Cornwallis to believe that it was headed for the upper fords of the Dan River, and from there intended to cross into Virginia. At Abbott's Creek near Lexington Greene halted to obtain definite information of Cornwallis' movements.[62] Morgan, with a detachment and the wagons, pushed on to Guilford Court House, which he reached on February 5.[63]

Greene wrote to Huger from Abbott's Creek that he intended if he could find a good position to prepare for the enemy's attack. "From Lord Cornwallis pushing disposition, and the contempt he has for our army, we may precipitate him into some capital misfortune. If Cornwallis knows his true interest he will pursue our army. If he can disperse that, he will complete the destruction of the state; and without it he will do nothing to effect."[64]

Cornwallis evidently agreed with this conclusion. Baffled by the height of the water at Trading Ford, and lacking boats, his Lordship spent two days in Salisbury collecting provisions and securing intelligence. Most of the latter proved to be wretched. Some of "our friends in canoes"[65] crossed over the Yadkin and informed Cornwallis that Morgan and Greene had decamped in a northerly direction. These or other friends also assured him that the lower fords of the Dan River were impracticable for foot or horse in the winter and that Greene could not possibly collect enough flats at these places to ferry his army across.[66] Cornwallis therefore concluded that Greene would make for the upper

fords of the Dan where the river was, even in winter, quite
shallow and easily passed. Secure in this conviction, the
British commander, on February 6, set out for Shallow Ford
on the Catawba ten miles above Trading Ford, which the
American army had left on the fourth. A crossing at Shallow
Ford involved a considerable swing to the west of Greene
but would also place the British closer to the upper fords of
the Dan.[67] This would make it all the easier to intercept
Greene on his race to the river.

Greene waited at Abbott's Ford until he received word at
one in the morning of February 8 [7][68] that Cornwallis had
taken the bait. Then he set out for Guilford Court House,
where he arrived on the same day. Here he met bitter dis-
appointment. Arnold's inroads in Virginia had prevented the
recruits which Steuben had hoped to send him from starting
out. And although by now it was known that the British
force landed at Wilmington was not Arnold's and presented
no immediate threat to the interior, the militia of the Piedmont were so occupied with hurrying their families out of
Cornwallis' line of march, and so dispirited by Davidson's
death, that they could not be induced to embody in any
number.[69] Of the North Carolina men with Morgan's force,
there remained now scarcely eighty, and there was every
evidence that they, too, were preparing to depart.

Yet there were still several reasons why Greene considered offering Cornwallis battle. For one thing, he believed
Cornwallis so anxious for it that he would accept the challenge even under circumstances disadvantageous to himself.
For another, the British were now penetrating a part of the
country which they had always believed, with some truth, to
be weighted in favor of the British cause. Greene dreaded
what a protracted retreat on his part would do to depress the
Patriots (of which he already had unhappy evidence) and
raise the enthusiasm of the Loyalists.[70] He expected Huger's
division of the army next day. Pending its arrival, Greene

reconnoitered the ground about Guilford Court House and made his plans for the disposition of his troops should a battle take place there.[71]

Whatever the outcome of the situation might be, Greene had no intention of crossing the Dan at the upper fords. If he crossed the river where it was fordable, there would be little to prevent Cornwallis, with his superiority in artillery and regular troops, from crossing on the heels of the Americans. If the British commander did so, he would be on the direct route to the depot where the prisoners taken at Cowpens had been secured. Not only that, he would be in reach of the stockade where the Convention Troops of Burgoyne's army were incarcerated.[72] It is true that these latter had been much depleted as a result of careless handling, whereby many of them had been permitted to escape. Nevertheless, those remaining, together with the Cowpens prisoners, would make a most formidable addition to Cornwallis' strength should the British general succeed in releasing them.

However, it was to Greene's advantage to have the British set out in the direction they thought Greene would take, for it meant that Cornwallis' pressing disposition was leading him ever farther and farther from his base of supplies and from the American army, while giving Greene the opportunity to join his forces together and, if possible, prepare to challenge the enemy or elude him. Means for the latter measure lay in readiness. Colonel Carrington, Greene's Quartermaster General, met him at Guilford with the welcome information that ample boats were concealed along the Dan in the vicinity of Boyd's and Irwin's ferries for the transport of the whole American army.[73] William Richardson Davie, the Commissary General, also arrived at Guilford. For the first time since leaving Charlotte, Greene had the weight of two of the most onerous departments of any army lifted from his own shoulders.[74] Another welcome arrival was Colonel Pickens, returned from escorting the prisoners to

Virginia. Pickens had few militia with him, but all of them had been with him since before Cowpens and so were almost in the nature of veterans.[75]

Huger and his troops reached Guilford on February 9. The regulars who had been with Morgan through the Cowpens campaign were far from parade ground neat as to clothing and equipment, but the sight of Huger's barefoot battalions made even them gasp.[76] When Morgan set out for the country west of the Catawba in December, he had naturally been provided with the best that the American army offered, which was little enough, since he would be operating in the field. The camp of repose on the Pee Dee, it was hoped, would be supplied with new equipment before it also took the field. The hope had been very slightly realized. The chaotic state of the nation's finances and Arnold's ravaging of Virginia had attended to that. Consequently Huger's men had marched one hundred miles under circumstances described as requiring the utmost patience,[77] as noble a masterpiece of understatement as ever was. The men's body clothing was much worn; a great part of the troops were without shoes; there was but one blanket for four men.[78] The harness of the sorry horses on the wagon teams matched the clothing of the men. It was broken in many places and mended with bits of rope or old rag or anything else that human ingenuity and patience could improvise.[79] Yet these men had come over frozen roads and cart tracks, in heavy rains, through deep creeks, over sagging bridges, "sometimes without meat, often without flour, and always without spirituous liquors."[80] Nobody had deserted.[81]

The only outfit in the whole line that had any semblance of military bearing was the Legion of Lee. Even in its case the fine white breeches of the dragoons had suffered sadly from contact with red mud, and the men were bone-tired from their forced march to catch up with Huger.[82] Lee had not wanted to come. He seems already to have conceived the plan, which he executed so brilliantly a few months later, of subduing the small British posts in South Carolina and Georgia piecemeal.[83] Misled perhaps by Greene's letter of January 26 suggesting an attempt on the British rear, on February 3 he showed a complete misunderstanding of the true situation by actually asking for reinforcements from Huger's army.[84] However, an urgent letter from Greene's aide, Major Burnet,[85] apprised him of the state of affairs and dashed whatever hopes the young Virginian may have had of action to the southward for the present. Pushing the Legion northwest, Lee joined the march from the Pee Dee and was now available and eager for action.

Morgan upon his arrival at Guilford had secured promise of four thousand pounds of salt pork together with bacon, corn meal, and forage.[86] Carrington had managed to procure a shipment of shirts, shoes, and "over Halls."[87] The army was fed and the clothing distributed as equitably as possible, but the shoes in particular proved to be but half enough.[88] Greene surveyed the situation and called one of his rare councils of war.[89]

The ground at Guilford, Greene felt, offered an ideal field for battle. But the returns of the American army showed a total of all ranks of only 2,036; of these only 1,426 were seasoned Continental troops; the rest were recruits, plus the militia of Pickens and the few reluctant North Carolinians from the late Davidson's district. Of these not a few were sick, and all were much fatigued. Cornwallis' force was estimated at three thousand excellent troops including three hundred dragoons and mounted infantry.[90] The decision of the council of war was unanimous against offering battle. If Cornwallis' objective was to destroy the American army, let the attainment of that objective be made as difficult as possible. Arrangements were made accordingly.

Pickens was directed to go back and hang on to the skirts of the enemy, to harry their foraging parties, to cut off their intelligence service, and to arouse the local militia against them. It was the kind of service in which the southern partisans were peculiarly adept. It cost them little but seriously disrupted the usefulness of the enemy cavalry, groups of which were constantly necessary to protect all detachments engaged in procuring food and stores. Cornwallis, by his own action in burning his supplies, had made it imperative that such detachments should operate.

The earl now lay at Salem twenty-five miles from Guilford, where the "mild and hospitable"[91] Moravian inhabitants had made him free of the fruits of their well cultivated plantations. In order to entice the British from this pleasant larder and to encourage Cornwallis in his belief that the Americans intended to cross at the Dan's upper fords, Greene detached seven hundred of his best troops as a light corps. This corps included all the cavalry under Colonel William Washington plus Lieutenant Colonel Lee's Legion, 280 Continental infantry under Howard, and 60 Virginia riflemen.[92] The detachment was to act as a cover for the retreat of the main army, interposing a screen between it and the British, keeping ever close to their pursuers, as the men of the light troops broke down bridges, blockaded fords, and in every way harassed and delayed the pursuit, while yet leading Cornwallis always toward the upper fords of the Dan. Behind this shield Greene and Huger would march to Irwin's and Boyd's ferries lower downstream.[93] Once the main army was safe, the light corps would join it.

The command of these troops was offered to General Morgan, but by this time the Old Wagoner was in a truly pitiable condition. He had written Greene on February 6: "To add to my misfortune, I am violently attacked with the piles. . . ."[94] Having ordered delivery of the foodstuffs, Morgan asked permission to retire from the army.[95]

Lee in his memoirs intimates that Greene was reluctant to grant the request; indeed the younger officer goes so far as to imply that there was some doubt as to the genuineness of Morgan's illness.[96] That Greene had any such notion is certainly not evident in his order of February 10 granting Morgan leave of absence.[97] However, Greene was a man who drove himself very hard; as a natural consequence he may have expected others to do likewise. Sciatica is a paroxysmal ailment. Between bouts of pain the victim appears normal enough. Whatever Greene's private thoughts may have been, he seems to have directed, or assented, that Lee approach Morgan in an attempt to persuade him to reconsider his resolution. Lee talked to Morgan at some length urging him to accept the proffered command. When ordinary arguments failed, Lee suggested that the general's retirement at such a hazardous time might reflect upon his patriotism, or be attributed to a conviction on his part that the American cause was already lost, or even cast aspersions on the general's courage or ability.[98]

"These observations," said Lee later, "appeared to touch the feelings of Morgan; for a moment he paused; then discovered a faint inclination to go through with the impending conflict; but finally returned to his original decision."[99] Perhaps this is as fair evidence as any of how ill Morgan really was. The old Morgan of the French war, of Battletown days, or Quebec would have knocked the young cock-of-the-walk flat for his insults.

With Morgan out of the picture, the command of the light corps devolved upon Colonel Otho Holland Williams, a gentleman as versatile as he was charming. On February 10 Greene and the main army left Guilford Court House, pursuing the direct route to the lower Dan. Kosciuszko preceded them with a small party prepared to protect the boats secured at the river and to throw up a light breastwork at the ferry to cover the passage of the army.[100] Later in the day, after giving his superior a few miles start of him, Williams with the light troops, slanted off on a course to the left which would put him on a road running north between the British army and the main body of the Americans.[101]

Cornwallis in the act of making a demonstration toward Hillsboro and the American stores he believed to be stockpiled there,[102] soon became aware of the force in front of him. Exactly as was intended, he took it to be the rear guard of the whole American army. He promptly ceased his movement toward Hillsboro and directed his army to the upper fords of the Dan, thinking thus to keep Greene from his objective;[103] the race for the Dan was now on in earnest.

The distance from Guilford Court House to the Dan River is slightly over seventy miles, but the wretched roads traveled by the armies lay through the red clay region of the Piedmont. In February, the worst season of the year in this area, the clay is deep and slimy by day, a heavy mire which clogs the wheels of wagons and swallows the hooves of horses. During the freezing nights, the ruts and furrows harden to a rough surface with edges sharp enough to cut bare feet and lame an unshod horse. Yet, almost inconceivably under these conditions, pursuer and pursued managed at times to make as much as thirty miles a day.[104]

Once satisfied that Cornwallis was aware of him, Williams on his "old horse Liberty"[105] directed his men north. Cornwallis, clawing after what he fondly thought was the whole American army, detached a mobile force under General O'Hara to destroy Williams,[106] whom he fancied to be the rear guard. The commander of the light troops kept them between Cornwallis and Greene. They were never far ahead of O'Hara, hunter and quarry striking and snapping at one another at fords, in defiles, and over broken bridges. Lee, with the rear guard, kept in sight of O'Hara's advance all day.

"The duty, severe in the day, became more so at night," said Lee.[107] It was necessary at night to employ many patrols and strong pickets, not only to protect the light troops but to prevent the enemy from circling round the relatively small group to place himself between Williams and Greene, a maneuver which would be fatal to the Americans since it would allow Cornwallis to discover himself duped. Half of the troops were alternately on night duty so that each man during the four days of the retreat got six hours of sleep in the forty-eight, if he were lucky. Of those technically free, one at every campfire had to remain on his legs to tend the fire since there were no tents and only one blanket for every four men. An exception in the matter of blankets was the Legion of Lee which luxuriated in one cover for every three men and also in the advantage that every man was booted and breeched.[108]

Each morning everyone turned out at three o'clock in order to get far enough ahead of the enemy, which had been visible at sundown, to prepare the one meal of the day. Lee says that this meal was hurried and scanty, but adds cheerfully that "it was very nutritious and good in quality, being bacon and corn meal."[109]

Although better clad than the Americans, the British were quite as tired and hungry and equally exposed to the elements. Yet, said Cornwallis: "Nothing could exceed the patience and alacrity of the officers and soldiers under every species of hardship and fatigue."[110]

On the afternoon of the 13th Cornwallis diverged from his line of march on a road paralleling that of Williams' route and came on to the road Williams' troops were following. Toward sunset he stumbled on Lee and his men, who had missed breakfast that morning and were engaged in preparing an evening meal.[111] Cheated of supper as they had been of breakfast, the Legion leaped to horse and escaped after a chase across a mile-wide plain. Cornwallis continued in pursuit until after nightfall. Lee had come up with Williams, and the retreat continued in the dark over uneven ground, both armies feeling their way.[112]

About eight o'clock Lee and Williams saw ahead the

fires of a large encampment. Immediately assuming it to be
Greene, whom they had thought far in front, they were heart-
sick. The only alternative to disaster for the whole American
army was for the light troops to throw themselves in the
face of the enemy and hold long enough for Greene to
escape.[113] This resolve was at once communicated to Williams. His heart was by no means against such a sacrifice, but
his cooler head led him to consult Greene's last dispatch.
This indicated that the fires seen must be on the site of a
camp Greene had left two days before. Such proved to be
the case. Friendly hands had kept the fires alight against the
coming of the decoys.[114]

Williams and his men could not stop to enjoy them; for
Cornwallis, with O'Hara in the lead, was nipping at their
heels. When word came that the British commander had at
last paused for breath, Williams' troops rested two or three
hours and again pushed on. Shortly after noon of February
14 about fourteen miles from the Dan, a jubilant courier met
them with a message from Greene: " The greater part of the
wagons are over, and the troops are crossing."[115] An hour or
two later a second courier brought the heartwarming news:
"All our troops are over.... I am ready to receive you and
give you a hearty welcome."[116] Both messages were dated
February 13. At the latter message the men of the light corps
set up such a hearty cheer that O'Hara with the British van,
following hard, heard the sound and suspected that the game
was up.[117]

By evening of February 14, with Cornwallis still in pursuit, the light troops started to cross the Dan. The men were
loaded in boats, but the luckless horses were turned into the
flood to swim for it. Some in panic swam back to the Carolina
shore and made for the woods. Lee sent the weary men to
round them up. When all were secured, he and the rear
troop crossed the Dan in the last boat.[118]

"All our exertions," said Cornwallis, "were in vain. For

upon our arrival at Boyd's Ferry on February 15 we learned that his rear guard had got over the night before.... More flats had been collected than had been represented to me as possible."[119]

"Every measure of the Americans, during the march from the Catawba to Virginia, was judiciously designed and vigorously executed...."[120] The words are Tarleton's.

On the night of February 14 on the north bank of Dan River, the American army slept—all of it, that is, but Greene. He was writing dispatches to Washington, to Steuben, to Jefferson.[121] He did not intend to leave Cornwallis in possession of the Carolinas if he could help it.

"LIKE A BEAR WITH HIS STERN IN A CORNER"[1]

From the time that Cornwallis, on January 19, 1781, plunged north after the fleeing Morgan until the British commander wrote his reports to Clinton and Germain following the battle of Guilford Court House in mid-March, the British southern army was, insofar as British headquarters in New York and His Majesty's government in London were concerned, swallowed up voiceless in the wilderness. The only news which reached New York came from rebel sources.

Stationed at New York was Major Frederick Mackenzie of the Royal Welsh Fusiliers, a literal-minded Scot who enlivened the boredom of garrison duty by keeping a diary. In it he noted the condition of the wind and weather and such public events as occurred each day. If there had been no event of significance, Mackenzie nonetheless scrupulously recorded temperature and wind direction. On February 11, 1781, a frosty day with the wind from the northwest, he reported that "a person ... from Elisabethtown saw a letter from a person in Virginia to one in Philadelphia which mentioned that Lord Cornwallis ... had attacked the rebel army under General Greene in Carolina ... defeated it and taken 1600 prisoners."[2] Nothing of the kind, of course, had happened. The first news of Cowpens reached New York by a coasting vessel on February 14 in surprisingly correct detail,[3] to be confirmed by Cornwallis' official report on February 16.[4]

From February 16 forward, however, the truth forms a very small part of the content of the rumors, most of which reached New York via Benedict Arnold in Virginia. That officer reported on February 5 that he had been unable to obtain any direct word from Cornwallis or Leslie but that "intelligence from the rebel camp says that Cornwallis is advancing to the northward, and that the rebel army is falling back."[5] This was true enough, but on February 25 General Arnold forwarded a report, the details of which were so far from the facts that one is constrained to suspect that the purveyor of the information knew the traitor's history and was deliberately misleading him out of spite. According to Arnold's report, someone from the rebels in Suffolk County had informed him that Cornwallis had crossed the Dan 60 miles above Halifax with 4000 infantry and 1000 cavalry and was on his march for Petersburg. Morgan and Greene with 3000 to 4000 men—chiefly militia—were retiring in disorder before him.[6] The British in Virginia proposed to make a junction with Cornwallis soon.[7]

The foregoing information was duly noted by Mackenzie in his diary. On March 11, a fine spring day with a southwest wind, the Scot recorded further exhilarating news: Cornwallis had backed Greene up against a swollen river in Virginia, annihilated his army, and made Greene prisoner.[8] The major was sceptical: "This account cannot be credited to the extent mentioned above."[9] The account may have been a much garbled version of Greene's crossing of the Dan.

Actually it was Lord Cornwallis on February 15, who raged frustrated on the edge of the flood of the Dan, once more unable to reach an enemy who sat comfortably on the opposite bank of yet another river. His Lordship can hardly be blamed for acquiring an aversion to this country "of large rivers and numberless creeks, many of which would be

reckoned large rivers in any other part of the world."[10] The
British commander was in an unenviable position. He had, to
be sure, pushed Greene out of North Carolina, but in so
doing he had marched his army 230 miles from its base of
supplies[11] and literally out of its shoes.[12] Moreover, although
there was now no organized American army in the field from
Virginia to Florida, the army the British had chased out was
still intact, unhurt, and, for the moment at least, completely
unassailable.[13]

Cornwallis rested a day on the banks of the Dan digesting
his cup of bitterness. "My force being ill-suited to enter by
that quarter so powerful a province as Virginia; and North
Carolina being in the utmost confusion; after giving the
troops a halt of a day, I proceeded by easy marches to Hills-
borough...."[14] His force was not only ill-suited to enter
Virginia; it was incapable of so doing, for Greene had all
the boats on the far side of the river. Furthermore, part of
the confusion in North Carolina, as his Lordship was shortly
to discover, was occasioned by Andrew Pickens, with seven
hundred new raised militia, who was threatening the British
left flank.[15] This able partisan was abetted by a force under
the militia general, Richard Caswell, not far from the British
right.[16]

Hillsboro is sixty-two miles from Boyd's Ferry on the
Dan where Greene had crossed. Cornwallis arrived there on
February 20 after crossing two branches of the Hycotee and
three creeks along his route.[17] Do what he might, he could
not escape the waters. At Hillsboro he issued a sonorous
proclamation: "Whereas it has pleased Divine Providence to
prosper the operations of his Majesty's arms in driving the
rebel army out of this province...."[18] The proclamation
invited all the loyal subjects of George III to flock to the
banner of his commander in Carolina "with their arms and
ten days provisions." However loyal they might be, Cornwallis could neither feed nor equip them.[19]

This fact, coupled with the distressed and meager appearance of the King's troops, which had presumably been brought to Loyalist support,[20] somewhat dampened the enthusiasm of the Tories of the Hillsboro area.[21] Nevertheless, the country about the little town and southeastward from it toward the coast did contain a considerable proportion of British sympathizers. Stimulated by Greene's evacuation of the state and by Cornwallis' presence, they began gathering in large numbers. In one day officers for seven independent companies came in.[22] Lee wrote Greene that they positively swarmed into Hillsboro with a delusion which was "excessive."[23] For three days Cornwallis had high hopes that he had at long last found "our friends." Then suddenly the movement of well-wishers slackened, diminished to a trickle, then ceased altogether.[24] On February 24 Cornwallis learned why. Greene had recrossed the Dan.[25]

The only way to destroy Nathanael Greene was to destroy him utterly, not simply to chase him out of the Carolinas. The Quaker general had dedicated himself to free America from tyranny. While he lived, he would not deviate from this resolve. He was a stubborn man with a goal. He was also intelligent, and therefore dangerous. On February 18 Greene ordered Lee and the Legion to recross the Dan to form a junction with Pickens, to harass the enemy and to ascertain and report his movements.[26] Lee reported that evening that Cornwallis was en route to Hillsboro.[27] On the 19th Lee had successfully passed the Dan and was encamped twenty-five miles from Hillsboro observing the flocking of the Tories.[28] He was also endeavoring to join Pickens. Should Cornwallis move from Hillsboro toward Cross Creek in an attempt to get supplies from the British post at Wilmington, Lee proposed to throw himself and Pickens in the enemy's front to delay him until Greene could come up.[29] Meanwhile he had written his commander, "I think you had better get in motion."[30]

Greene could not immediately get in motion, but on February 20 he sent Otho Williams, with the same light troops he had led in the Dan retreat, back across the river. They were to act in concert with Lee and Pickens and do everything in their power to prevent the British from withdrawing to Cross Creek or Wilmington.[31] To prevent the Tories in Cross Creek from embodying, General Alexander Lillington of the North Carolina militia and General Caswell were directed to activate a partisan force between Cross Creek and Wilmington in order to awe the Scotch Highlander inhabitants of the area with memories of Moore's Creek Bridge.[32]

Like Cornwallis, Greene had his frustrations. He had lured Cornwallis from his base of supplies and ground down his army. Surely now, while his adversary was weakened, was the time to strike. But Greene had not the manpower. Most of his militia and not a few of his Continentals, their time expired, had left him.[33] He hoped for reinforcements, indeed expected them daily. Yet they did not come. In an hour of desperate danger, all efforts to provide assistance became choked in a snarl of red tape, misunderstanding, and folly. The legislature of North Carolina took it upon themselves to countermand the orders of a body of militia on its way to the Dan and divert it to Wilmington. The Virginia militia of the counties bordering the Dan, seeing the enemy at their doors, rushed forward to volunteer, but their county lieutenants told them they had not been called according to law and dismissed them.[34] Steuben had managed to raise twenty-six hundred militia and four hundred new Continentals, but a rumor that Cornwallis was retreating to Wilmington caused the baron to halt the militia and send forward only the Continentals under Colonel Richard Campbell.[35] Colonel William Campbell of King's Mountain was expected daily with one thousand mountaineers, but they had yet to arrive.[36] Greene faced a dilemma. He might have stayed north of the Dan until he was strong enough to seek out Cornwallis and attack him. But if he did, Cornwallis might be so reinforced by jubilant Tories as to obviate Greene's increased complement. Or the British general might withdraw beyond Greene's reach. The enlistment terms of the militia were short at best. Marches of over one hundred miles could consume their time in travel. Moreover, many of them had no scruples about going home if they got tired out with difficulties or found the distance between them and fireside lengthening unduly.[37] In addition, Greene had no wish that Lee carry out his proposal to sacrifice the Legion to forestall Cornwallis' retreat. Aside from any question of Greene's personal friendship for Lee, the loss of the Legion would mean the loss of the eyes and ears of Greene's reconnaissance. Therefore, on February 23, 1781, Greene and an army of less than sixteen hundred recrossed the Dan. He had been reinforced by six hundred Virginia riflemen under General Edward Stevens.[38] Until more troops joined, Greene now planned a war of maneuver. He wrote to Jefferson, "I have been obliged to effect that by finesse which I dare not attempt by force."[39]

Meanwhile Lee and Pickens had been active. Pickens, who had been operating in the vicinity of Guilford Court House, moved to join Lee.[40] On the evening of February 21 he was within ten miles of Cornwallis' camp at Hillsboro. Before the British had any suspicion of an enemy's presence, a detachment of forty volunteers under Colonel McCall attacked a subaltern's picket, killed or wounded eight men, and carried off the luckless subaltern, nine soldiers, and some horses. "We had," Pickens wrote Greene, "not a man hurted."[41]

The above bit of impertinence within three miles of his camp induced Cornwallis to dispatch Tarleton and the Green Horse on February 23 to the country between the Haw and Deep rivers, some fifteen miles from Hillsboro.[42] The earl was still unaware of Greene's and Lee's movements and sanguine about enlisting the Loyalists. He knew that a considerable body of them was assembling beyond the Haw. Tarleton had orders to assist the volunteers and quell any effort of what Cornwallis took to be rebel partisans to prevent the Tories from gathering.[43] Tarleton entered upon this task with his usual enthusiasm.

Lee and Pickens had joined forces the morning of February 23 and were themselves moving toward the Haw for the reason that they had learned that the disaffected in that area were preparing to send great supplies to the British at Hillsboro.[44] The Americans soon got wind of the fact that a British force had advanced toward the Haw fields. Taking it to be a foraging party, they moved in cautious pursuit, pausing to pick up guides and sending exploring parties of cavalry toward the Haw. In midafternoon of February 24 they arrived at General Butler's farm, which they believed to be the object of the supposed foragers. Here Pickens and Lee learned that the number in the British party was "considerable, their objects extensive and their commander Lt. Col. Tarleton."[45]

The informants at Butler's farm told the Americans that Tarleton had crossed the Haw and encamped for the night at Mr. Hall's, four miles west of the river. He there expected to be joined by 350 North Carolina Loyalists under Colonel John Pyle together with a party of Colonel Hamilton's regiment.[46] Here Lieutenant Colonel Lee in his report to Greene says that *he* decided to cross the Haw in order to prevent the junction of Pyle and Tarleton. Lee and Pickens were greatly inferior in numbers to a combination of the British and Tories but might, with luck, succeed against them if they could attack each group separately. Since Pickens had been a brigadier general since Cowpens, it may reasonably be presumed that he had some share in Lee's decision, in spite of Lee's neglect to mention him.

In any case, the American pursuit reached Hall's place about five o'clock in the afternoon of February 24, 1781, only to find that Tarleton was four miles to their right at Major O'Neal's. Balked once more, the American force moved on rapidly—Lee and the cavalry in the front, Pickens with the mounted militia bringing up the rear. When they had marched three miles, they came up with Colonel Pyle's column of 350 Carolinians and the small group from Colonel Hamilton's regiment. This party was on its way to join Tarleton.[47]

By this time in the February afternoon in this wooded country, the light was failing.[48] Lee's Legion and Tarleton's Horse were both uniformed in tight-fitting short green jackets and plumed helmets. The prize Lee sought was not a hodge-podge collection of "deluded" back countrymen but Banastre Tarleton and his dragoons.[49] Morgan had severely mauled Tarleton at Cowpens; Lee might destroy him. With remarkable audacity and presence of mind, Lee took advantage of the similarity in uniforms and passed himself and his troops off as reinforcements for Tarleton.[50] Would Colonel Pyle and his men please draw aside to let the British troops pass to their destination? The awed provincials, with many protestations of loyalty, agreeably drew up on the right side of the road to give the supposed British free way.[51]

Lee and his Legion, with sabers drawn in salute, trotted along the line of mounted Tories to its head where Colonel Pyle was stationed.[52] As the number of the Legion nearly equalled that of Pyle's group, Lee had reached a point in the road opposite Pyle when the militia of Pickens came in view of the rear of the Loyalist column.

Apparently there had been a failure to fully communicate to Pickens the meaning of Lee's strategem. Perhaps there had been no communication at all because of the suddeness of the rencounter in a narrow country road heavily wooded on both sides. Whatever the way of it, a serious oversight had occurred. Needless to say, neither Patriot nor Tory militia were at any time uniformed. Consequently, as a distinguishing mark, the custom had developed that the Patriot militia wore in their hats or caps a green twig; Tories wore a red rag rosette.[53] Pickens' men all wore green twigs, and these had not been removed.[54] The Loyalists at the rear of the Tory line recognized Picken's corps as American because of this device and gave the alarm. Captain Eggleston of the Legion at the rear of the cavalry immediately ordered a charge, alerting the Legion troops ahead. It will be recollected that Lee's men already had their sabers drawn as if in salute. The rifles of Pyle's men were aslant over their shoulders. Before they could bring them to the ready, the legionnaires with their unsheathed sabers were upon them, slashing and cutting. "In ten minutes the whole body of the enemy was routed; the greater part was left on the ground dead and wounded. . . . The night came on and we necessarily deferred further operation."[55]

Lee and Pickens, overtaken by darkness, deferred their attack on Tarleton until dawn. By then it was too late. Cornwallis, having learned of Greene's recrossing of the Dan and tormented by visions of another Cowpens, sent three separate expresses to Tarleton on February 24 ordering his immediate recall to the main army.[56] It was an order which Tarleton obeyed with alacrity. "The capricious goddess [Fortune]," said Lee, "gave us Pyles and saved Tarleton."[57]

There was much subsequent criticism of Lee for his action. This was after the war. At the time there was only rejoicing.[58] The effect of this stroke on the will of the Tories to embody was the chief cause of satisfaction.

However, it was the inimitable Tarleton himself, who some days later gave the deathblow to Loyalist enthusiasm in the neighborhood. A party of Tories on the march to join the British standard was halted by a nervous picket. When they were unable to give the countersign of the day, the picket opened fire. The Tories fell back and huddled in the road, discussing how they should proceed. Suddenly, without warning, a detachment of dragoons under Tarleton charged them and cut to pieces all but the fleetest of foot. Later, discovering his mistake, the cavalry commander sent the dragoons to collect the scattered Loyalists, "but without effect"[59] —a development hardly to be wondered at in the circumstances. After that nobody wanted to have anything to do with anyone wearing a green jacket.

Meanwhile, Cornwallis had found his position at Hillsboro untenable. After recalling Tarleton on the evening of the Pyle massacre, he marched from Hillsboro southwest across the Haw to a position on Alamance Creek[60] at a junction of roads leading east to Hillsboro, west to Guilford Court House, and downriver to Cross Creek.[61] The downriver road was an avenue of escape if necessary. Ostensibly the commander's reason for leaving Hillsboro was to place himself nearer the enemy and in better posture to protect "our friends."[62] The truth is Cornwallis had worn his welcome out. Although the official state capitol, Hillsboro was no more than a village in size. When the British arrived there were supplies of salt beef, some pork, and a few hogs on the hoof in town, but these were soon exhausted. The only cattle in the neighborhood were draft oxen, which Cornwallis promised not to slaughter, except of necessity, since the animals were needed for the spring plowing.[63] Necessity arose, however, and several oxen were butchered, most of them the property of Loyalists. Ultimately Stedman, the civilian commissary, with an armed guard, was obliged to go from house to house and requisition supplies from the inhabitants, including all their spare shoes.[64] Not surprisingly, Cornwallis complained that he found himself "amongst timid friends and adjoining to inveterate rebels."[65] He decided to seek more healthful quarters.

In order to confuse any who might be watching him, the

British general made a feint and crossed the Eno south of Hillsboro as though on his way to Cross Creek. There he took ground on the evening of February 24, 1781, and waited for Tarleton to join him.[66] As he had surmised, Cornwallis was being watched with great care. Otho Williams knew within hours of the British move. "Lord Cornwallis grows apprehensive," he reported to Greene, "He moved out of town in a Hasty Quick Manner."[67]

On the 28th Williams reported that Cornwallis had backtracked and was probably on the west side of the Haw. Williams believed the earl was playing hide-and-seek with a view to bring action for which the American army was not ready. Williams was prepared to harass the enemy until Greene was ready. "Our present situation Appears to me not to be a bad one tho' not so agreeable as I could wish."[68] Cornwallis, however, went into position on Alamance Creek and there remained. Williams, Lee, and Pickens circled about him between five and ten miles off, awaiting opportunity. Williams wrote Greene: "While Lord Cornwallis keeps his position like a Bear with his Stern in a corner, I cannot attack him but at tooth and nail."[69]

The light troops were not strong enough to attack at tooth and nail. Neither was Greene, yet. So the war of maneuver—and of nerves—continued. Within a course of some twenty miles the Haw River receives three tributaries from the westward. The southernmost of these is the Alamance, where Cornwallis lay. North of it about twenty miles is Troublesome Creek. Between the two streams runs Reedy Fork, which empties into the Haw roughly midway of Troublesome and the Alamance. For two weeks the slender bulk of the main army operated between Speedwell's Iron Works on Reedy Fork and Boyd's Mill on Troublesome. The American commander constantly shifted his position, never remaining two nights in the same spot, never telling anyone where the night's encampment was to be until the hour for halting had arrived.[70]

The light troops under Williams, which now included Lee's Legion, William Washington's cavalry, Pickens' militia, three hundred mountaineers with Colonel William Preston of Virginia, and about one hundred more under Colonel William Campbell of King's Mountain,[71] acted as a screen between Greene and Cornwallis. Quite as restless as Greene, they were in continual motion, harassing, probing, intercepting supplies, cutting communications. To the wretched Tories in the neighborhood and to the immobilized Cornwallis, it seemed as though several armies were moving at once over the triangular area between the Troublesome, the Haw, and the Alamance, ready to attack at any quarter, but eluding every attempt to close with them.[72]

Tarleton and the British Legion were moving about in the same way for similar purposes.[73] On the night of March 3 Williams detailed Captain Kirkwood's company and thirty riflemen under Captain Baker to annoy the Green Horse. Kirkwood and Baker succeeded in destroying several men of an enemy picket, who were carelessly gathered round a bright camp fire, and in taking two prisoners.[74] Although nothing more was accomplished, Williams had the satisfaction of reporting to Greene next day that the interruption Captain Kirkwood gave the picket "appeared to be an inducement to Lt. Col. Tarleton to leave his Camp with seeming haste this morning early. A considerable quantity of Flour was left in hogsheads and in small parsells, kittles left over the fires, plates and other furniture, with a few cast Horses . . ."[75]

No doubt the flour was soon consumed, but in this lean and hungry land there was never enough of anything. The two weeks of waiting until Greene had sufficient reinforcements to challenge Cornwallis were a time of ragged nerves, of frustration, of hunger, sleeplessness, and petty vexations for both armies. Otho Williams, who loved and understood his fellow man so much that he forgave Gates for Camden,[76] suddenly had trouble with everyone. Of lean body himself and almost ascetic of visage, he could not understand the obstreperous riflemen newly under his command. "They cannot fast with good grace," he complained fretfully.[77] He even became waspish with Greene[78]—and then immediately contrite[79]—because of Greene's repetitious orders to attack the enemy whenever opportunity offered. He quarreled with Lee for commandeering for the Legion's sole use food and spirits sent for the light troops as a whole.[80]

Andrew Pickens also had as much as he wanted—and all that his men could stomach—of vexations and troubles. The hard core of his militia had been in the field without surcease since shortly after Charleston fell. They had not been paid in months, and most of them had not a second shirt to their backs. The new-raised back country militia Pickens had succeeded in collecting were outraged and deserting in droves because of Lee's action in dismounting them. Lee claimed that they did their fighting on foot anyway. Their good horses were needed as replacements for the Legion; the poor ones could be sent home and thus relieve the pressure on forage.[81] Rather understandably, the back country riflemen did not share the young Tidewater Virginian's viewpoint. "It has become a bone of contention for them," wrote Pickens to Greene. Then he added, mildly but firmly, "I must confess I want to see what becomes of Cornwallis, but should it be thought most advisable by you, I again repeat that I had rather return."[82] As noted earlier, neither Greene nor anyone else had authority to constrain the militia against their determination if their time was expended. On March 8 Greene ordered Pickens and his South Carolina and Georgia troops south to cooperate with Sumter.

However, during this time of stress Greene received what he afterwards said was the greatest compliment of his life. Customarily when the marchings and countermarchings of the day were over, he spent the evening in his tent at his paper work. After a few hours sleep, he was up again to make the rounds of the sentinels. One dark morning he passed the tent of a Virginia colonel; from it issued loud and comfortable snores. Greene entered the tent, shook the colonel by the shoulder and inquired how he could sleep so soundly at this hour just before dawn, the very time for surprise by the enemy. The officer opened his eyes, looked at his commander drowsily and said, "Why, General, I knew that you were awake." Then he turned over and fell asleep again like a good child.[83]

On March 6 the irritated and hungry Cornwallis struck back at the light troops who had routed Tarleton from his flour and "kittles" on March 3. Despite the defective quality of the British intelligence,[84] Cornwallis had managed to learn that sizeable Virginia reinforcements were on the march to join Greene. He wished, if possible, to bring Greene to action before their arrival.[85] At Wetzell's Mills on Reedy Fork lay a considerable quantity of cornmeal. Greene's provision wagons had been dispatched to carry it off.[86] Taking advantage of a heavy morning fog, Cornwallis hit hard with a view to surprise Williams and the light troops, who were covering the mill. Possibly if he could hurt Williams sufficiently, he could bring Greene, who was not far off, into the action.

The surprise did not come off. Williams was soon aware of the British movement on his left.[87] He hastily moved his troops to Wetzell's Mills, arriving there before Cornwallis' advance. Posting his troops on the north side of Reedy Fork, he was able to hold off the British until the loaded wagons with the precious meal got away.[88] Then he withdrew with but slight loss, although obliged to leave some of his wounded behind.[89] The British pursued for nearly five miles but found themselves much harassed by flanking parties under Lee and Washington. It had become obvious that the skirmish had resulted neither in cornmeal nor in action with Greene.[90] Accordingly the British prudently withdrew. The affair at Wetzell's Mills was chiefly notable for the miraculous escape of Lieutenant Colonel Webster. Webster on horseback led the British across the ford on Reedy Fork toward Williams' troops on the north bank. Lee had posted twenty-five crack riflemen of William Campbell's mountain men in a log house on the stream bank with orders to pick off the lead officers. All twenty-five of them drew bead on Webster, conspicuous by his position and the strength of his voice giving orders. Yet not a bullet touched him.[91] Death was willing to wait for the brave colonel a few weeks longer.

The game of cat and mouse that had seemed so long was drawing to a close. Even before the affair at Wetzell's Mills, orders had been dispatched to the light troops to prepare three days' cooked provisions in order to be in readiness for instant action.[92] However, several days more elapsed before Greene felt that he was strong as he could hope to be. After several notes heralding his approach,[93] Colonel Richard Campbell arrived from Virginia with four hundred new Continentals. Two brigades of militia, numbering 1,060, arrived from North Carolina under Brigadier John Butler and Colonel Pinkentham Eaton. One thousand six hundred and ninety-three Virginia militia also marched in and were organized into two brigades under Brigadiers Robert Lawson and Edward Stevens. On March 10 Williams' light troops were recalled and incorporated into the main army. Greene spent the next three days on the reorganization necessitated by his increased complement. Then he set out for the ground he had selected as a battlefield six weeks before on his flight to the Dan. On March 14 the American southern army took post at Guilford Court House.[94]

"I trust," Greene wrote Jefferson, "I shall be able to prescribe the limits of the enemy's depredations, and at least dispose of the army in such a manner as to encumber him with a number of wounded men."[95]

"EVEN FROM THE REBEL

ACCOUNT . . . A VICTORY"[1]

On March 17, 1781, Charles, second Earl Cornwallis, wrote Lord George Germain: "I have the satisfaction to inform your Lordship that His Majesty's troops under my command obtained a signal victory on the 15th instant over the Rebel Army commanded by General Greene."[2]

Major General Nathanael Greene wrote the Commander-in-Chief, George Washington: "My letter will inform you of an unsuccessful action with Lord Cornwallis on the 15th."[3]

Colonel Otho Williams wrote his brother Elie that the southern army had "once more" come off second best in a general action, but added cheerfully that Williams' "old horse Liberty" behaved "delightfully" in the battle.[4]

Somewhat ambiguously Major Mackenzie in New York noted in his diary: "Greene had been indefatigable in collecting troops and leading them to be defeated."[5]

With rather more prespicacity than anyone noted above Charles James Fox observed: "Another such victory would destroy the British Army."[6] The shade of Pyrrhus, King of Epirus, who had had considerable experience at Heraclea in 280 B.C., could have enlightened Mr. Fox still further. For all intents and purposes Cornwallis was destroyed at Guilford. The road from Guilford Court House led, with only minor meanderings, to Yorktown or, as Sir Henry Clinton felicitously put it, "to that burying ground which you had chosen."[7]

Let us then examine the action which Sir Henry, rather more mollified than usual with the behavior of his problem subordinate, acknowledged as "even from the Rebel Account ... a Victory."[8]

After the affair at Wetzell's Mills deprived him of the cornmeal he had hoped to obtain there, Cornwallis realized that he must open communciations with Major Craig at Wilmington. His army was in want of every necessity, and the food supply of the country had been almost completely exhausted by the depredations of the opposing armies.[9] Accordingly the earl moved from his camp on the Alamance and took position at the Quaker Meeting House at New Garden on the forks of the Deep River on March 13, 1781.[10] He was able to obtain some scanty subsistence from the gentle-mannered Friends in the neighborhood. While his hungry men consumed it, Cornwallis sent urgent messages to Craig to ship supplies by boat to Cross Creek to which place the army might have to retire.[11]

New Garden was less than twelve miles southwest of Guilford Court House. Consequently when Greene on March 14 took his post there with his whole army, his action was equivalent to throwing down the gauntlet or tossing a hat into the ring. It was a challenge which Cornwallis eagerly accepted. So straitened was he now for foodstuffs that his only alternative to closing with Greene was to retreat to Cross Creek or to the seacoast. The British commander did not hesitate over his choice. On the evening of March 14 he sent off Colonel Hamilton with the wagons and baggage to Bells' Mills on Deep River. At daybreak on March 15 Cornwallis marched with the rest of his corps to meet the enemy or attack him in his encampment.[12] The men marched breakfastless, not from any harsh disposition of their commander, but simply because there was no breakfast to feed them.[13]

Meanwhile, Greene had chosen his ground with care. Guilford Court House was an admirable field for a battle—for the formal, eighteenth century type of battle Greene seems to have had in mind. The court house itself stood on the brow of a domesticated hill in the midst of a howling wilderness.[14] The considerable cleared area around it, however, lay fallow. The few houses of the little village of Martinsville to the northeast had been deserted by their inhabitants, and the court house also was empty.[15] From the court house southward the ground sloped abruptly through half a mile of oak wood to an undulating valley in which there was a small stream. On the downslope edge of the oak wood were several fields of varying size which had been planted to corn the preceding summer. Portions of a zigzag rail fence still stood between the fields and the sapling trees on the edge of the wood. The area surrounding the fields was open and relatively treeless, a kind of rolling meadow[16] with small eminences of rising ground here and there.

The Great Road from Salisbury to Hillsboro,[17] over which Cornwallis must approach, entered the meadow from the southwest through a narrow defile shouldered by rising ground covered with dense coverts of copse.[18] After passing this defile, which was close to a half mile in length, the road wound a little east of north, intersecting the old corn fields and climbing the slope through the wood to the court house on the brow of the hill. Anyone situated on the rising ground from the little vale to the height above had a nearly clear view of the valley floor, for the trees at this season of the year were still in bud. It was much the same view the audience has in a Greek theatre. The defile entering the open space might be likened to the central players' entrance in such a theatre.

When Greene marched his army into camp at Guilford on the afternoon of March 14, 1781, there was still light enough remaining to enable him to make a second survey of

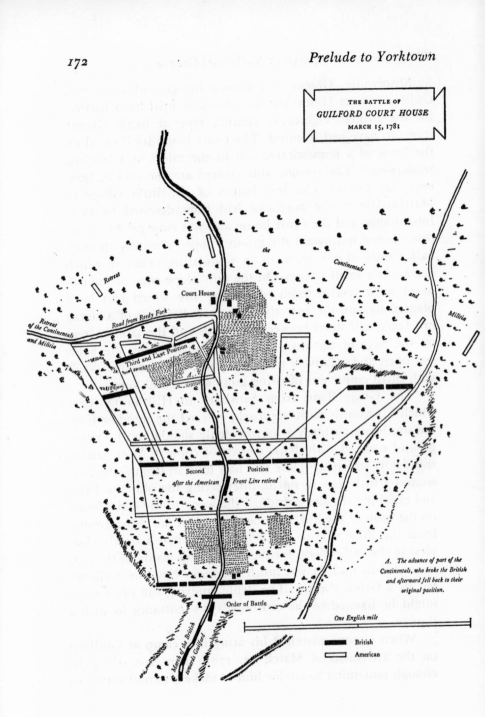

THE BATTLE OF
GUILFORD COURT HOUSE
MARCH 15, 1781

Retreat

the

Continentals

Court House

Road from Reedy Fork

Retreat
of the Continentals

and Militia

and

Militia

Third and Last Position

A.

Second   Position
after the American Front Line retired

*A. The advance of part of the
Continentals, who broke the British
and afterward fell back to their
original position.*

Order of Battle

March of the British
toward Guilford

One English mile

British

American

the ground he had selected six weeks before.[19] He did this with his usual thoroughness and then summoned his officers and gave out the order of battle.[20]

Greene's army at this time comprised the following units: Otho Williams' brigade of the 1st and 2nd Maryland regiments, which included some Delaware infantry, 630 rank and file; Brigadier General Isaac Huger's 4th and 5th Continental regiments, 778 rank and file; the infantry of Lee's Legion, 82 men; and Kirkwood's light infantry, 110 men, making a total of 1600 regular infantry. In addition there were four brigades of militia: two from North Carolina of 500 men each under Brigadier Generals Pinketham Eaton and John Butler; two from Virginia of about 600 men each under Brigadier Generals Robert Lawson and Edward Stevens. There were two corps of riflemen numbering 400 under Colonels Charles Lynch and Richard Campbell plus the scant 100 under Williams Campbell of King's Mountain. The cavalry consisted of Lee's 75 horsemen and William Washington's 86 light dragoons. The artillery—four six-pounders—was served by 60 artillerists and matrosses under Captains Anthony Singleton and Samuel Finley. In grand total Greene had a force of something less than 5000[21] despite Cornwallis' estimate of it at 9000-10,000.[22]

Although 1490 infantry were rated as regulars of the Continental line,[23] only 630 war-worn veterans of Maryland and Delaware had ever before been in battle. It was impossible to predict how the untried Virginia Continentals would react to bullets and bayonets. Of the riflemen, many had stood the test of King's Mountain, but they were, as always, an independent lot. All of them were volunteers, bound for no stated time and free to leave at a moment's notice, or simply at their own pleasure.[24] As for the militia, their behavior was ever as unpredictable as their experience was varied. At this stage of the war a majority of them had probably been in the field half a dozen times, but this did not

necessarily mean that they had seen action. Many of them
had merely tramped briefly up and down the countryside,
consuming rations, engaging perhaps in a small skirmish or
two, such as the one at Cowan's Ford, and speedily returning
home "to kiss their wives and sweethearts," as Greene acidly
put it.[25] In the back country, where hunting was as much a
part of daily living as farming, the militia, even the boys,
were fine marksmen. However, deer, bear, and possum
seldom return fire. By and large, most militiamen found a
show of determination on the part of the enemy quite un-
nerving. Yet among them were not a few time-expired Continentals.[26] Some of the North Carolinians had fought under
Morgan at Cowpens.[27]

Greene had been in correspondence with Morgan. Morgan wrote: "If they [the militia] fight you'll beat Cornwallis,
if not he will beat you.... Put [them] ... in the centre with
some picked troops in the rear with orders to shoot down the
first man that runs."[28]

Greene planned his dispositions accordingly and so informed his officers the evening of March 14. When and if
Cornwallis accepted the challenge—and Greene had no
doubt he would accept it—Greene proposed to form his army
as follows: the North Carolina militia would constitute the
first line posted behind the rail fence at the back edge of
last summer's corn fields with nine hundred yards of open
ground between them and the mouth of the defile from
which Cornwallis must emerge. Three hundred yards back
of the Carolinians in the shelter of the budding oaks the
Virginia militia would take post. The third and Continental
line would form on the brow of the court house hill, 550
yards in the rear of the Virginians. Lee's post would be on
the American left on an eminence just back of the flank of
the first line. Washington and his cavalry would protect the
American right flank. It was a disposition roughly similar to
that of Cowpens, but the distance between the lines was

much greater. Instead of the sharpshooters Morgan had deployed ahead of his first line at Cowpens, Greene had Singleton and two of the six-pounders stationed in the center of the Carolinian first line where it was bisected by the Salisbury Road. Singleton would thus be ready to move the guns forward on the road and open on the enemy when the time came. The two remaining guns were in the center of the third Continental line. This line, because of the conformation of the hill, was actually posted to the American right of the Salisbury Road at an angle to the second line in the wood. Just back of it the road to Reedy Fork ran at right angles to the Salisbury Road, affording an avenue of retreat should the fortunes of the day go against the Americans. Across the road just in front of the court house was Greene's command post. There was no reserve; the entire army was in the lines.[29]

Having determined that his officers understood perfectly what their positions would be on the morrow, Greene sent the baggage off to the old camp at the Iron Works on Troublesome Creek, now designated as a rendezvous in case of defeat.[30] Lee with his Legion, supported by William Campbell and his rifles, was constituted a reconnaissance group.[31] Lee, accordingly, late in the evening of March 14 ordered Lieutenant Heard with a small party of dragoons to place himself near the British camp and to report at intervals any unusual occurrences there.[32]

After Heard with his contingent had clattered off into the night, the men of the army slept or sleeplessly awaited the morning, in conformity with the state of their nerves. The greater part of the rank and file knew little of what portended. On the whole a feeling of hope and confidence prevailed.[33] As Major St. George Tucker wrote his beloved Fanny: "We little folk walk about with a bandage over our eyes and with wool in our ears."[34]

In the small hours of the morning of March 15 the alert Heard reported that all efforts to approach closely to the enemy camp had proved abortive because of far-flung British patrols.[35] In a later message Heard said that the sound of rumbling wheels convinced him that a general movement was in progress.[36] Greene promptly ordered Lee and the balance of the reconnaissance force forward.

As noted earlier, Cornwallis marched at dawn, Tarleton and his dragoons probing ahead.[37] About mid-morning, some four miles from Guilford, Lee and Tarleton met. There ensued a sharp, running skirmish, the details of which vary considerably, depending upon who is recounting them. Cornwallis says that Tarleton "defeated" Lee.[38] Greene says Captain Armstrong of Lee's Legion charged Tarleton and "cut down near 30 dragoons."[39] Tarleton says he drove Lee back and took prisoners.[40] Lee says that Tarleton sounded a retreat and Lee took prisoners, "Not a single American soldier or horse injured."[41]

In such cases the historian may perhaps accept what he sees fit. There *was* a skirmish. The sound of firing was heard in the American camp.[42] It appeared to be so near that Greene at once prepared for battle.[43] It should be noted as well, that neither Lee nor Tarleton was expected to expend his force in destruction. They were acting as reconnaissance troops. Their duty was to discover the enemy's movements and report them back to their commanders with as little loss as possible to their own body. Retreat was not only prudent but necessary and expected of both groups. As it was, the British may be considered to have suffered more than the Americans. A rifle ball struck Tarleton in the right hand, painfully maiming the first and middle fingers.[44] Tarleton's tenacity was such, however, that he refused to consider himself disabled. He fought through the rest of the day with his right arm in a sling, his bridle reins held in the left.[45] He was quite defenseless and vulnerable. For better or worse, courage is not a quality limited wholly to Galahads.

Lee returned to Guilford toward noon and placed his

Legion, with Campbell's rifles, in its assigned position on the American left.[46] The rest of the army was already in line or rapidly occupying the assigned posts. The North Carolinians were behind the rail fence at the edge of the corn field. Captain Singleton moved his two six-pounders a few paces ahead of this first line. The muzzles of the guns were trained on the opening of the defile from which the head of the British column would emerge. This opening was long range for such artillery. It would be some time after the British appeared before the cannon could be used to any purpose.

Quite incredibly, there was no outpost in the defile itself, although surely marksmen stationed in the dense copses on the shoulders could have done much damage to the enemy column constricted in the narrow half-mile stretch of road.

Back three hundred yards from the Carolinians in the oak wood stood the Virginia militia with Stevens and Lawson. Some of them were uneasily aware of the grim-faced sentinels posted at intervals in their rear.[47] Stevens had had the mortification of seeing his militia flee Camden at the first volley.[48] He was taking no chances this time. He had followed Morgan's advice to the letter.[49] The sentinels had orders to shoot down the first Virginia militiaman to run.

On the brow of the court house hill was the third line of Continentals on the north side of the Salisbury Road. This third line could see the open ground in the vale but could not see the first and second lines.[50]

When all arrangements were complete, Greene passed along the first line of militia.[51] The day has been variously described as cold, cool, and hot.[52] In short, it was March, when, in regard to weather anything can happen within a few hours. There is general agreement that at this noontide hour the air was clear with a bright sun and no wind worth mentioning, but there had been frost the night before. It is probable that the midday sun was warm. Greene was a florid man with a tendency toward weight. It is remembered that he held his hat in one hand and mopped the perspiration from his forehead with the other as he asked the militia for two or three rounds: "Then you may fall back, boys."[53] His voice was clear and firm,[54] pleasant but unemotional with a slight nasal twang alien to the ears of the Carolina backwoodsmen.[55]

Lee followed Greene along the line, his dashing horsemanship contrasting unfavorably with Greene's awkward countryman's seat.[56] The young Virginian sought to ease any nervousness the militia might entertain. He "rode along the line from one end to the other, exhorting them to stand firm and not to be afraid of the British, for he swore that he had whipped them three times that morning and could do it again."[57] The militia heard him with an enthusiasm somewhat tempered by the fact that he was known to them chiefly as the officer who commandeered their horses as remounts for his cavalry.[58]

In short, there was at Guilford no grizzled giant with a stentorian voice more sonorous than brass or steel, no Old Wagoner riding the lines at a gallop, calling men by name and making them feel that he loved and depended on them. Greene with his aides plodded back to the post on the brow of the hill while Lee trotted to position on the left flank. The militia at their fence rails were alone; it is possible that they felt lonely.[59] Major Richard Harrison, leaning on the fence, ingeniously used his domestic problems as a counterirritant for his present unease. March 15 was the day that his Ann was due to present him with a child. Faced awfully with life and death, he pulled pencil and paper from his pocket: "This is the very day that I hope will be given me a creature capable of enjoying what its father hopes to deserve and earn—the sweets of Liberty and Grace."[60]

The British meanwhile reached the point on the Salisbury Road where it crossed the stream rather prosaically known as Horse Creek. Today the creek is bridged, but at that time Cornwallis' men as usual had to get their feet wet. After fording the stream they marched into the unguarded defile. It was nearly one-thirty when the head of the British column debouched into the open valley. They could be seen for nearly a mile defiling on the double, "their scarlet uniforms and burnished arms contrasting strongly with the somber countryside . . . barren of leaves and grass."[61] "An army with banners and a most gorgeous array."[62]

The right of the British line consisted of the Hessian Regiment von Bose, whose men wore tall, conical leather hats with a brass device just over the forehead. At a distance such a device appeared to be the man's face, the real face obscured by the chin strap. Thus a man of moderate height appeared six feet tall, a six-footer a giant. This, of course, was precisely the object of the design. With the Hessians were Fraser's Highlanders in tartan with their bagpipes.[63] The left of the line under Colonel Webster, who had escaped the picked riflemen at Wetzell's Mills, was composed of the red-coated Welsh Fusiliers and the 33rd Regiment of grenadiers in tall bearskin shakos, the 2nd battalion of Guards in support. In the rear of the column in the road glinted the plumed brass helmets of Tarleton's horse.[64] Underneath all this panoply, of course, were tired and hungry men who marched twelve miles without breakfast and with holes in their boots.

As soon as he thought the van within range, Singleton in the road ahead of the first line opened fire with his two six-pounders. Lieutenant McLeod of the British artillery pushed three guns forward and replied. The cannonade continued for more than twenty minutes with little damage done on either side. The experienced Cornwallis neatly calculated the intervals in Singleton's fire and deployed his troops between blasts. Thus the cannonade for the inexperienced militia must have been twenty minutes of stomach-tightening noise during which the unruffled British led charmed lives.

The Carolinians could see only too clearly ahead of them as the shot whistled over their heads, but they had no way of knowing whether the Virginians in the woods, three hundred long yards to their rear, were hurt or not.

At the end of twenty minutes Singleton withdrew his guns to the second line in the wood.[65] McLeod's guns also fell silent. From the British ranks sounded a pulse-quickening beating of drums and squealing of fifes. Against a dun-colored backdrop the enemy marched into the cleared fields in front of the Carolinians, moving forward deliberately, as if on parade,[66] a broad, shining line, blood-red under the sun.

Here the record becomes confused. Lee says: "To our infinite distress and mortification the North Carolina militia took to flight."[67] Greene wrote later to Washington: "They left the most advantageous position I ever saw, without scarcely firing a gun."[68] Simms states: "A single discharge from the whole line may have been delivered."[69] Since the North Carolinians numbered one thousand, this would seem to be verified by Ward's statement that "then a thousand rifles spoke."[70]

However, there was an eyewitness to this affair, whose judgment in other matters is sound.[71] Sergeant Roger Lamb of the Welsh Fusiliers was no recruit. He was twenty-seven years of age in 1781, had been in the British service since the age of seventeen and on active duty in America since 1776. As Lamb points out, what the Americans failed to realize was that while the British troops in the valley were conspicuously visible to them, the Rebel troops were by no means so to the British. The Carolina militia behind the unpainted rail fence blended with the leafless wood rising behind them. To the British moving in slanting sunlight north and east, the old corn field, the rail fence, and the wood back of it were all one drab color. The militia were un-uniformed, and at this season the green twigs they wore in their hats came of necessity from the few pine trees that grew among the oaks on the hill. Hence the green was not very vivid. The only bit of color afforded was their battle flag, but in the windless hush it drooped inconspicuously on its staff in the care of Maciyah Bullock. Therefore Lamb tells us:

After the brigade formed across the open ground, the colonel [Webster] rode on to the front and gave the word, "Charge!" Instantly the move was made, in excellent order, in a smart run, with arms charged. When arrived within forty yards of the enemy's line, it was perceived that their whole force had their arms presented and resting on the rail fence, the common partitions in all America. They were taking aim with the nicest precision.... At this awful moment a general pause took place; both parties surveyed each other with the most anxious suspense. Nothing speaks the general more than seizing on decisive moments: Colonel Webster rode forward in the front ... and said with more even than his usual commanding voice, "Come on, my brave Fuzileers!"[72]

Colonel Webster appears to have been possessed of the kind of far-carrying voice which may be deplorable in the drawing room but is very useful on the field of battle. Lamb reports that it acted like an inspiration and the men rushed forward *"amidst the enemy's fire; dreadful was the havoc on both sides."*[73] The British fusil did not have the range of the American rifle. Consequently the fusiliers were obliged to move forward some yards before they could return the fire. When they did return, they delivered one volley and charged with the bayonet. *"At last,"* says Lamb, "the Americans gave way, and the brigade advanced to attack the second line."[74]

It would appear that the North Carolinians did put up some resistance, even perhaps in some cases the three volleys which were all that had been requested of them. Green troops who will stand for a bayonet charge when they themselves have no bayonets must be rare in history.[75] However, three volleys or none, when they did break it was a rout. Brigadiers Eaton and Butler and other officers of every grade vainly attempted to hold them. Colonel Davie, the Commissary General, and Major Harrison, the expectant father, shouted and cursed at them to no effect. Lee left his post and spurred among them, threatening to fall upon them with his cavalry. "All was vain; so thoroughly confounded were these unhappy men, that, throwing away arms, knapsacks, and even canteens, they rushed like a torrent headlong through the woods."[76]

A very few of them, all belonging to Pinketham Eaton's brigade, joined the militia under William Campbell and, with the infantry of the Legion, bravely held their ground against the oncoming foe.[77] The rest poured like a herd of berserk steers through the second Virginia line. General Stevens had the wit to tell his men that the retreat of the Carolinians was part of a plan.[78] Therefore the Virginians opened ranks to let them pass, but not without jeers and taunts at their undisciplined haste.[79]

The defection of the first line center had not spread to the supporting corps on the American right and left. Thus the British advance to the second line found itself the object of "a most destructive fire"[80] from Kirkwood and Lynch on the American right and the Legion infantry and Campbell's rifles on the left. The steady fire enfiladed the British lines in such a way that a bullet missing the first man was quite likely to hit another farther down the line. To meet this hazard the British jaegers and the 33rd Regiment wheeled to the left on Kirkwood and Lynch while the Regiment von Bose and the Highlanders turned on Lee and Campbell. This left a gap in the British center which was filled by the grenadiers and the 2nd battalion of the Guards.[81]

The cleared ground had been left behind. The fighting was now in the woods where the forest-wise frontiersmen had all the advantage, and the cavalry of both sides were all but useless. Cornwallis ordered Tarleton to keep in compact order in the road and not to charge without positive orders unless he saw that some British corps was in evident danger of defeat.[82] The battle had now become general, but because of the wood and the broken terrain, which was everywhere intersected by ravines and gullies of varying breadth and depth, those engaged knew very little of what was happening except just ahead or to their immediate right and left.[83] Kirkwood and Lynch managed to fall back with Washington's support and take a position on the right of the Virginia militia. Campbell attempted to do likewise on the left, but the Regiment von Bose struck across his front and cut him off from the Virginians. He and Lee were forced farther and farther to their left until they finally found themselves on a height of ground to the southward of the main battle. They continued at this point to oppose the Hessians in a contest entirely separated from the main engagement.[84]

Cornwallis, having re-formed, advanced on Greene's second line. The Virginians, under General Stevens' exhortations and mindful of the sentinels in their rear, quitted themselves well. Tarleton, who had contemptuously noted the retreat of the first line, remarked that "at this place [the second line] the action became more severe."[85] Covering themselves with trees, the Virginians kept up a galling fire which severely damaged the British ranks. Gradually, however, the right of the line, that to the right of the Salisbury Road, swung back until it was at a right angle to the Virginia left.[86] General Stevens took an unlucky ball in his thigh and was carried from the field. The British took advantage of the confusion attendant on the loss of the commander to infiltrate the rear of this right section of the Virginians. When the militia discovered themselves beset fore and aft, they yielded to nearly as abject a panic as that which had afflicted the Carolinians. Major St. George Tucker and his brother Beverley were able to rally sixty or seventy of them,[87] but the rest fled to the shelter of the third Continental line. Washington with his cavalry covered their retreat.[88]

The Virginia militia on the left held out a little longer until Cornwallis himself led a charge against them, when they began to fade back to the third line.[89] Meanwhile Colonel Webster with the 23rd Regiment, which had routed Stevens' militia, found no one between himself and the right half of the Continental line, which had not yet taken part in the battle. He decided to bypass the remnants of the second line, now unsupported by Washington's horse, and engage the third line. Here Webster was so sharply received by the veteran 1st Maryland under Colonel John Gunby and Lieutenant Colonel John Eager Howard of Cowpens, together with Hawes' Virginia Continentals and Kirkwood's light infantry, that he was obliged to fall back across the ravine.[90] Here he posted himself on an eminence and waited the approach of the rest of the British line, which struggled amid gullies, thickets, and imprecations to reach the open ground of the court house height.[91]

The 2nd battalion of the Guards was the first to gain the cleared ground and immediately swept to attack the 2nd Maryland Regiment formed in the field to the left of the road.[92] The 2nd Maryland was far superior[93] in numbers to the Guards and was supported by Captain Finley with two six-pounders. Otho Williams, confidently expecting his second regiment to behave with the courage displayed so shortly before by the first, hastened toward it with the idea of combining his whole force to resist the attack.[94] He was disappointed. The 2nd Maryland was composed largely of recruits in their first battle. Their nerves gave way at the crucial moment, and they fled, abandoning Finley and the guns.[95] Stuart with the Guards (O'Hara, the commander, had been wounded) pursued them, seizing the guns as he went.[96]

Gunby with the 1st Maryland, freed by Webster's retreat across the ravine, wheeled on the Guards and retook the guns.[97] Simultaneously Washington, having witnessed the inglorious retreat of the 2nd Maryland, charged furiously into the melée, followed by John Eager Howard and his infantry with fixed bayonets.[98] There was wild fighting. Flared-nostriled horses, men with teeth bared like angry dogs, plunging sabers, lunging bayonets, swinging musket butts tangled in a seemingly inextricable mass in a hand-to-hand struggle to the death. Stuart of the Guards was killed. Lovell of the Guards fell to the ground on the edge of the melée and prudently remained there.[99] Peter Francisco, the giant dragoon in Washington's corps, cut down eleven men with his broadsword but was checked when one of the Guards pinned Francisco's leg to his horse with a bayonet. This strange ward of Patrick Henry's assisted his assailant to withdraw the bayonet, then brought his sword down on the man's skull and cleft it to the shoulders.[100]

Cornwallis and the wounded O'Hara watched the affray from the Salisbury Road. Cornwallis decided on a desperate remedy. Lieutenant McLeod had just come up with two three-pounders. Over O'Hara's protests the British commander directed McLeod to load the guns with grapeshot and open fire on the struggling mass.[101] O'Hara pleaded that the fire would kill friend and foe alike. The earl was aware of this, but it was also obvious to him that if something were not done to separate the British and Americans, the whole 2nd battalion of Guards would be killed or taken prisoner.[102] McLeod fired. The tangled mass of men and animals gradually drew apart. The men on their feet reeled as though dazed or drunken. As their faces again assumed a semblance of humanity, they looked about them with wonder and horror at a world in which trees still budded, clouds scurried across a graying sky under a waning sun, and blood sullied the trampled earth. Old soldiers will tell you that there is a smell about such encounters. It is not the odor of blood or of gunpowder or of dead men. It is simply the smell of battle, unmistakable and curiously lingering.[103]

Nathanael Greene from his post in front of the court house had seen the whole affair. As general in command, as challenger of Cornwallis, and as a man who was to the best of his ability honest with himself, he knew quite well who had instigated the carnage. The realization of death afflicted is not easy for any commander to take. One may at least speculate that a man who had been a Quaker for thirty years and a general for only six might find the acceptance of his role of violence more difficult than is common. Few of us ever escape the conditioning of our youth.

Meanwhile the 71st Regiment and the grenadiers of the Guards had extricated themselves from the ravines in which they had been floundering in time to witness the effect of Cornwallis' grapeshot.[104] They emerged from the wood on the American left opposite the court house. O'Hara, his wound dressed, exerted himself to rally the remnants of the 2nd battalion. Webster now recrossed the ravine with the 23rd Regiment to threaten the American right. Tarleton arrived on the Salisbury Road with a portion of his cavalry.[105] "The enemy," said Cornwallis, "were soon put to flight."[106]

Said Greene: "They having turned our left flank, got into the rear of the Virginia brigade and appearing to be gaining on our right, which would have encircled the whole of our Continental troops, I thought it most advisable to order a retreat.... We lost our artillery and two ammunition waggons."[107]

The artillery horses were all dead. Greene would not risk the delay entailed in hauling off the guns and ammunition wagons by hand. Leaving Huger[108] with the Virginia Continentals to hold the enemy in check, the American general retreated in good order three miles to Reedy Fork. There he halted to collect stragglers and wait for Lee, who did not appear.[109] Believing that Cornwallis might be in pursuit, Greene then proceeded ten miles to the old camp at the Iron Works on Troublesome Creek, the army marching all night in a pouring rain. Greene had accomplished his announced intention. He had encumbered the enemy with a number of wounded men.[110] But the weary weeks of little sleep and the events of the day had taken their toll even of his resolution. When the army was safely bivouacked, Greene fainted.[111]

Cornwallis was left in possession of the field. He could legitimately claim a victory, but its cost was excessive. Of the 1,900 men who went into battle under him,[112] more than a fourth were casualties—93 dead and 439 wounded.[113] Four officers were killed, 24 others wounded, many of them mortally. Of these was the gallant Colonel Webster, whose stout heart earned him a slow and painful end. The regiment hardest hit by officer casualties was the Guards. Nine of their number fell, most of them in the melée on the court house hill.[114]

Greene's casualties were much less in proportion to his numbers—78 killed and 156 wounded. Those listed as missing, however, did more honor to their prudence and fleetness of foot than their courage—161 Continentals and 885 militia. Of the latter, 563 were North Carolinians, more than 50 percent of the total of 1,000. On the credit side the Carolinians had six killed and five wounded.[115]

The battleground at Guilford on the night of March 15 was not a happy place. The sun that had shone so brightly at noon was obscured at three o'clock that afternoon. Shortly after Greene began his retreat the skies opened. Rain fell in torrents all night long and the darkness was intense. The tired and hungry men still fit for duty did what they could to succor the wounded, but it was inadequate. There were no tents, no shelter, no proper surgical supplies, nor even any food. Supper was as non-existent as breakfast had been. The morning of March 16 saw fifty men, whose wounds had not in themselves been mortal, dead of exposure. After forty-eight hungry hours, Cornwallis' foragers and cattle drovers were able to supply sick, wounded, and well with just four ounces of flour and four ounces of lean beef per man. The victor of Guilford wrote his battle report amid the groans of the dying.[116]

"LEFT THEIR DEAD UNBURIED ON THE GROUND"[1]

Greene sent his surgeon, Dr. Wallace, to Cornwallis' camp on Guilford battlefield to care for the American casualties in British hands and forwarded some of his own small store of provisions and medical supplies for their use.[2] The two exhausted armies lay within ten miles of each other for two days licking their wounds. It was a time of growing optimism in the American camp as reports came in indicating the magnitude of Cornwallis' hurt.[3] Conversely for the British it was a period of growing despondency. Lee's Legion hung on the fringes of the camp.[4] No foraging party was safe, no provision train unmolested.[5]

On the third day after the battle[6] the British abandoned the camp at Guilford and marched to New Garden. There Cornwallis installed seventy of his most seriously wounded in the Quaker Meeting House and committed them to Greene's humanity.[7] He then set out, with the rest of the wounded swinging painfully in horse litters, for Cross Creek where he believed supplies had been sent for him from Wilmington.[8] En route he issued a proclamation:

WHEREAS by the blessing of Almighty God, his Majesty's arms have been crowned with signal success, by the compleat victory obtained over the Rebel forces on the 15th instant, I have thought proper to call upon all loyal

subjects to stand forth, and take an active part in restoring
good order and government....[9]

He might better have saved his breath. The prudence
of the Loyalists overcame whatever devotion they had for the
king. These Tories had hardly had time to spread the glad
tidings that Greene was chased across the Dan before Greene
was back again. When they had sought to embody, Lee had
cut the party under Pyle to ribbons.[10] Tarleton's savage attack on another group of volunteers was still a vivid memory.
"Food and intelligence they gave cheerfully, but reserved
their swords and rifles for a more propitious occasion."[11]
"Many," said Cornwallis disgustedly, "rode into camp, shook
me by the hand, said they were glad to see us, and to hear
that we had beat Greene, then rode home again. I could not
get 100 men in all the Regulators' country to stay with us
even as militia."[12]

Lee, not to be outdone, issued a proclamation of his own
to the Whigs[13] and set off in pursuit of the British. Greene
immediately prepared to follow.[14] As he could not afford to
be encumbered with his own and the enemy's wounded, he
wrote a letter to the Quaker inhabitants of the countryside.
He mentioned that he had been brought up a Quaker, and
he urged the Quakers to care for the wounded of both sides.
That way they would be showing no partisanship. The pacific
folk complied and provided the hospitals with every comfort
in their power.[15]

As soon as it was determined that Cornwallis was not for
the Yadkin but headed southeast, Greene broke camp on
March 20 and followed him. Greene did not yet know
whether the British general intended to make for Cross
Creek and Wilmington or whether he proposed to march to
the Pee Dee[16] and to return by that route to South Carolina.
Nevertheless, the American general was at pains to do everything in his power to slow the enemy's progress. Lee and the

Legion continued to hang on the flanks and rear of the British. Colonel Malmedy, who had been engaged in intercepting the British supply trains in the Quaker Church area since March 18,[17] was ordered to join General Lillington in the country between Cross Creek and Wilmington.[18] Lillington's partisans had the duties of preventing any junction of Craig's forces from Wilmington with Cornwallis and of discouraging any Tory rising in an area known to favor the British cause.[19]

Meanwhile, Greene pressed on through heavy rains and over muddy roads in pursuit of his quarry. On March 22 he was at Buffalo Creek,[20] and on the 26th near Rigdon's Ford on Deep River.[21] He had been delayed a day by the need to bring up ammunition. The country through which the army was now passing was deeply disaffected. Provisions were scant, Tories numerous.[22] The militia, hungry for meat and nervous of their neighbors, had recklessly wasted powder and ball taking pot shots at game and the disaffected.[23]

On March 27 came evil news. The North Carolina and Virginia militia with Greene had been enlisted for only six weeks. They had now been with the army twenty-three days. Greene knew that at best he had perhaps two more weeks to employ them against Cornwallis. He felt that he could manage this with luck, for Cornwallis, encumbered with wounded, was not many miles ahead, despite the wait for ammunition. However, on the 27th Greene discovered with dismay that the militia counted their six weeks as measured from the day of their gathering in the different counties, not from the day they joined the army. Furthermore, the men counted the time consumed in returning home as part of their six weeks stint. This meant that the majority of them had only about four days remaining.[24] In vain Greene pleaded with them. The men were determined to stand up for what they considered their rights. The few who consented to remain did so on the condition that it was at their own pleasure; they were free to leave at any time. "Upon such a precarious footing," Greene wrote Jefferson," . . . no measure can be taken with certainty."[25]

Nonetheless, he pushed on hoping to bring Cornwallis to battle before the militia left him.[26] Word came that the British were at Ramsey's Mill on Deep River twelve miles below Rigdon's Ford and still on the same side of the river as Greene.[27] The Americans reached the mill on March 28 to find that Cornwallis had bridged the river, crossed to the far side and moved some miles southward. "They left with the greatest precipitation so much so as to leave their dead unburied on the ground. I wish we had provisions to enable us to continue our pursuit."[28]

Lee and his Legion had moved into the camp as Cornwallis' rear guard drew off, and thus prevented them from destroying the bridge as Cornwallis had ordered.[29] The bridge, therefore, was available for Greene's use, but he was is such straits for provisions that many of the men had fainted from hunger on the march.[30] In the slaughter pens in the hastily evacuated camp were some quarters of lean beef. The starving men hastily devoured them half-cooked and then, their hunger still unslaked, consumed the offal that had been thrown aside for the turkey buzzards.[31]

For days Greene had had the greatest difficulty in obtaining provisions. The same Tories who supplied Cornwallis shot down the American foraging parties and refused to furnish any intelligence concerning the British army.[32] Lee, maneuvering in Cornwallis' rear, was the sole source of information.[33] Furthermore on April 2 the last of the militia would leave. Greene's force then would consist of about fourteen hundred men. He had to come to some decision as to how to employ them. He knew that Cornwallis was weak, but so was Greene. One thing was certain, he could not pursue Cornwallis into the pine barrens between Ramsey's Mill and Cross Creek without provisions. A crow would find it difficult to live off those bleak sand hills, let alone an army. Greene determined to rest his men a few days at the mill and collect provisions.[34] During the halt he made his decision. On March 29 he wrote Washington: "I am determined to carry the war immediately into South Carolina. The enemy will be obliged to follow us, or give up his posts in that state. If the former takes place, it will draw the war out of this state. . . . If they leave their posts [in South Carolina] to fall, they must lose more than they can gain here. If we continue in this state the enemy will hold their possessions in both."[35]

Greene added that he was sure that the move would be unexpected by the enemy and stated, *"I intend it shall be as little known as possible."*[36]

On March 30 Greene wrote to Sumter informing the Gamecock of his intentions, telling him to alert Marion and Pickens and adjuring him that *"the object must be secret to all except the generals."*[37] He also wrote Lillington, preparing him perhaps for a surprise by saying, "You shall be further supported, as far as . . . *consistent with the great plan of operations."*[38] A day or two later Greene wrote James Emmet, an officer of Lillington's corps who had been supplying him with intelligence from Cross Creek: "Don't be surprised if my movements don't correspond with your ideas of military propriety. War is an intricate business. . . . Nothing shall be left unattempted to give protection to this Country, *but the manner can only be known to myself."*[39]

Evidently Greene also wrote Lee, confiding his intentions, for on April 2, Lee replied: "As you have been pleased to honor me with your confidence, I take the liberty to communicate to you my sentiments respecting your plan of operations. I am decidedly of the opinion with you, that nothing is left for you but to imitate the example of Scipio Africanus."[40]

At the risk of tedium, the steps in Greene's decision to move south have been outlined in detail for the purpose of questioning an old fallacy accepted by some historians—namely, that it was Lee who instigated the plan. It has been noted before that Greene rarely held councils of war. There is absolutely no evidence that he did so on this occasion; indeed, the adjurations to secrecy in the letters quoted above point to the contrary. Otho Williams, as Deputy Adjutant General, was responsible for many official records of the southern campaign. Were these available they might shed light on whether or not there was any discussion by Greene with his senior officers on his decision. Unfortunately these papers were subsequently lost at sea,[41] a circumstance Henry Lee was perfectly aware of when he wrote his *Memoirs,* for Williams had informed him of it in a personal letter in the spring of 1792.[42]

There is no doubt that Lee does imply in the *Memoirs* that he was responsible for Greene's plan.[43] Yet he does so in curiously uncharacteristic fashion. The book, written in the third person, is—in all other sections save this one—not in the least reticent in stating that "Lt. Col. Lee" did this and "Lt. Col. Lee" did that. In fact, this officer seems ubiquitous. But in the passage referring to the plan to move south Lee— if it is Lee who is implied—hides modestly behind the sobriquet "the proposer."[44] According to Lee there was "much deliberation" over whether to continue the pursuit of Cornwallis to Wilmington or to adopt some alternative action. "The proposer" then suggested the move south. Many arguments were advanced pro and con, most of the conservative and unimaginative persons involved favoring a continuation of the pursuit, again according to Lee. Indeed, Lee's account, which goes on for some five pages of text, constrains one to believe that everyone in camp down to the lowest private no class had his say in the matter. This in itself is utterly out of keeping with Greene's usual habit.

At length, says the *Memoirs,* Greene, having listened critically to all arguments, accepted that of "the proposer" and immediately commenced operations. "The Legion of Lee . . . was ordered to move on the subsequent morning (6th April), and the army was put in motion the following day."[45]

This, of course, is absurd. Greene had commenced operations on March 29 when he wrote to Washington. We have letters of March 29 and 30 and April 3 and 4 ordering up supplies—rum, shoes, stockings, and the necessitous "overhauls," which the men were again naked for want of.[46] Furthermore, we have letters between Lee and Greene for April 2, 3, 4, and 5,[47] which prove that Lee was not even in the American camp on those days. He was attending to his duties of hanging on Cornwallis' coat-tails, and there is every reason to believe he had been doing so since March 29.

Greene's letter of April 4 to Lee informs him that the American army will march the following morning at seven o'clock. Lee, however, will take a different route, make a feint toward Cross Creek to alarm Cornwallis, and then join Marion on the Santee. Greene closes the letter significantly: "Remember that you command men, and that their Powers may not keep pace with your ambition. I have entire confidence in your prudence."[48] Lee replied: "You have my best prayers."[49]

Before we leave the subject, let us say that it is within the bounds of possibility that Lee and Greene separately arrived at the same strategy. Robert E. Lee in an editorial in the 1870 edition of his father's work states that Dr. Matthew Irvine, Lee's cavalry surgeon and a family friend, brought Lee's suggestion to Greene.[50] However, there is no evidence that the doctor did this as early as March 29 when Greene wrote to Washington of his decision. Lee's letter of April 2, quoted above, would appear to prove that Lee heard of the plan from Greene and decidedly agreed with it. In any case, the affair cannot have occurred as Lee recounted it in his *Memoirs*.

There is an interesting bit of evidence that as early as March 23 Greene seriously considered the move south should he not succeed in catching up with Cornwallis. On March 23 he wrote Jefferson from Buffalo Creek asking the Governor of Virginia to send him fifteen hundred militia from the back counties to serve for three months instead of the customary six weeks. "Their forces will be immediately wanted."[51] On April 6 he again wrote Jefferson: "I am on the march for South Carolina. *I had the present plan in contemplation at the time I wrote for the upper country militia.*"[52]

There is no reason to doubt this. The obvious course after Guilford was to pursue Cornwallis and destroy him. But Greene could never rely on the obvious; he could not afford to. It is very well for a commander with ample resources of men and equipment to conceive a plan, examine it for flaws, reshape it to seeming perfection, and then proceed to carry it out. That is what Cornwallis did—to his ultimate ruin. But Greene never had ample resources. Most of the time he had barefoot men, broken harness, spavined horses, an empty war chest, and too little ammunition. "I have been obliged to practice that by finesse, which I dare not attempt by force."[53] "I will equip a flying army . . . and make a kind of partizan war."[54] "I am of a Spanish disposition, always the most serious when there is the greatest run of good fortune, for fear of some ill-fated stroke."[55]

A commander in Greene's position could not have only one objective, one plan. He must maneuver, dodge, tease, lead on, side-step. In short, he must think of every possibility in advance and assume that most of the possibilities were those of disaster. As has been noted often before, Greene had made it his business to know the country of the Carolinas. He knew that Cornwallis had the start of him, and he knew that if he could not reach the British before they reached the pine barrens, pursuit must falter or fail.[56] Therefore, he must have considered what then would be the best way to retrieve his fortunes and those of his army. Like Lee and Hamilton, Greene was familiar with the Punic Wars. He had been playing the part of Fabius for a long time. He may not have expected that Cornwallis would refuse to play Hannibal.

On Monday, April 2, the last of the militia were dismissed.[57] April 3 the men were told to "wash and clean themselves, to get their arms in good order, and be prepared to march at a short warning."[58] On April 5 Greene set his face for Camden and Lord Rawdon.[59]

Greene was to win no decisive battles in South Carolina any more than he had won one at Guilford Court House. His genius lay in his mastery of maneuver. He had the ability to conduct himself with serenity under discouragement and pressure. He had the temperament for dealing with partisan leaders and provisioners, with governors and assemblies,[60] and with the manifold irritations arising from the constant lack of every necessity. He was an excellent planner, but he seems to have been unable to realize the fruition of his plans in actual tactical operations on the field of battle through lack of self-assurance and personal force.

Why? Greene showed Cornwallis a war of maneuver which his Lordship was never able to comprehend.[61] Yet he was unable to defeat the British commander at Guilford despite his advantage of superior numbers and choice of terrain. There were, of course, many factors at Guilford which had no apparent bearing on Greene's qualities as a leader—the flight of the North Carolina militia, the collapse of the 2nd Maryland, the failure of Lee to make contact with the Continentals when he withdrew from his support of Campbell's rifles. In short, according to John Fortescue, the historian of the British army, there was at Guilford and in Greene's subsequent battles an element of bad luck.[62]

Fortescue admits that Cornwallis was no match for Greene. However, in the British historian's evaluation of Greene as a general he says that the American commander possessed "patience, resolution, and profound common sense, qualities which go far toward making a great commander,"[63] but that he lacked "the faculty of leadership." In attempting to analyze the explanation for this lack the best Fortescue can do is to say that, unlike Washington, Greene did not "have the advantage of being a gentleman." Even Fortescue seems to find this a bit absurd, for he goes on to add, somewhat testily, that he realizes that "this is now [1902] supposed to be no advantage," but that Washington considered it essential and Fortescue is content to abide by his opinion.[64]

The usual explanation given for Greene's decision to retreat at Guilford is that he dared not risk the commitment of his whole army in what was at best only a chance of victory.[65] The writer suggested earlier the possibility that Greene was sickened at the sight of the slaughter for which he as commander was responsible, and wished to make an end to it, and that his fainting fit after the battle was indicative of an emotional strain. This, of course, is speculation, but it is hazarded as legitimate speculation. Fifty years of practical experience with professional military men have disclosed to the writer that many, even of those of what may be called belligerent disposition, are appalled at the realization that men have died under their orders. Greene was not belligerent by nature. As was earlier pointed out, he was a Quaker for many years before he was a soldier. In short, he entered military service in full maturity with his reactions of non-violence well established, however much he may have sought to rationalize a change to violent means for the sake of a cause.

There are, however, two factors less speculative which may help to explain Greene's seeming lack of self-assurance and personal force on the battlefield. The first is the fact that, revering Washington as he indubitably did,[66] he modeled his conduct on that of the Commander-in-Chief. Fortescue was correct in saying that Greene was not a gentleman in the aristocratic British sense of the term. The war had brought him from obscurity as a rural Rhode Island businessman to a commission as brigadier general in the army besieging Boston in 1775. There he met General Washington, whose impeccable manners and dignity made a lasting impression on the self-educated young Rhode Islander. Despite their disparity of background the two men had several characteristics in common[67]—notably integrity, prudence, and a certain reticence or aloofness of manner. This last attribute makes it unfortunate that Greene should have modeled his outward deportment on that of Washington. Washington has been accused of coldness, but, as Fortescue said, he had the advantage of being a gentleman with superb carriage, magnificent horsemanship, and presence in the archaic sense of the word. Greene had none of these. He was inclined to corpulence, limped in one leg, and had a slight squint in one eye. Neither man was easy to know. The men who did know Greene, the Continental troops and officers who served with him over a period, trusted and respected him. The militia, in all probability, did not.

Greene in emulating Washington with the sincerest form of flattery was, nevertheless, acting a part—and not wholly successfully, as he must have been intelligent enough to realize. The militia could see the mask but not the man behind it. Moreover, Greene, was by nature constitutionally incapable of Morgan's rapport with men. To be sure, he had a great respect for the dignity of mankind—for justice and human rights and natural law.[68] But this is a very different thing from appreciating man as man in all his cowardly, indomitable, ludicrous, magnificent, fornicating, noble, dastardly, sublime, ridiculous, wholly untrustworthy and unpredictable reality—as Morgan did. Morgan did not trust militia, but he made use of them by employing his knowledge of men and human motivations; the militia served him well. Greene did not trust militia and did not like them; they knew it and served him ill. Militia, like other men, have organs, dimensions, senses, affections, passions—and a faculty for observation. Greene expressed his opinion of them so caustically that his friend Joseph Reed advised him to look upon them as he would upon an undesired wife: "Be to their faults a little blind and to their virtues very kind."[69] In brief, Greene lacked one essential for leadership—the loyalty of a part of his men.

Thus these two factors—the fact that Greene, perhaps unwittingly, was acting a part alien to him[70] and the fact that he did not trust or understand all of the men under him—may account for a lack of confidence on the battlefield. Yet they are not the whole answer; there is no whole answer. For milleniums men have sought to define leadership. That a leader must have the qualities listed by Fortescue of patience, resolution, and common sense is generally agreed. To these are added such things as courage, efficiency, and imagination. Greene possessed all of them. Lest it seem here that we have overstressed outward appearance, it should be noticed that flamboyance of physique is no prerequisite or guarantee of leadership. Any military man knows that leaders come in all sizes, shapes, heights, and divisions of girth from rotund to spare. However, Aristotle in his *Nicomacheaen Ethics* made an observation which may have some bearing: "Brave men act for honor's sake, but passion aids them."[71] Greene was by nature reticent and self-restrained and had adopted a manner which accentuated these qualities to a point that might have appeared as disinterest.

Still we have not reached the answer, for there is no answer to be reached. All those who have sought to define leadership are agreed on two things: first, in addition to the qualities listed as desirable, and obviating some of them, there is a final quality which remains an imponderable; second, whether or not a man has the imponderable quality cannot be predicted in advance, despite jousts, drills, military academies, tomes on strategy, or treatises on tactics. The proof is on the field of battle, and only there. Morgan possessed the imponderable, as demonstrated at Quebec, Saratoga, and Cowpens; Greene, so far as he ever proved, did not.

In the long run it made no difference to the outcome of the campaign in North Carolina. For Cornwallis pursued his own particular *via dolorosa* to its ultimate destination. Greene's halt at Ramsey's Mill and the harassment of the British by Lee's Legion left the British commander puzzled as to Greene's intent. Fearing that the Americans were still following him, Cornwallis increased his pace to sixteen to eighteen miles a day to the enhanced suffering of his wounded.[72] He arrived in Cross Creek on April 1. "I found to my great mortification and contrary to all former accounts that it was impossible to secure . . . provisions and there was not four days forage within twenty miles. Navigation of the Cape Fear River was totally impracticable."[73] The army remained a day in Cross Creek.[74] The loyal Highlanders there did what they could for them, but resources were little enough.

On April 2 the British pressed on by the road the hundred miles to Wilmington, evil fortune dogging their steps. "The English according to their custom have left the Small pox behind them."[75] At the little village of Elizabethtown[76] brave Colonel Webster died. He had come nearly two weeks and 160 miles by horse litter with suppurating wounds of an arm and leg. Death must have been a welcome relief. Said Tarleton: "He united all the virtues of civil life to the gallantry and professional knowledge of a soldier."[77] Cornwallis buried him with every honor and found time to write to the officer's aged father in Edinburgh: "You have for your support, the assistance of religion, good sense, and the experience of the uncertainty of human happiness. You have for your satisfaction, that your son fell nobly in the cause of his country, honored and lamented by his fellow soldiers. . . ."[78]

With Generals O'Hara and Howard and several officers of lesser rank swaying painfully in their litters, the sorry procession reached Wilmington on April 7.[79] There Cornwallis learned that Greene had marched on April 5 for Camden. He dispatched expresses to warn Lord Rawdon, but these never arrived at their destination.[80] Cornwallis saw that his exhausted army could never reach Camden ahead of Greene. By the time that it did, if Greene had already defeated Rawdon, Cornwallis would be too late to help. If Rawdon had defeated Greene, he would need no assistance from Cornwallis.[81]

Cornwallis had had enough of Greene and the Carolinas. He wrote Sir Henry Clinton on April 10: "I cannot help expressing my wishes that the Chesapeake may become the seat of the war. . . ."[82] To his old friend General Phillips on the same day he sent another letter:

I have had a most difficult and dangerous campaign and was obliged to fight a battle 200 miles from any communication against an enemy seven times my number. The fate was long doubtful. . . . The idea of our friends rising in any number and to any purpose totally failed, as I expected, and here I am, getting rid of my wounded and refitting my troops at Wilmington. . . . Now, my dear friend, what is our plan? Without one we cannot succeed, and I assure you that I am quite tired of marching about the country in quest of adventures. If we mean an offensive war in America, we must abandon New York and bring our whole force into Virginia; we then have a stake to fight for, and a successful battle may give us America.[83]

It was not the first time that Cornwallis had expressed himself to the effect that Virginia was the key to the rebellious thirteen colonies. Events proved his view correct. However, like Croesus of Lydia before him, Lord Cornwallis grievously misconstrued the Delphic oracle. Washington and Rochambeau won at Yorktown, not the British. The Greeks would have described this as the hand of Moira, or fate; Washington deemed it Providence.[84]

NOTES

The following abbreviations have been used throughout the notes:

GW—The Writings of George Washington from the Original Manuscript Sources, 1745-1799, edited by John C. Fitzpatrick

JCC—Journals of the Continental Congress

NYHS—New York Historical Society

NYPL—New York Public Library

PCC—Papers of the Continental Congress

SHSW—State Historical Society of Wisconsin

TJ—The Papers of Thomas Jefferson, edited by Julian P. Boyd

WCL—William Clements Library, University of Michigan

Complete references to these and all titles cited in the notes will be found in the bibliography.

NOTES

CHAPTER 1

1. Lyman C. Draper, *King's Mountain and Its Heroes*, pp. 239-42.
2. Verner W. Crane, *The Southern Frontier*, pp. 3, 5, 11.
3. *Ibid.*, p. 22.
4. David Duncan Wallace, *South Carolina: A Short History*, p. 228.
5. Oliver Chitwood, *A History of Colonial America*, p. 422; John Richard Alden, *The South in the Revolution*, pp. 42-43.
6. Melville Herskovits, *Dahomey: An Ancient West African Kingdom*, II, 63-65.
7. Wallace, *South Carolina*, p. 183.
8. Richard Walsh, *Charleston's Sons of Liberty*, p. 19.
9. Wallace, *South Carolina*, p. 264.
10. Walsh, *Charleston's Sons*, p. 19.
11. Alden, *South in Revolution*, p. 9.
12. Charles Woodmason, *The Carolina Backcountry on the Eve of the Revolution*, p. 13. According to Woodmason, who describes himself as an Anglican Itinerant, "They complained of being eaten up by Itinerant Teachers, Preachers, and Imposters from New England and Pennsylvania—Baptists, New Lights, Presbyterians, Independants, and an hundred other Sects—So that one day You might hear this System of Doctrine—the next day another—next day another retrograde to both—Thus by the Variety of Taylors who would pretend to know the best fashion in which Christ's Coat is to be worn none will put it on."
13. Wallace, *South Carolina*, p. 264.
14. Otho Williams to Nathanael Greene, Feb. 26, 1781, Greene Papers, WCL.
15. Lord Cornwallis to General William Phillips, Apr. 10, 1781, Clinton Papers, WCL.
16. Greene to Jefferson, Mar. 23, 1781, *TJ*, V, 215. See also Greene Papers, WCL.
17. George Washington Greene, *Life of Major General Nathanael Greene* III, 227 n.

CHAPTER 2

1. Sir Henry Clinton, *American Rebellion*, edited by William B. Willcox, p. 171.

2. Christopher Ward, *The War of the Revolution*, II, 703; David Ramsay, *History of the American Revolution*, II, 202; William Gordon, *History of the Rise, Progress and Establishment of the Independence of the United States of America*, III, 51.

3. "Articles of Capitulation Between Their Excellencies Sir Henry Clinton, Mariot Arbuthnot, Esq., and Major-General Benjamin Lincoln, Article 4th," in Henry Lee, *Memoirs of the War in the Southern Department of the United States*, pp. 158-59.

4. David Duncan Wallace, *South Carolina: A Short History*, p. 295.

5. *Ibid.*, p. 283.

6. Clinton, *Rebellion*, pp. 179-81. Clinton claims that the army never go a penny of this wealth, that the navy took three-quarters under the contention that "*it alone are authorized to by law share prize money.*" The remainder was held by the King's agents. Italics are Clinton's. He was much given to italics when heated—which was most of the time.

7. Clinton, *Rebellion*, pp. 166-69; Lee, *Memoirs*, p. 154; Ward, *Revolution*, II, 702.

8. Ward says 154 miles but is contradicted by Tarleton, Lee, and Greene. Tarleton rode the course and should know its length.

9. Tarleton was given to such misrepresentations, apparently as a matter of policy. "On his route he [Tarleton] ordered the inhabitants to collect great quantities of provisions for the King's troops, whose numbers he magnified in order to awe the militia" (Banastre Tarleton, *A History of the Campaigns of 1780-1781 in the Southern Provinces of North America*, pp. 287-88).

10. John Marshall, *Life of George Washington*, III, 179-81; Ward, *Revolution*, II, 705-6; Clinton, *Rebellion*, p. 176; Lee, *Memoirs*, pp. 164-65. Lee's account differs in some details from that of the others.

11. The British encouraged this belief as far as possible. They spread the rumor that Congress had determined to abandon the two southern states (Wallace, *South Carolina*, p. 297).

12. Clinton, *Rebellion*, p. 175. Italics in original.

13. *Ibid.*, pp. 171, 177, 439-40.

14. *Ibid.*, p. 186. Italics are Clinton's.

15. Ramsay, *History*, II, 319.

16. Wallace, *South Carolina*, p. 298.

17. Robert D. Bass, *The Green Dragoon*, p. 205.

18. Sumter Papers, SHSW (Draper Collection, 7VV, 105). The letter from Governor Rutledge, dated October 6, 1780, notifying Sumter of his commission as brigadier general, directed him to embody all of the militia of South Carolina and hold them in readiness to cooperate with the Continentals. It added: "You will supply the men whom you assemble in such manner as may render the most effectual service to the State. This must, in great measure, depend on circumstances, and your own judgment." Subsequent evidence seems to indicate that Sumter relied almost exclusively on his own judgment. His cooperation with the Continentals was never of a very high order.

19. Wallace, *South Carolina*, p. 298; Robert D. Bass, *Gamecock: Life and Campaigns of Thomas Sumter, passim.*

20. Lee, *Memoirs*, pp. 174-75.

21. George Washington Greene, *Life of Major General Nathanael Greene,* III, 21.

22. Wallace, *South Carolina*, p. 300; Bruce Lancaster, *American Heritage Book of the Revolution*, p. 324.

23. Gordon, *America*, III, 113; Ward, *Revolution*, II, 733; Lancaster, *Heritage*, p. 326.

24. Lee, *Memoirs*, p. 174.

25. *Ibid.*, p. 585.

26. *Dictionary of American Biography*, XIV, 559.

27. *Ibid.*

28. George Washington, *Writings*, ed. John C. Fitzpatrick, XVIII, 197-98; 226.

29. Gordon, *America*, III, 72; Greene, *Life*, III, 15; Ward, *Revolution*, II, 712 ff.

30. William Johnson, *Sketches of the Life and Correspondence of Nathanael Greene*, I, 485.

31. Ward, *Revolution*, II, 712-13; *DAB*, X, 253; Lee, *Memoirs*, p. 575.

32. Marshall, *Washington*, III, 186; Ward, *Revolution*, II, 717; Greene, *Life*, III, 16.

33. Ward, *Revolution*, II, 718.

34. Greene, *Life*, III, 15.

35. Ward, *Revolution*, II, 718; Otho Williams, "Narrative of the Campaign of 1780," in Johnson, *Greene*, I, 510; and William Gilmore Simms, *Life of Nathanael Greene*, p. 359.

36. Ward, *Revolution*, II, 735.

37. *Ibid.*, pp. 521-42.

38. For accounts of Saratoga favorable to Gates see Bernhard Knollenberg, *Washington and the Revolution;* and Lynn Montross, *Rag, Tag and Bobtail.*

39. Lee, *Memoirs*, pp. 575 ff.

40. Greene, *Life*, III, 18-19.

41. *Ibid.*, p. 26; Gordon, *America*, III, 100; Williams, "Narrative."

42. Williams, "Narrative."

43. *Ibid.;* Gordon, *America*, III, 103; Greene, *Life*, III, 29. Gordon and Greene lean heavily on Williams in their accounts of the battle.

44. Williams, "Narrative."

45. *Ibid.*

46. *Ibid.*

47. Ward, *Revolution*, II, 730.

CHAPTER 3

1. *GW*, XX, 182.

2. Samuel Huntington to Greene, Oct. 31, 1780. Greene Papers, WCL.

3. *Journals of the Continental Congress*, XVII, 697.

4. George Washington Greene, *Life of Major General Nathanael Greene,* II, 158.

5. William Johnson, *Sketches of the Life and Correspondence of Nathanael Greene*, II, 485 ff.; *GW*, XX, 215.

6. Greene, *Life*, II, 158.

7. *Ibid.*, p. 316.

8. Edmund Cody Burnett, *The Continental Congress*, p. 463; Greene, *Life*, II, 324; *JCC*, XVII, 690, 697; Lynn Montross, *The Reluctant Rebels*, p. 53.

9. Burnett, *Congress*, p. 463; Greene, *Life*, II, 327.

10. Bernhard Knollenberg, *Washington and the Revolution*, pp. 112 ff.

11. Douglas Southall Freeman, *George Washington: A Biography*, IV, Chapter XXIII, Greene, *Life*, II, 283 ff.

12. *GW*, XIX, 366-69.

13. *JCC*, XVII, 797.

14. *Ibid.*

15. Harold C. Syrett, ed., *The Papers of Alexander Hamilton*, II, 440-41.

16. Greene to Washington, Sept. 26, 1780, Green Papers, WCL.

17. Greene, *Life*, II, 282-83.

18. James T. Flexner, *The Traitor and the Spy*, p. 387; John C. Miller, *Alexander Hamilton: Portrait in Paradox*, p. 71.

19. Johnson, *Greene*, II, 485 ff.

20. Henry Lee, *Campaign of 1781 in the Carolinas*, p. xxiv.

21. *GW*, XX, 125-26.

22. Arnold to Clinton, Apr. 16, 1781, Clinton Papers, WCL. Arnold replied to a letter from Sir Henry regarding West Point that he was "intirely unacquainted with the repairs or additions" made to the works since he saw them the previous September: "At that time they were in a very defenseless state."

23. Greene to Henry Knox, Oct. 11, 1780, Greene Papers, WCL.

24. Greene, *Life*, III, 485.

25. Richard B. Morris, *Alexander Hamilton and the Founding of the Nation*, p. 39.

26. Knollenberg, *Washington*, p. 169.

27. Christopher Ward, *The War of the Revolution*, II, 730.

28. Greene, *Life*, III, 31.

29. Ward, *Revolution*, II, 735; Greene, *Life*, III, 105.

30. *JCC*, XVII, 809 ff.

31. Otho Williams, "Narrative of the Campaign of 1780."

32. *JCC*, XVIII, 906.

33. *Ibid.*

34. Ward, *Revolution*, II, 748.

35. *GW*, XX, 182.

36. *Ibid.*

37. *Ibid*, p. 189, n.

38. Greene, *Life*, II, 373.

39. *GW*, XX, 215-16.

40. David Ramsay, *History of the American Revolution*, III, 294.

CHAPTER 4

1. Cornwallis to Clinton, Dec. 3, 1780, in Benjamin F. Stevens, *The Campaign in Virginia, 1781: An Exact Reprint of Six Rare Pamphlets on the Clinton-Cornwallis Controversy*, I, 302.

2. Henry Lee, *Memoirs*, p. 187.

3. Christopher Ward, *The War of the Revolution*, II, 733; Lee, *Memoirs*, p. 185.

4. William Gordon, *History of the Rise, Progress and Establishment of the Independence of the United States of America*, III, 99; Lee, *Memoirs*, p. 179; Ward, *Revolution*, II, 722; Williard M. Wallace, *Appeal to Arms*, p. 215. Wallace describes this detachment as 400 regular troops. This is not in agreement with other sources. It will be recalled that de Kalb had marched south with only 1,400 regular troops. Subsequently the army had been increased by the addition of Armand's Legion, made up mostly of foreigners and deserters from the British army (Lee, *Memoirs*, p. 181) and the Virginia and North Carolina militia under Stevens and Caswell respectively. Surely even Gates would not have been so foolhardy as to detach 400 regulars, roughly one-quarter of his Continental strength.

5. David Ramsay, *History of the American Revolution*, II, 219; Sir Henry Clinton, *American Rebellion*, p. 222.

6. Ward, *Revolution*, II, 708-9; Robert D. Bass, *Gamecock: Life and Campaigns of Thomas Sumter, passim.*

7. Lee, *Memoirs*, p. 174.

8. Gordon, *America*, III, 113; Lee, *Memoirs*, p. 175.

9. William Richardson Davie, "Supply Service Under Nathanael Greene, 1780-1781," *Greene Papers*, WCL. (This is not Davie's manuscript, but a typed carbon copy included in the Greene Papers. G. W. Greene apparently had access to the original, or some form of it, for he refers to it in his work.) It is not easy to evaluate the depths of Sumter's patriotism. He was suspected, apparently without proof, of Tory leanings early in the war, which delayed the issuance of his Continental commission (David Duncan Wallace, *South Carolina: A Short History*, p. 282; Bass, *Gamecock*, p. 172). He was described by one who knew him well as "avaricious, indomitable, taciturn, sarcastic—exceedingly so." He had a great contempt for Colonel Henry Lee, who was a strict disciplinarian, while Sumter was simply a fighter—not much for discipline. His men were lawless and hard to control. According to the traditions of the country he always secured his portion of the spoils of war, in common with his men. Sumter Papers, SHSW (Draper Manuscripts, 14, VV, 194). It is noteworthy that, while Marion and Pickens both, at various phases of their careers, formed a part of the Continental line during Greene's southern Campaign, Sumter never, from the time he took the field after Charleston fell, served under any other man's command than his own. Sumter's Law, passed after the war in 1784, was aimed at legalizing his illegalities in the matter of pillaging. Sumter survived full of years and honors to the age of ninety-eight and was the last surviving general officer of the Revolutionary War.

10. Lee, *Memoirs*, p. 578; Davie, "Supply," Greene Papers, WCL.

11. Lee, *Memoirs*, p. 188.

12. Kenneth Roberts, *The Battle of Cowpens*, p. 45.

13. Gordon, *America*, III, 107; Ramsay, *History*, II, 219. Since Gordon and Ramsay use identical wording, it seems evident that Ramsay borrowed from Gordon, but the physician gives the man of God no credit.

14. Ward, *Revolution*, II, 733; Wallace, *Appeal*, p. 215.

15. Banastre Tarleton, *A History of the Campaigns of 1780-1781 in the*

Southern Provinces of North America, pp. 114-119; Clinton, *Rebellion,* p. 225; Ward, *Revolution,* II, 734; Lee, *Memoirs,* pp. 188-89.

16. Clinton, *Rebellion,* p. 225.

17. Gordon, *America,* III, 112.

18. Stevens, *Controversy,* I, 302-3; Ward, *Revolution,* II, 739; Roberts, *Cowpens,* pp. 28, 59.

19. Gordon, *America,* III, 113.

20. Stevens, *Controversy,* I, 259.

21. *Ibid.,* p. 260.

22. Louis C. Duncan, "Medical Men in the American Revolution," *Army Medical Bulletin,* No. 25.

23. Stevens, *Controversy,* I, 261.

24. Clinton, *Rebellion,* p. 225; Stevens, *Controversy,* I, 262.

25. Ramsay, *History,* II, 222; Lee, *Memoirs,* p. 193; Clinton, *Rebellion,* p. 226.

26. Robert D. Bass, *The Green Dragoon,* p. 106; Ward, *Revolution,* II, 738; Lee, *Memoirs,* p. 195.

27. Tarleton, *Campaigns,* p. 162.

28. Lee, *Memoirs,* pp. 105-6; Ward, *Revolution,* II, 738.

29. Lee, *Memoirs,* p. 196; Ward, *Revolution,* II, 739; Bass, *Dragoon,* p. 107.

30. After the bewildering manner of southern rivers, the Catawba is simply the Wateree in its upper reaches above the Waxhaws.

31. Cornwallis to Clinton, Dec. 3, 1780, Clinton Papers, WCL.

32. Ward, *Revolution,* II, 659.

33. Gordon, *America,* III, 117.

34. "Account of Colonel Isaac Shelby," *North Carolina State Records,* XV, 105-8.

35. *Ibid.*

36. *Ibid.*

37. Lord Francis Rawdon to General Alexander Leslie, Oct. 24, 1780, Clinton Papers, WCL. Italics mine.

38. Shelby, "Account."

39. *Ibid.*

40. Clinton, *Rebellion,* pp. 227, 456, 458; Tarleton, *Campaigns,* p. 165; Bass, *Dragoon,* p. 108. The timing is hopelessly confused in the various accounts. Tarleton, convalescent from yellow fever, was for a time unable to sit a horse. Before he was strong enough to travel, Major Hanger, who had taken command of the Legion in his place, was in turn seized with the fever and lay for weeks near death. This may be reason enough for Cornwallis' delay. Sir Henry, of course, with his antipathy for Cornwallis, attempted to accuse him of culpability (Clinton, *Rebellion,* p. 227). By October 10 it was too late for unlucky "poor Ferguson."

41. Shelby, "Account."

42. Draper, *King's Mountain,* pp. 223-24.

43. Shelby, "Account."

44. *Ibid.*

45. Lee to Greene, Mar. 1, 1781, Greene Papers, WCL.

46. Shelby, "Account."

47. Ramsay, *History,* II, 229. Ramsay as a physician had a professional interest in this phenomenon.

48. James Collins, "Autobiography of a Revolutionary Soldier," in Henry Steele Commager and Richard B. Morris, *Spirit of 'Seventy-Six*, II, 1145.
49. George F. Scheer and Hugh F. Rankin, *Rebels and Redcoats*, p. 420.
50. Ward, *Revolution*, II, 744.
51. Shelby, "Account."
52. Scheer and Rankin, *Rebels*, p. 421; Howard H. Peckham, *The War for Independence*, p. 149.
53. Tarleton, *Campaigns*, pp. 162-64.
54. Ward, *Revolution*, II, 745; *GW*, XX, 258.
55. Clinton, *Rebellion*, p. 224.
56. *Ibid.*, pp. 226-28.
57. *GW*, XX, 258.
58. *JCC*, XVIII, 1048.
59. *GW*, XX, 148, 216, 217, 230.

CHAPTER 5

1. *GW*, XX, 321 n.
2. Lynn Montross, *Reluctant Rebels*, p. 266.
3. Douglas Southall Freeman, *George Washington*, III, overleaf p. 435.
4. Greene, *Life*, III, 35-36.
5. *Ibid.*, 62-63.
6. Montross, *Reluctant Rebels*, Chapter, 20, *passim*.
7. *JCC*, XVIII, 995.
8. *Ibid.*
9. John W. Wright, "Some Notes on the Continental Army," *William and Mary College Quarterly Historical Magazine*," 2nd Series, Vol. XI (April, 1931), 81-105. This was Washington's interpretation of Congress' instructions. Being Washington he scrupulously followed it. Later, in 1777, Congress stated that it had intended no such restriction in the first place.
10. *JCC*, XVIII, 995.
11. *Ibid.*
12. Christopher Ward, *The War of the Revolution*, II, 149; George Washington Greene, *Life of Major General Nathanael Greene*, III, 39-43.
13. Greene, *Life*, III, 52.
14. *JCC*, XVIII, 963, 985, 997.
15. Greene, *Life*, III, 52.
16. *Ibid.*, p. 51.
17. Greene, *Life*, III, 57; Theodore Thayer, *Nathanael Greene: Strategist of the American Revolution*, p. 287; Greene to Jefferson, Feb. 15, 1781, Feb. 29, 1781; Mar. 10, 1781, *TJ*, IV, 615-16; V, 22; V, 111. (See also Greene Papers, WCL). The relationship between Greene and Jefferson was not entirely happy. In these letters Greene taxed Jefferson with sending militia so ill-equipped as to be unemployable and of counting the contributions in men from Virginia by "paper" armies since the quotas actually received were never so large as the returns on paper. Jefferson, in his turn, seems to have had some fear that Greene's army might pose such a threat as the armies of the

Roman barrack emperors did in the latter Roman Empire. In a letter of Feb.
18, 1781 (*TJ*, IV, 647), Jefferson proposed to send a friend of his, Major
McGill, to Greene's headquarters for the ostensible purpose of keeping
Jefferson informed of events which Greene's multiplicity of business might
prevent him from relaying to the governor of Virginia. Jefferson's letter would
appear to be in reply to an ill-advised statement in Greene's letter of Feb. 15:
"The Army is all that the States have to depend on for their political
existence." To a man of Jefferson's temperament this might seem to propose
a threat of military dictatorship. With regard to McGill, Greene replied on
Feb. 29 that the necessity of military secrecy would make it "utterly impossible" to furnish the major with facts in time to make them useful to Jefferson.
He added that should anything develop immediately concerning Virginia,
"I shall do myself the honor to write to you, or send it through the channel
of Major Maggill as circumstances may be." In brief, Greene was in command
of the army, and he did not intend that politicians should interfere with
his movements. This is a hassle as old as governments and armies.

18. Within a few weeks of this time Arnold entered Virginia unopposed
because of Jefferson's failure to make preparations against invasion despite
warning from Washington that Arnold might be on his way. See Chapter 10.

19. Jefferson to Henry Lee, May 15, 1826, in Henry Lee, *Memoirs*, pp.
315-16. Jefferson states in this letter that he was "without Military education"
and therefore left military matters to "persons of the art." Otho Williams
observed that "the Governor of Virginia is said to boast that he is no military
man" (Williams to James McHenry, Jan. 23, 1781, *Calendar of the General
Otho Holland Williams Papers*, Maryland Historical Society).

20. Greene, *Life*, III, 55.

21. Sir Henry Clinton, *American Rebellion*, p. 229; Cornwallis to Clinton,
Dec. 22, 1780, Clinton Papers, WCL. According to Cornwallis' letter, Leslie
arrived in Charleston on Dec. 14.

22. William Johnson, *Sketches of the Life and Correspondence of
Nathanael Greene*, II, 440. Greene's letters in his collected papers and as
quoted in secondary works abundantly bear this out.

23. *GW*, XX, 183.

24. *Ibid.*, p. 321, n.

25. *Ibid.*, p. 183.

26. Lee, *Memoirs*, p. 249; Greene, *Life*, III, 72; Benson J. Lossing, *Pictorial
Field-Book of the Revolution*, II, 398. Greene's admiration for Washington
was such that he named his first child George Washington Greene and his
second Martha Washington Greene. After the war he left his native New
England and settled in Georgia where he was in the process of establishing
himself as a planter upon his untimely death.

27. Greene, *Life*, III, 67.

28. George F. Scheer and Hugh F. Rankin, *Rebels and Redcoats*, p. 436.

29. Lossing, *Field-Book*, II, 390.

30. Otho Williams, "Narrative," in Johnson, *Greene*.

31. William Gordon, *History of the Rise, Progress and Establishment of the
Independence of the United States of America*, III, 112-13; Greene, *Life*, III,
82.

32. *JCC*, XVIII, 906.

33. Greene, *Life*, III, 82.

34. Lee, *Memoirs*, p. 216. Gates was never tried. On May 21, 1781, by Congressional resolve, he returned to Washington's command where he served honorably for the balance of the war, although he never again saw combat.

35. Ward, *Revolution*, II, 749; Gordon, *America*, III, 157; Greene, *Life*, III, 68-70; David Ramsay, *History of the American Revolution*, II, 296; Lee, *Memoirs*, p. 220; Clinton, *Rebellion*, p. 245. The numbers vary slightly in the various sources but on the whole are in remarkable agreement.

36. Johnson, *Greene*, I, 393.

37. Greene, *Life*, III, 71.

38. *Ibid.*, p. 73.

39. Greene, *Life*, III, 75-77; Davie, "Supply Service," Greene Papers, WCL.

40. Marion to Greene, Jan. 1, 1781, Greene Papers, WCL.

41. Greene, *Life*, III, 81.

42. Marion-Greene letters, Dec., 1780-Jan., 1781, Greene Papers, WCL.

43. Montross, *Rag, Tag*, pp. 217-18.

44. Gordon, *America*, III, 157; Greene, *Life*, III, 85.

45. Ward, *Revolution*, II, 750.

46. *GW*, XX, 239; *JCC*, XVIII, 960.

47. Johnson, *Greene*, I, 401.

48. Thayer, *Greene*, p. 24; Greene, *Life*, I, 57; Wright, "Some Notes on the Continental Army," pp. 81-105.

49. Ward, *Revolution*, II, 751.

50. Greene to Joseph Reed, Aug. 6, 1781, in Johnson, *Greene*, II, 467.

51. Williams to Greene, Feb. 25, 1781, Greene Papers, WCL.

52. Ward, *Revolution*, II, 751.

53. Gordon, *America*, III, 159.

54. Ward, *Revolution*, II, 752; Greene, *Life*, III, 91; Gordon, *America*, III, 159. It should not be forgotten that the southern theatre included the states from Delaware to Georgia by the terms in which Congress bestowed the command on Greene. By those terms also he was permitted to call on the executives of the various states included for aid and assistance. If some of his letters to these personages appear demanding and peremptorial, it must be remembered that he was only carrying out the terms of his commission.

55. Cornwallis to Clinton, Jan. 6, 1781, Clinton Papers, WCL.

56. Clinton, *Rebellion*, p. 245.

57. Banastre Tarleton, *A History of the Campaigns of 1780-1781 in the Southern Provinces of North America*, p. 214.

58. Cornwallis to Clinton, Dec. 22, 1780, Clinton Papers, WCL.

59. Marion to Greene, Jan. 1, 1781, Greene Papers, WCL.

60. Greene to Morgan, Jan. 19, 1781, *Ibid.*

61. Ward, *Revolution*, II, 751-54.

62. Brown to Cornwallis, Dec. 17, 1780, Clinton Papers, WCL.

63. Robert D. Bass, *The Green Dragoon*, p. 141.

64. North Callahan, *Daniel Morgan*, pp. 202-3. Callahan gives as his source for this incident, which will be elaborated in an ensuing chapter, the Lyman C. Draper Manuscripts, Wisconsin Historical Society.

65. Ward, *Revolution*, II, 754; Kenneth Roberts, *The Battle of Cowpens*, p. 31.

CHAPTER 6

1. Henry Lee, *Memoirs*, p. 34.
2. George Washington Greene, *Life of Major General Nathanael Greene*, III, 92.
3. Greene Papers, WCL, 1780-1781.
4. Charles M. Lefferts, *Uniforms of the American, British, French and German Armies in the War of the American Revolution*, Plate XVIII, facing page 48.
5. Joseph Reed to Nathanael Greene, March 29, 1781, Greene Papers, WCL.
6. Jared Sparks, *Correspondence of the American Revolution*, III, 190.
7. *Ibid.*
8. William Johnson, *Sketches of the Life and Correspondence of Nathanael Greene*, I, 344; William Gordon, *History of the Rise, Progress and Establishment of the United States of America*, III, 160; Howard H. Peckham, *The War for Independence*, p. 150; Lee, *Memoirs*, pp. 32, 223. The exact numerical strength of the Legion upon arrival is debatable. Lee himself says that its full strength was 350, but declares that it was never complete. At one place in his *Memoirs* he counts it as 250, at another as 280 upon arrival in Greene's camp. The proportion of horse to foot is also variously given in different sources. Johnson says there was an equal proportion of horse to foot. This seems reasonable in view of Lee's statement that on the march, to expedite progress, the cavalrymen frequently mounted the foot soldiers on their horses' rumps and carried them over the miles. He makes much of this as proof of what fine horses he had procured from Virginia by contrast with the miserable "tackies" on which Tarleton was forced to mount his dragoons. Now 140 horsemen could carry 140 infantry soldiers in the manner described. But the notion of 120 horsemen attempting so to transport 180 footmen—a proportion of horse to foot sometimes given—presents a ludicrous picture, regardless of how fine the horseflesh.
9. Robert D. Bass, *The Green Dragoon*, p. 15.
10. Greene, *Life*, III, 110-12; Lee, *Memoirs*, pp. 16-24.
11. Lee, *Memoirs*, p. 22; *GW*, XVII, 220.
12. *GW*, XX, 223.
13. *GW*, XX, 223 n.; Lee, *Memoirs*, Chapter XXX, *passim*. This is a cloak-and-dagger story *par excellence*. Carl Van Doren retells it in his *Secret History of the American Revolution*. The most detailed modern account of this incident, based on manuscript sources and British Headquarters maps is George F. Scheer's "The Sergeant Major's Strange Mission," *American Heritage*, VIII (October, 1957).
14. Greene, *Life*, III, 111.
15. Greene, *Life*, III, 110; Washington Irving, *Life of Washington*, I, 16; Burton J. Hendrick, *The Lees of Virginia*, p. 332.
16. Lee, *Memoirs*, p. 221.
17. Lee to Greene, 1780-1782, *passim.*, Greene Papers, WCL.
18. Lee, *Memoirs*, p. 583; Christopher Ward, *The War of the Revolution*, II, 767; Peckham, *Independence*, p. 153; Henry Lee, *Campaign of 1781 in the Carolinas*, pp. xi-xiii
19. Lee, *Memoirs*, p. 223; Greene, *Life*, III, 133, Gordon, *America*, III, 150.
20. Lee, *Memoirs*, pp. 32-34. Robert E. Lee in his introduction to the

third (1870) edition of his father's *Memoirs* includes several letters from Light Horse Harry to friends in the north, recording his first impressions of the conditions of the southern army, which condition evidently dismayed him. The letter to Wayne is one of these.

21. Gordon, *America*, III, 160; Greene, *Life*, III, 113. Gordon says Jan. 13; Greene says Jan. 16.

22. Lee, *Memoirs*, p. 174, n.

23. Lee to Greene, Jan. 23, 1781, Greene Papers, WCL.

24. Lee, *Memoirs*, p. 225.

25. Lee to Greene, Jan. 23, 1781, Greene Papers, WCL.

26. Greene to Abner Nash, Governor of North Carolina, Feb. 3, 1781, Greene Papers, WCL.

27. Marion to Greene, Jan. 27, 1781, Greene Papers, WCL.

CHAPTER 7

1. Morgan's account of his military career, No. 1084, Morgan Papers, Myers Collection, NYPL.

2. Morgan to Greene, Dec. 31, 1780, Greene Papers, WCL.

3. Greene to Morgan, Dec. 16, 1780, No. 867, Morgan Papers, Myers Collection, NYPL.

4. Morgan to Greene, Dec. 31, 1780, Greene Papers, WCL; Morgan to Greene, Jan. 4, 1781, No. 944, Morgan Papers, Myers Collection, NYPL. This incident sometimes cited as Hammond's Store.

5. Sir Henry Clinton, *American Rebellion*, p. 245; Cornwallis to Clinton, Jan. 18, 1781, Clinton Papers, WCL.

6. Greene to Sumter, Feb. 3, 1781, Greene Papers, WCL.

7. Morgan to Greene, Jan. 15, 1781, Greene Papers, WCL.

8. Greene to Morgan, Jan. 19, 1781, Greene Papers, WCL.

9. Morgan to Greene, Dec. 31, 1780, Greene Papers, WCL.

10. *Ibid.*

11. *Ibid.*

12. North Callahan, *Daniel Morgan*, p. 171.

13. Morgan's account of his career, No. 1084, Morgan Papers, Myers Collection, NYPL.

14. Greene, *Life*, III, 99-100; Henry Lee, *Memoirs*, p. 580; James Graham, *The Life of General Daniel Morgan*, p. 50; Callahan, *Morgan*, p. 62; Benson J. Lossing, *Pictorial Field-Book of the American Revolution*, II, 431; Don Higginbotham, *Daniel Morgan: Revolutionary Rifleman*, p. 9.

15. Higginbotham, *Daniel Morgan*, p. 11.

16. Christopher Ward, *The War of the Revolution*, I, 167-80; Graham, *Morgan*, pp. 465-66; Kenneth Roberts (ed.), *March to Quebec, passim*.

17. Morgan's account of his career, No. 1084, Morgan Papers, Myers Collection, NYPL, (Italics added); Higginbotham, *Daniel Morgan*, p. 46.

18. Greene to Morgan, Dec. 29, 1780, Greene Papers, WCL.

19. Callahan, *Morgan*, pp. 202-03. Callahan cites this story as coming from the Draper Manuscripts, but does not give the volume or page. There was reputedly a nine-year-old drummer boy at Cowpens whom Morgan, after the battle, picked up and kissed on both cheeks, whether from sheer exuberance

or for other reason is not clear (Higginbotham, *Daniel Morgan*, p. 142). Lyman C. Draper collected an enormous amount of material of the anecdote or "human interest" variety, some of which may be of dubious historical value. Nevertheless, it appears likely that Morgan was not unaware of specific British interest in him after the affair of Fair Forest (or Hammond's Store). On Jan. 26, 1781, he wrote his friend William Snickers, describing the Fair Forest incident, and said: "On this Lord Cornwallis detached Tarleton and nine hundered chosen Troops, the flower of his Army, with his Legion, on the West side of the Broad River to Attack me in front...." In brief, Morgan seems to have been cognizant of the fact that Tarleton was on the march long before he actually knew that the Britisher was in his immediate vicinity (Morgan to Wm. Snickers, Jan. 26, 1781, Gates Papers, courtesy of the New York Historical Society, New York City).

20. *GW*, XX, 223-24, 253, 255, 276, 355.
21. Morgan to Greene, Jan. 19, 1781, in Graham, *Morgan*, pp. 467-70.
22. Morgan to Greene, Jan. 15, 1781, in William Johnson, *Sketches of the Life and Correspondence of Nathanael Greene*, II, 370-71.
23. *Ibid.*
24. *Ibid.*
25. *Ibid.*
26. *Ibid.*
27. Robert D. Bass, *The Green Dragoon*, p. 141.
28. Cornwallis to Clinton, Jan. 6, 1781, Clinton Papers, WCL.
29. Banastre Tarleton, *A History of the Campaigns of 1780-1781 in the Southern Provinces of North America*, p. 218.
30. *Ibid.*, pp. 247-48.
31. *Ibid.*
32. *Ibid.*, pp. 248-49.
33. *Ibid.*, pp. 218-20.
34. Bass, *Dragoon*, p. 151.

CHAPTER 8

1. Morgan to Greene, Jan. 19, 1781, "Battle Report" in James Graham, *The Life of General Daniel Morgan*, pp. 309-12; 467-70.
2. *Ibid.*
3. Banastre Tarleton, *A History of the Campaigns of 1780-1781 in the Southern Provinces of North America*, p. 220.
4. Don Higginbotham, *Daniel Morgan*, p. 132: "I would not have had a swamp in the view of my militia on any consideration; they would have made for it, and nothing could have detained them from it. And as to covering my wings, I knew my adversary, and was perfectly sure I should have nothing but downright fighting. As to retreat, it was the very thing I wished to cut off all hope of. I would have thanked Tarleton had he surrounded me with his cavalry. It would have been better than placing my own men in the rear to shoot down those who broke from the ranks. When men are forced to fight, they will sell their lives dearly.... Had I crossed the river, one half of the militia would immediately have abandoned me."

5. Morgan to Wm. Snickers, Jan. 26, 1781, Gates Papers, NYHS: "As matters were circumstanced, no time was to be lost, I prepared for Battle."

6. George Washington Greene, *Life of Major General Nathanael Greene,* III, 139; Henry Lee, *Memoirs,* p. 225.

7. Robert D. Bass, *The Green Dragoon,* pp. 150-51.

8. Morgan to Greene, Dec. 31, 1780, Green Papers, WCL.

9. Greene, *Life,* III, 139; Lee, *Memoirs,* p. 226 n.; George F. Scheer and Hugh F. Rankin, *Rebels and Redcoats,* p. 428; Kenneth Roberts, *The Battle of Cowpens,* p. 74. Pickens had been with Morgan earlier but had been temporarily detached to bring in the new militia.

10. Benson J. Lossing, *Pictorial Field-Book of the American Revolution,* II, 430, n.; Roberts, *Cowpens,* p. 67.

11. Morgan to Greene, Jan. 19, 1781, *Battle Report.*

12. Lee, *Memoirs,* p. 226.

13. Tarleton, *Campaigns,* p. 214; Greene, *Life,* III, 141-42; Lee, *Memoirs,* p. 226; Lossing, *Field-Book,* II, 430; Higginbotham, *Daniel Morgan* p. 131.

14. Greene, *Life,* III, 141; Christopher Ward, *The War of the Revolution,* II, 756; Willard M. Wallace, *Appeal to Arms,* p. 233.

15. North Callahan, *Daniel Morgan,* p. 50.

16. Greene, *Life,* III, 141; William Johnson, *Sketches of the Life and Correspondence of Nathanael Greene,* I, 176.

17. Lee, *Memoirs,* p. 226, n., John Eager Howard's description of a portion of the battle.

18. Graham, *Morgan,* p. 291.

19. Roberts, *Cowpens,* p. 78.

20. Thomas Young, "Memoir of . . . a Revolutionary Patriot of South Carolina," in Scheer and Rankin, *Rebels,* p. 428; cf. SHSW, Draper Manuscripts, 14 VV, 167-83.

21. Graham, *Morgan,* p. 289.

22. Johnson, *Greene,* I, 382.

23. Lee, *Memoirs,* p. 226. King's Mountain seems to be the place Lee had in mind when he discussed Morgan's—to Lee—ill-advised choice of a battleground. Lee wrote: "Had Morgan crossed this river [the Broad] and approached the mountain, he would have gained a position disadvantageous for cavalry, but convenient for riflemen." This is true enough, but Lee completely ignores the time factor here. Tarleton, as will presently appear, had gained five miles on Morgan since the previous morning. In 20 more miles he would certainly have caught up with him even if Morgan had crossed the river. Moreover, despite its advantages over the Cowpens against a cavalry attack, King's Mountain would have been a grisly field indeed to fight upon. The bones of Ferguson's men were not much more than three months buried, and, as noted earlier, the wolves had made their own uses of the shallow graves, as had the hogs of the neighboring farms.

24. Graham, *Morgan,* pp. 295-96.

25. Young, "Memoir."

26. Graham, *Morgan,* pp. 295-96; Lee, *Memoirs,* p. 227; Ward, *Revolution,* II, 757; Greene, *Life,* III, 142; Johnson, *Greene,* I, 377-78; Lossing, *Field-Book,* II, 433-34; Roberts, *Cowpens,* p. 73.

27. Morgan to Greene, Jan. 19, 1781, *Battle Report.*

28. Ward, *Revolution,* II, 758.

29. Kenneth Roberts, *The March to Quebec, passim.*

30. Young, "Memoir."

31. Graham, *Morgan*, p. 29.

32. Roberts, *Cowpens*, p. 75; Graham, *Morgan*, p. 30.

33. Young, "Memoir."

34. Scheer and Rankin, *Rebels*, p. 429; Howard H. Peckham, *The War for Independence*, p. 151.

35. Graham, *Morgan*, pp. 291, 300; Ward, *Revolution*, II, 755; Bass, *Dragoon*, p. 153; Tarleton, *Campaigns*, pp. 245-46; Roberts, *Cowpens*, pp. 59-60; Johnson, *Greene*, I, 374; Cornwallis to Clinton, Jan. 18, 1781, Clinton Papers, WCL.

36. Tarleton, *Campaigns*, p. 220.

37. *Ibid.*, p. 222. Cornwallis, writing to Clinton, was slightly more conservative, estimating Morgan's total force at 1,300 with the militia "fluctuating."

38. Tarleton, *Campaigns*, pp. 223-24.

39. *Ibid.*, pp. 215-16.

40. Graham, *Morgan*, p. 299; Ward, *Revolution*, II, 758; Johnson, *Greene*, I, 379; Greene, *Life*, III, 142-43.

41. Tarleton, *Campaigns*, pp. 215-16.

42. Graham, *Morgan*, p. 299; Ward, *Revolution*, II 758; Johnson, *Greene*, I, 380; Greene, *Life*, III, 143.

43. Charles Stedman, *The History of the Origin, Progress, and Termination of the American War*, II, 322; Gordon, *America*, III, 161; Ramsay, *History*, II, 299.

44. Tarleton, *Campaigns*, p. 216.

45. Morgan to Greene, Jan. 19, 1781, *Battle Report.*

46. Young, "Memoir."

47. *Ibid.*

48. Ward, *Revolution*, II, 760; Graham, *Morgan*, p. 301; Johnson, *Greene*, I, 380.

49. *Ibid.*

50. James Collins, "Autobiography of a Revolutionary Soldier," in Henry Steele Commager and Richard B. Morris (eds.), *The Spirit of 'Seventy-Six*, II, 1156.

51. Lyman C. Draper, *King's Mountain and Its Heroes*, pp. 285-86, n.

52. Graham, *Morgan*, p. 301; Ward, *Revolution*, II, 760; Johnson, *Greene*, I, 380; Morgan to Greene, Jan. 19, 1781, *Battle Report.*

53. Tarleton, *Campaigns*, p. 216.

54. Bass, *Dragoon*, p. 157; Graham, *Morgan*, p. 301.

55. Collins, "Autobiography."

56. Ward, *Revolution*, II, 760-61; Roberts, *Cowpens*, p. 91.

57. Draper, *King's Mountain*, p. 285.

58. Graham, *Morgan*, p. 295; Roberts, *Cowpens*, p. 89.

59. Ward, *Revolution*, II, 761; Graham, *Morgan*, p. 302; Roberts, *Cowpens*, p. 92.

60. Henry Lee, *Campaign of 1781 in the Carolinas*, pp. 97, n. - 98, n.

61. *Ibid.*

62. *Ibid.*

63. Ward, *Revolution*, II, 761; Graham, *Morgan*, p. 303; Johnson, *Greene*, I, 381.

64. Graham, *Morgan*, p. 304; Ward, *Revolution*, II, 761.

65. Tarleton, *Campaigns*, p. 217.

66. Lee, *Campaign of 1781*, pp. 97, n. - 98, n.

67. Lossing, *Field-Book*, II, 435; Lee, *Memoirs*, p. 587.

68. Graham, *Morgan*, p. 303; Roberts, *Cowpens*, p. 93; Johnson, *Greene*, I, 381.

69. Tarleton, *Campaigns*, p. 217.

70. Johnson, *Greene*, I, 381.

71. Young, "Memoir."

72. Tarleton, *Campaigns*, p. 217.

73. General James Jackson to General Daniel Morgan, Jan. 20, 1795, in Graham, *Morgan*, p. 472.

74. Ward, *Revolution*, II, 761; Graham, *Morgan*, p. 305; Johnson, *Greene*, I, 383.

75. Tarleton, *Campaigns*, p. 218; Higginbotham, *Daniel Morgan*, p. 141.

76. Cornwallis to Clinton, Jan. 18, 1781, Clinton Papers, WCL.

77. Lee, *Campaign of 1781*, pp. 97 n. - 98 n.

78. Johnson, *Greene*, I, 382, n.; Graham, *Morgan*, p. 306; Bass, *Dragoon*, p. 159.

79. Lee, *Campaign, 1781*, pp. 97, n. - 98, n.

80. Ward, *Revolution*, II, 761; Johnson, *Greene*, I, 382; Graham, *Morgan*, p. 304.

81. Morgan to Greene, Jan. 19, 1781, *Battle Report*.

82. Tarleton, *Campaigns*, p. 218.

83. Johnson, *Greene*, I, 384.

84. Graham, *Morgan*, p. 291.

85. Tarleton, *Campaigns*, p. 218.

86. Graham, *Morgan*, p. 307. The day, however, was not entirely over for Thomas Young, who had so observantly noted Morgan's morale-building of the previous night and the beautiful advance of the British line at sunrise. Mounted on a captured British charger, Young joined Major Jolly's volunteer mounted militia in pursuit of Tarleton. Young was ambushed by some stragglers from Tarleton's dragoons. Resolved to sell his life as dearly as possible, the boy wielded his sword with a will. In a few minutes he had a finger on his left hand split, his sword arm cut, saber cuts on both shoulders, and finally a cut across the forehead which blinded him in his own blood and temporarily laid him low. The British troopers bound his wounds and conveyed him to Tarleton, by whom he rode for several miles. Tarleton, Young reported, was "a very fine-looking man, with a rather proud bearing, but very gentlemanly in his manners." The British cavalryman endeavored to pump his prisoner. Had Morgan received [Continental] reinforcements? Not yet, lied Young, but he expected them any minute. He added casually that Morgan did have two volunteer companies of mounted militia, "But you know militia won't fight." "By God," replied Tarleton bitterly, "they did today though!" During the night Young and a fellow prisoner succeeded in escaping their captors. The boy arrived home the following evening and—understandably enough—spent the "next eight or ten days in bed with a fever" following what had been probably the longest and most eventful forty-eight hours of his life (SHSW, Draper Manuscripts, 14 VV, 180-81).

87. Ward, *Revolution*, II, 762; Graham, *Morgan*, p. 308; Edward Stevens to Thomas Jefferson, Jan. 24, 1781, *TJ*, IV, 440-41.

88. Scheer and Rankin, *Rebels*, p. 432.

89. Morgan to Greene, Jan. 19, 1781, *Battle Report*.

90. *Ibid.* To his friend William Snickers, Morgan wrote in less formal vein that he had given Tarleton "a devil of a whipping, a more compleat victory was never obtained." Morgan to Wm. Snickers, Jan. 26, 1781, Gates Papers, NYHS.

CHAPTER 9

1. Henry Steele Commager and Richard B. Morris, *The Spirit of 'Seventy-Six*, II, 1246-47.

2. William Johnson, *Sketches of the Life and Correspondence of Nathanael Greene*, I, 385.

3. James Graham, *The Life of General Daniel Morgan*, p. 325.

4. Morgan to Greene, Jan. 15, 1781, in Johnson, *Greene*, I, 370.

5. Graham, *Morgan*, p. 325; Johnson, *Greene*, I, 386.

6. Graham, *Morgan*, p. 326; Johnson, *Greene*, I, 386; Christopher Ward, *The War of the Revolution*, II, 764.

7. Robert D. Bass, *The Green Dragoon*, pp. 158, 164.

8. Morgan to Greene, Jan. 23, 1781, in Graham, *Morgan*, p. 330.

9. Greene, *Life*, III, 78; Ward, *Revolution*, II, 744-45.

10. Graham, *Morgan*, p. 325; Ward, *Revolution*, II, 764; Greene, *Life*, III, 149.

11. See note 2 above.

12. Bass, *Dragoon*, p. 160; Cornwallis to Clinton, Jan. 18, 1781, Clinton Papers WCL.

13. *Ibid.*

14. Bass, *Dragoon*, p. 161.

15. *Ibid.*

16. Banastre Tarleton, *A History of the Campaigns of 1780-1781 in the Southern Provinces of North America*, pp. 248-49.

17. Graham, *Morgan*, p. 326; Bass, *Dragoon*, p. 160.

18. Cornwallis to Clinton, Jan. 18, 1781, Clinton Papers, WCL.

19. Cornwallis to Clinton, Dec. 22, 1780, *Ibid.*

20. Cornwallis to Clinton, Dec. 3, 1780, in Benjamin Franklin Stevens (ed.), *The Campaign in Virginia, 1781*, I, 302-4.

21. Cornwallis to Clinton, Jan. 18, 1781, Clinton Papers, WCL.

22. Tarleton, *Campaigns*, p. 222.

23. Graham, *Morgan*, p. 327; Johnson, *Greene*, I, 388; Ward, *Revolution*, II, 764.

24. Ward, *Revolution*, II, 765.

25. Graham, *Morgan*, pp. 327-28.

26. Morgan to Greene, Jan. 23, 1781, Greene Papers, WCL.

27. *Ibid.*

28. Extract from the notebook of Otho Holland Williams, Jan. 23, 1781, No. 84, *Calendar of the General Otho Holland Williams Papers in the Maryland Historical Society;* George F. Scheer and Hugh F. Rankin, *Rebels and Redcoats*, p. 434. There is a curious discrepancy as to the exact date of the receipt of the news of Cowpens. Ward, *Revolution*, II, 766, gives Jan. 25 as

does Graham, *Morgan*, p. 343, and Johnson, *Greene*, I, 391. George Washington Greene, *Life of Major General Nathanel Greene*, III, 151, says Jan. 24. In the Cowpens section of his biography of Morgan, Graham leans heavily on Johnson's earlier work, and in this case has apparently borrowed the other's error. The evidence in Williams' notebook, a primary source, would seem to carry conviction. Williams was Greene's deputy adjutant general at the time. He had been trained as a clerk and held the position of county clerk in Frederick, Maryland, before entering the army. It does not appear likely that he would have made an error in so important an event as the date of the receipt of the news of Cowpens, for all his other reports indicate that he was a precise and careful person, who wrote a beautiful hand. There are numerous letters from Greene to Washington (*GW*, XXI, 223), to Steuben (Greene, *Life*, III, 151 n.), and to Samuel Huntington (Greene Papers, WCL). These letters are all dated Jan. 24 and detail the news of the victory at Cowpens. This indicates the Jan. 25 date to be incorrect. Moreover, Morgan wrote his battle report to Greene on Jan 19. Unless Giles had been very grievously delayed en route he should surely have reached the camp on the Pee Dee by Jan. 23.

29. Williams to Morgan, Jan. 25, 1781, No. 1072, Morgan Papers, Myers Collection, NYPL.

30. Greene, *Life*, III, 152; Johnson, *Greene*, I, 391-92.

31. Greene to Samuel Huntington, Jan. 24, 1781, Greene Papers, WCL.

32. Greene, *Life*, III, 152.

33. Morgan to Greene, Dec. 31, 1780, Greene Papers, WCL.

34. Greene to Lee, Jan. 26, 1781, in Henry Lee, *Campaign of 1781 in the Carolinas*, pp. viii-ix.

35. Greene, *Life*, III, 153.

36. Johnson, *Greene*, I, 398-99.

37. See note 26 above.

38. Greene, *Life*, III, 152; Johnson, *Greene*, I, 394.

39. Morgan to Greene, Jan. 24, 1781, in Graham, *Morgan*, p. 354; see also Morgan to Williams, Jan. 24, 1781, No. 86, *Calendar of Williams Papers*.

40. Morgan to Greene, Sunrise, Jan. 25, 1781, in Graham, *Morgan*, p. 335.

41. Morgan to Greene, 2 o'clock p.m., Jan. 25, 1781, in *ibid.*

42. Johnson, *Greene*, I, 394; William Gordon, *History of the Rise, Progress and Establishment of the Independence of the United States of America*, III, 163; Ward, *Revolution*, II, 766; Greene, *Life*, III, 153; Benson J. Lossing, *Pictorial Field-Book of the American Revolution*, II, 391.

43. *Ibid.*

44. Lossing, *Field-Book*, II, 394; Gordon, *America*, III, 163.

45. Morgan to Greene, midnight, Jan. 25, 1781, in Graham, *Morgan*, pp. 335-36.

46. Johnson, *Greene*, I, 403. There is some confusion as to the date of Greene's arrival on the Catawba. Gordon, *America*, III, 163, puts it on the 31st, as does Henry Lee, *Memoirs*, p. 233, and Lossing, *Field-Book*, II, 391. Greene, *Life*, III, 154, Graham, *Morgan*, p. 342, and Johnson, *Greene*, I, 403, all state it as Jan. 30. Inasmuch as Johnson also quotes at length a letter from Greene to Huger dated Jan. 30 at Sherrald's Ford the evidence would seem to be that he was in fact there that day.

47. Johnson, *Greene*, I, 388.

48. Ward, *Revolution*, II, 765.
49. Cornwallis to Germain, Mar. 17, 1781, Clinton Papers, WCL.
50. *Ibid.*
51. Tarleton, *Campaigns*, p. 222.
52. Sir Henry Clinton, *The American Rebellion*, p. 259.
53. Morgan to Greene, Jan. 25, 1781, in Graham, *Morgan*, pp. 335-36.
54. Morgan to Greene, Jan. 28, 1781, in *ibid.*, pp. 336-37.
55. Clinton, *Rebellion*, p. 260; Ward, *Revolution*, II, 765.
56. Lynn Montross, *Rag, Tag and Bobtail*, p. 271. Montross here recounts the typical contents of British portmanteaus as contrasted with those of the Americans, which he says contained maps, not playing cards, and military works, not novels and plays.
57. Ward, *Revolution*, II, 765.
58. Cornwallis to Germain, Mar. 17, 1781, Clinton Papers, WCL.
59. Lee, *Memoirs*, p. 232. Lee implies, although without giving an actual date, that the burning of the baggage, which he terms a wise resolution, took place immediately upon receipt of the news of Cowpens, when presumably it might have served some useful purpose.
60. Johnson, *Greene*, I, 407-8; Ward, *Revolution*, II, 765.
61. Johnson, *Greene*, I, 409; Graham, *Morgan*, pp. 338-39.
62. Graham, *Morgan*, p. 341.
63. Morgan to Greene, Jan. 29, 1781, in *ibid.*, p. 337.
64. Cornwallis to Germain, Mar. 17, 1781, Clinton Papers, WCL.
65. Morgan to Greene, Jan. 29, 1781, in Graham, *Morgan*, p. 337. Morgan was unaware that Greene was en route to join him until Greene arrived.
66. Ramsay, *History*, II, 303; Gordon, *America*, III, 163; Lee, *Memoirs*, p. 233.
67. Johnson, *Greene*, I, 389, 405-6. Italics Johnson's.
68. Bass, *Dragoon*, p. 161.
69. Charles Stedman, *The History of the Origin, Progress and Termination of the American War*, II, 325. Stedman was present during the campaign and had opportunity to observe this interesting situation at first hand.
70. Bass, *Dragoon*, p. 161.
71. Tarleton, *Campaigns*, pp. 221-22.
72. *Ibid.*, p. 252.
73. Johnson, *Greene*, I, 413; Graham, *Morgan*, p. 341.

CHAPTER 10

1. Henry Steele Commager and Richard B. Morris, *The Spirit of 'Seventy-Six*, II, 1246-47.
2. William Johnson, *Sketches of the Life and Correspondence of Nathanael Greene*, I, 407.
3. Greene to Huger, Jan. 30, 1781, in Johnson, *Greene*, I, 403-4.
4. Greene to William Campbell, Jan. 30, 1781, Greene Papers, WCL.
5. Greene to Huger, Jan. 30, 1781, in Johnson, *Greene*, I, 403-4.
6. Sir Henry Clinton, *The American Rebellion*, pp. 228, 263-64.
7. Greene to Huger, Jan. 30, 1781, in Johnson, *Greene*, I, 403-4
8. Christopher Ward, *The War of the Revolution*, II, 868.

9. Clinton to Benedict Arnold, Dec. 14, 1780, Clinton Papers, WCL.
10. *GW*, XX, 31, 147, 190.
11. Henry Lee, *Memoirs*, p. 298.
12. *TJ*, IV, 254.
13. *Ibid.*, p. 269.
14. *Ibid.*, p. 269.
15. Dumas Malone, *Jefferson, the Virginian*, p. 337. Malone adds that Jefferson "appears to have maintained his unruffled manner."
16. *TJ*, IV, 258.
17. Clinton, *Rebellion*, p. 237.
18. Ward, *Revolution*, II, 869.
19. Williams to Dr. James McHenry, Jan. 23, 1781, No. 85, *Calendar of the General Otho Holland Williams Papers, in the Maryland Historical Society*. Despite efforts on the part of his biographers, Jefferson's actions during the time of Arnold's invasion cannot be made to redound to his credit with any degree of conviction. Dumas Malone (*Jefferson, the Virginian*, pp. 336-44) attempts an *apologia* as does Julian Boyd (*TJ*, IV, 256-58). That Jefferson himself regarded this period in his life with chagrin is amply demonstrated by the three rather conflicting "diaries" of Arnold's invasion written by him in 1796?, 1805, and 1816 (*TJ*, IV, 258-66). The original "diary" purportedly written while the events were in progress has, as of the present, apparently been lost to posterity. However, it does not follow that criticism of Jefferson's capabilities in a military situation necessarily implies criticism of him as a statesman or man of letters. By his own account the man was militarily innocent, although whether he "boasted" of his ignorance, as the Federalist-inclined Otho Williams claims, is certainly debatable. On May 15, 1826, shortly before his death, Jefferson, evidently under the impression that Lee's *Memoirs* (which admittedly he had not read) contained more animadversions of his conduct as governor in 1780-1781 than they in fact do, wrote a letter to Light Horse Harry's son, Henry Lee, in a yet further attempt to extricate himself from blame for incompetence. The letter may be found in its entirety in the 1870 edition of Lee, *Memoirs*, pp. 316-18. Presumably it will also appear in the Boyd edited edition of the Jefferson Papers when that edition is complete. It says in part: "I was absent myself from Richmond [when Arnold entered the city], but always within observing distance of the enemy, three days only; during which I was never off my horse but to take food or rest; and was everywhere, where my presence could be of any service; and I may, with confidence, challenge any one to put his finger on the point of time when I was in a state of remissness from any duty of my station. But I was not with the army!—True: for, 1st, where was it? 2d. I was engaged in the important task of taking measures to collect an army and, without military education myself, instead of jeopardizing the public safety by pretending to take its command, of which I knew nothing, I had committed that to persons of the art—possessed of that military skill and experience of which I had none."
20. Johnson, *Greene*, I, 404.
21. *Ibid.*, p. 405.
22. Cornwallis to Germain, Mar. 17, 1781, Clinton Papers, WCL.
23. Johnson, *Greene*, I, 414.
24. Johnson, *Greene*, I, 414; George Washington Greene, *Life of Major*

General Nathanael Greene, III, 156-57; Ward, *Revolution*, II, 767. Estimates of the number of militia actually present vary from 300 to 800, so widely that it seems unlikely that an accurate count was ever made.

25. Johnson, *Greene*, I, 414; Greene, *Life*, III, 154; Ward, *Revolution*, II, 769.

26. Johnson, *Greene*, I, 422; Greene's order to militia, Feb. 1, 1781, Greene Papers, WCL.

27. Cornwallis to Germain, Mar. 17, 1781, Clinton Papers, WCL.

28. Johnson, *Greene*, I, 414.

29. Cornwallis to Germain, Mar. 17, 1781, Clinton Papers, WCL.

30. *Ibid.;* Banastre Tarleton, *A History of the Campaigns of 1780-81 in the Southern Province of North America*, p. 227.

31. *Ibid.*

32. *Ibid.*

33. Ward, *Revolution*, II, 767-68.

34. Robert Henry, "Narrative of the Battle of Cowan's Ford," in George F. Scheer and Hugh F. Rankin, *Rebels and Redcoats*, p. 436.

35. *Ibid.*

36. *Ibid.*

37. *Ibid.*

38. *Ibid.*, p. 437.

39. *Ibid.* Most authorities say the guide deliberately ran away. However, Henry knew Beal and claims to have seen him in the wagon ford. Just how a man could "flee away" in the middle of a turbulent ford with deep water on each side, an American force in front, and the greater part of the British southern army in column of fours at his back is something of a minor mystery in itself which none of the persons claiming that this happened has even attempted to explain (Cornwallis makes no mention of the incident). It seems more reasonable that the man did become confused in the flickering light and by the swollen state of the waters.

40. *Ibid.*

41. *Ibid.*

42. *Ibid.*, p. 438.

43. Cornwallis to Germain, Mar. 17, 1781, Clinton Papers WCL.

44. Johnson, *Greene*, I, 415; Ward, *Revolution*, II, 768.

45. Johnson, *Greene*, I, 415; Scheer and Rankin, *Rebels*, p. 438.

46. Scheer and Rankin, *Rebels*, p. 438.

47. Johnson, *Greene*, I, 414-15; Theodore Thayer, *Nathanael Greene: Strategist of the American Revolution*, pp. 312-13.

48. Charles Stedman, *The History of the Origin, Progress and Termination of the American War*, II, 329 n.

49. Cornwallis to Germain, Mar. 17, 1781, Clinton Papers, WCL; Tarleton, *Campaigns*, p. 270.

50. Johnson, *Greene*, I, 416; Greene, *Life*, III, 158; Ward, *Revolution*, II, 769; Tarleton, *Campaigns*, p. 270.

51. Johnson, *Greene*, I, 417; William Gilmore Simms, *Life of Greene*, p. 139; Greene, *Life*, III, 159; Lossing, *Field-Book*, II, 392 n; Ward, *Revolution*, II, 769; Thayer, *Greene*, p. 313. Insofar as the writer has been able to determine, the story first appeared in Johnson's life of Greene published in 1822. Neither Lee, Gordon, nor Ramsay, whose works are of earlier date, mention

it. Greene's papers in the Clements Library make no mention of it, but they are very thin for the whole period of Feb. 1 to Feb. 14, 1781. The movement of the army was too rapid to admit of time for correspondence, other than necessary orders and the like. It smacks of legend, but Lossing claims to have direct evidence for it from Mrs. Steele's descendants.

52. Cornwallis to Germain, Mar. 17, 1781, Clinton Papers WCL; Greene to Washington Feb. 10, 1781, *PCC*, National Archives, Microcopy 247, Roll 175, Item 155, Letters from Major General Nathanael Greene, 1776-85, I, 565-68.

53. Greene, *Life*, III, 159; Johnson, *Greene*, I, 416; Ward, *Revolution*, II, 769; Lossing, *Field-Book*, II, 394.

54. Johnson, *Greene*, I, 418.

55. Ward, *Revolution*, II, 771.

56. Johnson, *Greene*, I, 417; Ward, *Revolution*, II, 771.

57. Johnson, *Greene*, I, 419; Ward, *Revolution*, II, 771; Greene, *Life*, III, 161.

58. Johnson, *Greene*, I, 419.

59. Greene to Abner Nash, Feb. 3, 1781, Greene Papers, WCL.

60. *Ibid.*

61. Johnson, *Greene*, I, 426; Greene, *Life*, III, 162.

62. Greene to Huger, Feb. 1, 1781, in Johnson, *Greene*, I, 422.

63. Morgan to Greene, Feb. 6, 1781, in James Graham, *The Life of General Daniel Morgan*, pp. 354-55. Most authorities imply that Morgan and Greene remained together. However, Morgan's letter is headed Guilford Court House. Its contents imply that Morgan had been sent ahead to relieve the army of the burden of the wagons and to arrange for supplies for Huger's army. The letter would certainly not have been written had the two men remained together.

64. Greene, *Life*, III, 162; Johnson, *Greene*, I, 421; Ward, *Revolution*, II, 772.

65. Johnson, *Greene*, I, 420; Ward, *Revolution*, II, 772.

66. Greene, *Life*, III, 162; William Gordon, *History of the Rise, Progress and Establishment of the Independence of the United States of America*, III, 165.

67. Cornwallis to Germain, Mar. 17, 1781, Clinton Papers, WCL.

68. Ward, *Revolution*, II, 772.

69. Lee, *Memoirs*, p. 236; Gordon, *America*, III, 165; Johnson, *Greene*, I, 425.

70. Ward, *Revolution*, II, 773.

71. Greene, *Life*, III, 163; Johnson, *Greene*, I, 427-28.

72. Johnson, *Greene*, I, 426.

73. Johnson, *Greene*, I, 424; Graham, *Morgan*, p. 340.

74. Johnson, *Greene*, I, 422; *JCC*, XIX, 195-96, 229.

75. Johnson, *Greene*, I, 428-29; Greene, *Life*, III, 164.

76. Johnson, *Greene*, I, 428; Greene, *Life*, III, 165.

77. Johnson, *Greene*, I, 427.

78. Lee, *Memoirs*, p. 248, n.

79. Gordon, *America*, III, 166.

80. Ward, *Revolution*, II, 772; Scheer and Rankin, *Rebels*, p. 439.

81. Greene, *Life*, III, 166.

82. Gordon, *America*, III, 166.
83. *Ibid.*
84. Lee to Greene, Feb. 3, 1781, in Henry Lee, *The Campaign of 1781 in the Carolinas*, pp. xxvii-xxx.
85. I. Burnet to Lee, Feb. 2, 1781, in *ibid.*, pp. xxvii-xxviii.
86. Morgan to Greene, Feb. 6, 1781, in Graham, *Morgan*, p. 354.
87. Lee, *Memoirs*, p. 236; Johnson, *Greene*, I, 425.
88. *Ibid.*
89. James F. Armstrong to [Otho Holland Williams], Feb. 7, 1781, No. 89, *Calendar of Williams Papers*. The Council of War was a very small body, consisting of Greene, Otho Williams, Isaac Huger and Daniel Morgan; see *PCC*, National Archives, Microcopy 247, Roll 175, Item 155, Vol. I, 569.
90. Ward, *Revolution*, II, 772.
91. Johnson, *Greene*, I, 425; Ward, *Revolution*, II, 773.
92. Johnson, *Greene*, I, 426; Ward, *Revolution*, II, 722; Gordon, *America*, III, 166.
93. Ward, *Revolution*, II, 773; Lee, *Memoirs*, p. 236; Johnson, *Greene*, I, 429.
94. Morgan to Greene, Feb. 6, 1781, in Graham, *Morgan*, p. 354.
95. Ward, *Revolution*, II, 773.
96. Lee, *Memoirs*, p. 237.
97. Greene to Morgan, Feb. 10, 1781, No. 87, Morgan Papers, Myers Collection, NYPL. The full context of Greene's permission for Morgan to take leave of absence reads: "General Morgan of the Virginia Line has leave of absence until he recovers his health, so as to be able to take the field again." Greene did not have the authority to retire Morgan permanently or to accept his resignation; this would have been up to Washington or Congress.
98. Lee, *Memoirs*, p. 237.
99. *Ibid.*
100. *Ibid.*
101. *Ibid.*
102. Johnson, *Greene*, I, 431.
103. Lee, *Memoirs*, p. 237; Ward, *Revolution*, II, 773. Ward has Williams leaving on Feb. 8. Lee says Greene left first, leaving Williams on the ground. Lee, as we know, was with Williams' detachment. Thus he should be reasonably sure of what occurred. Greene was still at Guilford on February 10, for he wrote both Patrick Henry and Thomas Jefferson from that place asking for troops (Greene to Patrick Henry, Feb. 10, 1781, Greene Papers, WCL; Greene to Thomas Jefferson Feb. 10, 1781, *TJ*, IV, 576). On Feb. 11, Greene had left Guilford and was near Haw Bridge from whence he wrote three letters regarding supplies to Colonel John Gunby (Greene to Gunby, Feb. 11, 1781, Greene Papers, WCL).
104. Lee, *Memoirs*, p. 238; Ward, *Revolution*, II, 774.
105. Williams to Elie Williams, Mar. 16, 1781, *Calendar of Williams Papers*.
106. Greene, *Life*, III, 165-66; Ward, *Revolution*, II, 774.
107. Lee, *Memoirs*, p. 238.
108. *Ibid.*
109. *Ibid.*, p. 248.
110. Cornwallis to Germain, Mar. 17, 1781, Clinton Papers, WCL.
111. Lee, *Memoirs*, p. 244.

112. *Ibid.*, p. 245.
113. Lee, *Memoirs*, p. 245; Ward, *Revolution*, II, 775.
114. *Ibid.*
115. Ward, *Revolution*, II, 776.
116. Greene, *Life*, III, 173.
117. Gordon, *America*, III, 168.
118. Greene, *Life*, III, 173.
119. Cornwallis to Germain, Mar. 17, 1781, Clinton Papers, WCL.
120. Tarleton, *Campaigns*, p. 236.
121. Greene, *Life*, III, 174-75.

CHAPTER 11

1. Williams to Greene, Mar. 5, 1781, Greene Papers, WCL.
2. *Diary of Frederick Mackenzie*, Feb. 11, 1781.
3. *Ibid.*, Feb. 14, 1781.
4. Cornwallis to Clinton, Jan. 18, 1781, Clinton Papers, WCL.
5. Arnold to Clinton, Feb. 5, 1781, "Letter Book of Correspondence with Arbuthnot, Arnold, Leslie and Phillips," Clinton Papers, WCL.
6. Arnold to Clinton, *ibid.*
7. *Mackenzie Diary*, Mar. 5, 1781.
8. *Ibid.*
9. *Ibid.*
10. Cornwallis to Germain, Mar. 17, 1781, Clinton Papers, WCL.
11. Christopher Ward, *The War of the Revolution*, II, 777.
12. Lee to Greene, Feb. 23, 1781, Greene Papers, WCL.
13. Ward, *Revolution*, II, 777.
14. Cornwallis to Germain, Mar. 17, 1781, Clinton Papers, WCL.
15. Ward, *Revolution*, II, 777; Greene Papers, WCL.
16. Ward, *Revolution*, II, 777; William Gilmore Simms, *The Life of Nathanael Greene*, p. 166.
17. Sir Henry Clinton, *The American Rebellion*, p. 263.
18. Benjamin Franklin Stevens, *The Campaign in Virginia*, I, 327.
19. *Ibid.*
20. Clinton, *Rebellion*, p. 264. "They seemed," says Clinton, "to be more in need of assistance themselves than to be capable of offering any to others."
21. *Ibid.*
22. George Washington Greene, *The Life of Major General Nathanael Greene*, III, 177.
23. Lee to Greene, Feb. 23, 1781, Greene Papers, WCL.
24. Greene, *Life*, III, 177; William Gordon, *History of the Rise, Progress and Establishment of the Independence of the United States of America*, III, 162; William Johnson, *Sketches of the Life and Correspondence of Nathanael Greene*, I, 488.
25. *Ibid.*
26. Lee to Greene, Feb. 19, 1781, Greene Papers, WCL.
27. *Ibid.*
28. Lee to Greene, Feb. 20, 1781, *ibid.*
29. *Ibid.*

30. Lee to Greene, Feb. 18, 1781, *ibid.*

31. Ward, *Revolution,* II, 780; Johnson, *Greene,* I, 444; Gordon, *America,* III, 169.

32. Benson J. Lossing, *Pictorial Field-Book of the American Revolution,* II, 399 n.; Ward, *Revolution,* II, 663-64. Lillington and Caswell defeated the Scots at Moore's Creek in 1776.

33. Ward, *Revolution,* II, 778.

34. Greene, *Life,* III, 178; Ward, *Revolution,* II, 778.

35. Ward, *Revolution,* II, 780.

36. Lyman C. Draper, *King's Mountain and Its Heroes,* p. 391.

37. George F. Scheer and Hugh F. Rankin, *Rebels and Redcoats,* p. 443.

38. Ward, *Revolution,* II, 780.

39. Greene to Jefferson, Mar. 10, 1781, *TJ,* V, III; see also Greene Papers, WCL.

40. Lee to Greene, Feb. 10, 1781, Greene Papers, WCL.

41. Pickens to Greene, Feb. 23, 1781, *ibid.*

42. Cornwallis to Germain, Mar. 17, 1781, Clinton Papers, WCL.

43. *Ibid.*

44. Lee to Greene, Feb. 23, 1781, Greene Papers, WCL.

45. Lee to Greene, Feb. 26, 1781, *ibid.*

46. *Ibid.* Colonel Hamilton was in charge of Cornwallis' heavy baggage and occasionally of foraging. Pyle was a Loyalist; the origin of his titular rank is not clear, but it is probable that the Tory militia, like the Patriots, elected their officers.

47. *Ibid.*

48. Greene, *Life,* III, 181; Ward, *Revolution,* II, 779.

49. Lee to Greene, Feb. 26, 1781, Greene Papers, WCL.

50. *Ibid.*

51. *Ibid.;* Lee, *Memoirs,* p. 257; Ward, *Revolution,* II, 779.

52. Lee, *Memoirs,* p. 258; Ward, *Revolution,* II, 779.

53. Gordon, *America,* III, 170. The Tories are sometimes described as wearing a white paper cockade. Perhaps this depended upon the material available.

54. Greene, *Life,* III, 182.

55. Lee to Greene, Feb. 26, 1781, Greene Papers, WCL. This letter seems to have been misdated by Lee as midnight of Feb. 26. Lee had had a long hard day. The endorsement on the original bears the date Feb. 25, which would indicate the time it was received in Greene's camp. Lee in a letter to Williams gives the date of his encounter with Pyle as Feb. 24, 1781. (Lee to Williams, sunset, Feb. 26, 1781: "Pickens and myself fought a body of 350 North Carolina insurgents on the 24th, beat them, and pursued Tarleton." This note is in the Green Papers.) The date of Feb. 24 is borne out by Tarleton and Cornwallis (Banastre Tarleton, *A History of the Campaigns of 1780-1781 in the Southern Provinces of North America* p. 257; Cornwallis to Germain, Mar. 17, 1781, Clinton Papers, WCL). Henry Lee in his *Memoirs,* pp. 253-63, gives a much longer and more detailed account of his pursuit of Tarleton and encounter with Pyle, which has been much used by later historians. This account, however, has so many irreconcilable discrepancies with the account in Lee's letter to Greene written immediately after the action that it has been thought best to refer to it only where it has been

confirmed by documentary sources. Gordon (*America*, III, 170) has yet a different version, although one adhering more closely to Lee's letter. Ramsay, in his history, follows Gordon. There is no doubt that Lee's letter is authentic. His handwriting, which was atrocious, was also very distinctive, and legible with a reading glass and in a good light.

56. Cornwallis to Germain, Mar. 17, 1781, Clinton Papers, WCL.

57. Lee, *Memoirs*, p. 263.

58. Greene to Pickens, Feb. 26, 1781, Greene Papers, WCL. Pickens, as senior in rank, was in command of his own militia and the Legion, and it was to him that Greene addressed his letter with instructions that Pickens extend "warmest thanks to Col. Lee, and all the officers and soldiers under your command," for their action against Pyle.

59. Williams to Greene, Mar. 4, 1781, Greene Papers, WCL.

60. Cornwallis to Germain, Mar. 17, 1781, Clinton Papers, WCL.

61. Ward, *Revolution*, II, 780.

62. Cornwallis to Germain, Mar. 17, 1781, Clinton Papers, WCL.

63. Charles Stedman, *The History of the Origin, Progress and Termination of the American War*, II, 334-35.

64. *Ibid.*

65. Tarleton, *Campaigns*, p. 273.

66. *Ibid.*, p. 257.

67. Williams to Greene, Feb. 25, 1781, Greene Papers, WCL.

68. Williams to Greene, Feb. 28, 1781, *ibid.*

69. Williams to Greene, Mar. 5, 1781, *ibid.*

70. Greene, *Life*, III, 185-86; Ward, *Revolution*, II, 781.

71. Draper, *King's Mountain*, p. 391. Campbell, to his mortification, had been able to bring only a token force to Greene's aid. There was turmoil on the frontier from a British-instigated rising of the Cherokees.

72. Greene, *Life*, III, 187; Ward, *Revolution*, II, 781.

73. Ward, *Revolution*, II, 781.

74. Williams to Greene, Mar. 4, 1781, Greene Papers, WCL.

75. Williams to Greene, Mar. 4, 1781, *ibid.* These were two separate communications written the same day.

76. Williams to Morgan, Jan. 3, 1781, No. 1070, Morgan Papers, Myers Collection, NYPL. Williams wrote: "I shall quiet the old gentleman's [Gates] doubts by letter, for in whatever his conduct may appear to the world I always rather pitied than condemned his misfortunes...."

77. Williams to Greene, Feb. 25, 1781, Greene Papers, WCL.

78. Williams to Greene, Mar. 4, 1781, *ibid.*

79. Williams to Greene, Mar. 5, 1781, *ibid.*

80. Williams to Greene, Mar. 7, 1781, *ibid.* Although Williams at this time had more years left to him than Greene had to live—the colonel was yet to marry and sire a family—it is probable that his death was already upon him. He had been taken prisoner by the British in Nov., 1776 and confined until Jan., 1778, sharing a 16 ft. square cell with Ethan Allen ("Introduction," *Calendar of the General Otho Holland Williams Papers in the Maryland Historical Society*; Lee, *Memoirs*, pp. 592-93). It was generally felt that in his imprisonment he contracted the seeds of the tuberculosis that killed him in 1794. He had been complaining during the weeks before Guilford of pains in the chest and fever.

81. Lee to Greene, Mar. 1, 1781, Greene Papers, WCL.
82. Pickens to Greene, Mar. 5, 1781, *ibid.* Pickens did not ask to return home and cool his heels in idleness but to return to the field in South Carolina where he felt that he was better known and could do more good. Whether Pickens' enforced association with Lee had any bearing on his request is not known. Johnson says that Lee "seldom failed to disgust the state and militia officers whenever he was called upon to serve with them" (Johnson, *Greene,* II, 461). It is obvious, however, throughout Johnson's work that he is somewhat biased in Lee's disfavor.
83. Greene, *Life,* III, 186-87.
84. Cornwallis to Germain, Mar. 17, 1781, Clinton Papers, WCL.
85. *Ibid.*
86. Draper, *King's Mountain,* p. 392; Greene, *Life,* III, 188, n.
87. Williams to Greene, Mar. 7, 1781, Greene Papers, WCL.
88. Draper, *King's Mountain,* p. 392.
89. Williams to Greene, Mar. 7, 1781, Greene Papers, WCL.
90. Cornwallis to Germain, Mar. 17, 1781, Clinton Papers, WCL.
91. Lee, *Memoirs,* pp. 266-67; Ward, *Revolution,* II, 782; Tarleton, *Campaigns,* pp. 237-38. Lee and Tarleton make much of Wetzell's Mills, Lee particularly emphasizing the miraculous quality of Webster's escape from destruction. Greene calls the affair a small skirmish over stores (Greene, *Life,* III, 188, n.). The veterans of King's Mountain who took part in the incident regarded it entirely as a scrap over which side would get the cornmeal (Draper, *King's Mountain,* pp. 382-83). Williams in his official report makes it a matter of no great importance. Lee and Tarleton, in a manner after all eminently human, had difficulty in treating the aspects of history in which they were active participants in a wholly objective light.
92. I. Burnet [Greene's aide-de-camp] to Pickens, Mar. 5, 1781, Greene Papers, WCL.
93. Richard Campbell to Greene, Mar. 3, 1781, Greene Papers, WCL. Colonel Campbell was a phonetic speller with a southern drawl. He wrote from Taylor's "Ferra:" "This moment arived at this place with four hunderd men.... I was ordered by the barrin Steuben to Informe you emediatly.... I shall continnu my march the neariest and best route.... I have foure Hundred men and thirteen waggins with Six Hundred Stand of Armes."
94. Greene, *Life,* III, 189; Gordon, *America,* III, 173; Ward, *Revolution,* II, 783.
95. Greene to Jefferson, Mar. 10, 1781, *TJ,* V, III; see also Greene Papers, WCL.

CHAPTER 12

1. Clinton to Cornwallis, Apr. 13, 1781, Clinton Papers, WCL.
2. Cornwallis to Germain, Mar. 17, 1781, Clinton Papers, WCL.
3. Jared Sparks, *Correspondence of the American Revolution,* III, 266-68.
4. Otho Williams to Elie Williams, Mar. 16, 1781, *Calendar of the General Otho Holland Williams Papers in the Maryland Historical Society.*
5. *Dairy of Frederick Mackenzie,* Oct. 22, 1781.

6. Henry Steele Commager and Richard B. Morris, *The Spirit of 'Seventy-Six*, II, 1160.

7. Benjamin Franklin Stevens, *The Campaign in Virginia, 1781*, I, 71 n.

8. Clinton to Cornwallis, Apr. 13, 1781, Clinton Papers, WCL.

9. Cornwallis to Germain, Mar. 17, 1781, *ibid.*

10. *Ibid.*

11. *Ibid.*

12. *Ibid.*

13. William Johnson, *Sketches of the Life and Correspondence of Nathanael Greene*, II, 4.

14. George F. Scheer and Hugh F. Rankin, *Rebels and Redcoats*, p. 445; Greene to Samuel Huntington, Mar. 16, 1781, in Banastre Tarleton, *A History of the Campaigns of 1780-1781 in the Southern Provinces of North America*, notes to Chapter IV.

15. Benson J. Lossing, *Pictorial Field-Book of the American Revolution*, II, 405, n. Martinsville originally was the county seat of Guilford County. The county government was moved to Greensboro when it was founded in 1808 and named in Greene's honor. There is no known picture of the court house. When Lossing visited the battleground in 1850, only a broken chimney remained to indicate the site. Today even that is gone. The spot lies just outside the limits of the National Park Service Monument and is designated by an historical marker placed by a huge elm which is said to have been standing in Greene's time. Apparently the area was very sparsely inhabited in the eighteenth century, with heavy woods encompassing a few cleared fields (Simms, *Life of Greene*, pp. 183-84). Quaker influence was strong. True to the principles of their faith, these people shunned both armies, but tradition has it that as long as the guns sounded on March 15, groups of women of the Buffalo and Alamance congregations prayed for the safety of the Americans. "The battling hosts were surrounded by a cordon of praying women" (Lossing, *Field-Book*, II, 407, n.).

16. Cornwallis to Germain, Mar. 17, 1781, Clinton Papers, WCL.

17. Scheer and Rankin, *Rebels*, p. 445. The term "Great Road" is relative to the time. The road was marked on the maps and well traveled, but narrow and of unpaved red clay.

18. Johnson, *Greene*, II, 4-5.

19. George Washington Greene, *Life of Major General Nathanael Greene*, III, 192.

20. *Ibid.*

21. Christopher Ward, *The War of the Revolution*, II, 784; William Gordon, *History of the Rise, Progress and Establishment of the Independence of the United States of America*, III, 173.

22. Cornwallis to Germain, Mar. 17, 1781, Clinton Papers, WCL. Cornwallis need not necessarily have believed this figure. But he did know that he was outnumbered.

23. Ward, *Revolution*, II, 784.

24. Ward, *Revolution*, II, 785; Williams to Greene, Feb. 26, 1781, Greene Papers, WCL.

25. Greene to Joseph Reed, Mar. 18, 1781, in Commager and Morris, *Spirit of '76*, II, 1162. Greene's bitterness may have been enhanced by the

fact that it had been so long since he had an opportunity of doing anything of the kind.

26. As the war wore on, "voluntary proffer of service being no longer fashionable," (Henry Lee, *Memoirs,* p. 227, n.) the militia were drafted. Hence the custom developed—and continued through the Civil War—whereby the timid and wealthy were able to buy a substitute. Frequently the substitutes were former Continental soldiers who had served their enlistment time and been discharged only to find the pickings of civil life lean. Needless to say, the timid and poor found no such recourse from the draft. These presumably were the ones who fled at the first volley. Unfortunately panic is notoriously contagious.

27. Vincent Jones, Church of Jesus Christ of Latter-day Saints Genealogical Offices (personal communication). Mr. Jones reports that of about 100 applications for pension from Carolina militia veterans, which he had studied in another connection, perhaps a half dozen had fought at Cowpens and Guilford. This is too small a sample but is worthy of further research. All during the Revolution militiamen were called out for brief periods of emergency. It is entirely possible that men who stood fast at Cowpens were among those who fled at Guilford under different circumstances and leadership.

28. Morgan to Greene, Feb. 20, 1781, in James Graham, *The Life of General Daniel Morgan,* p. 370; Johnson, *Greene,* II, 6-7, n.

29. Greene to Samuel Huntington, Mar. 16, 1781, in Tarleton, *Campaigns,* Notes to Chapter IV; Lee, *Memoirs,* pp. 596-97. This is Greene's report to Congress of the battle at Guilford. The manuscript of this report is not in the Greene Papers in the Clements Library, but there are several other reports to Morgan, Joseph Reed, Abner Nash and others. These do not differ materially in detail from the report to Congress or to Washington, which appear in printed sources.

30. *Ibid.*
31. *Idem. Ibid.*
32. Lee, *Memoirs,* p. 272.
33. Greene, *Life,* III, 193.
34. St. George Tucker to Frances Bland Tucker, Mar. 13, 1781, in Scheer and Rankin, *Rebels,* p. 444.
35. Lee, *Memoirs,* p. 273.
36. *Ibid.*
37. Cornwallis to Germain, Mar. 17, 1781, Clinton Papers, WCL.
38. *Ibid.*
39. Greene to Huntington, Mar. 16, 1781, *Battle Report.*
40. Tarleton, *Campaigns,* p. 272.
41. Lee, *Memoirs,* p. 274.
42. Greene, *Life,* III, 193.
43. Lossing, *Field-Book,* II, 401; Johnson, *Greene,* II, 4.
44. Lee, *Memoirs,* p. 275, n.; Bass, *Dragoon,* p. 169. The wound was so severe that after the Guilford battle the British surgeon, Stewart, amputated the two mutilated fingers and part of the hand as well.
45. Bass, *Dragoon,* p. 170.
46. Greene to Huntington, Mar. 16, 1781, *Battle Report.*

47. Ward, *Revolution*, II, 786; Greene, *Life*, III, 195; Johnson, *Greene*, II, 5.

48. Greene, *Life*, III, 29, 195.

49. Morgan to Greene, Feb. 20, 1781, in Graham, *Morgan*, p. 370; Johnson, *Greene*, II, 6-7, n.; Emory Upton, *The Military Policy of the United States*, p. 56.

50. Ward, *Revolution*, II, 786-87. Since Greene's post was with the third line, he could not see much of what was occurring on his own front. He must have received messengers from time to time telling him of what occurred, and he was on the field in the court house area at one time at least (Greene to Mrs. Greene, Mar. 18, 1781, in Johnson, *Greene*, II, 22).

51. Greene, *Life*, III, 196; Lee, *Memoirs*, p. 274; Scheer and Rankin, *Rebels*, p. 445.

52. Lossing *Field-Book*, II, 402; Greene, *Life*, III, 193.

53. Greene, *Life*, III, 193; Ward, *Revolution*, II, 787.

54. Greene, *Life*, III, 196.

55. Colonel Richard Campbell was not the only phonetic speller of the Revolution. The New Englander, David How *(Diary of David How)*, spelled English as he spoke it. The nasal twang and the New England peculiarity of adding R to words ending in A and dropping it from words ending in R is evident.

56. Greene, like everyone else in those days, had ridden since childhood, but to him a horse was simply a means of conveyance. There is nowhere any comment on him as a notable equestrian as there so frequently is with respect to Lee and Washington. Moreover, Greene had a stiff right knee, the result of some childhood injury (Simms, *Life of Greene*, p. 21; Greene, *Life*, I, 81), which caused him to limp when he walked, made mounting difficult, and presented an awkward picture when he was riding a horse.

57. Scheer and Rankin, *Rebels*, p. 446. The source of this quotation is not given in the foregoing. It is not, however, in Lee's *Memoirs*.

58. See above, Chapter 11, note 81.

59. The 300 yards separating the North Carolina militia from the Virginia militia represents the length of three football fields. The militia could not have felt very closely supported.

60. Richard Harrison to Ann Harrison, Mar. 15, 1781, in Scheer and Rankin, *Rebels*, p. 447.

61. Lossing, *Field-Book*, II, 403.

62. Simms, *Life of Greene*, p. 188.

63. Cornwallis to Germain, Mar. 17, 1781, Clinton Papers, WCL. The contingent of the 71st defeated at Cowpens had lost its bags to Morgan, but the regiment contained more than one set.

64. *Ibid.*

65. Greene to Huntington, Mar. 16, 1781, *Battle Report.*

66. Ward, *Revolution*, II, 787.

67. Lee, *Memoirs*, p. 277.

68. Greene to Washington, Mar. 18, 1781, in Sparks, *Correspondence*, III, 266.

69. Simms, *Life of Greene*, p. 188.

70. Ward, *Revolution*, II, 787.

71. Greene in this was no eyewitness as the front line could not be seen

from his position. His information as to what happened must have come from Lee or one of the militia officers.

72. Roger Lamb, *An Original and Authentic Journal of Occurrences during the Late American War,* p. 361.

73. *Ibid.* Italics added.

74. *Ibid.* Italics added.

75. The technique in such cases requires that those attacked hold their ground, then sidestep the oncoming bayonets and club the assailants with the butts of their rifles. It is a procedure demanding remarkably steady nerves. There is no evidence that the North Carolina militia had ever been instructed in this technique.

76. Lee, *Memoirs,* pp. 277-78. They did not, however, throw away their flag. The flag is now on display at the National Park Service Museum at Guilford. It is the only United States flag now in existence that was carried in a battle in the Revolution. Its colors and design are unusual. There are 16 stripes of dark wine red and navy blue alternately. There are 13 navy blue stars on a white field, and the stars are 8-pointed. The whole flag measures approximately 3 by 5 feet. Maciyah Bullock, to whom the flag was entrusted, apparently saw it and himself safely home after the battle.

77. *Ibid.*

78. Gordon, *America,* III, 174.

79. Johnson, *Greene,* II, 9.

80. Cornwallis to Germain, Mar. 17, 1781, Clinton Papers, WCL.

81. Lee, *Memoirs,* p. 259.

82. *Ibid.*

83. This is very evident in Cornwallis' and Greene's battle reports. Greene's report to Congress is particularly thin. When he wrote it, he was a sick and beaten man. Cornwallis did not write his report to Germain until a day later, March 17, when he had had an opportunity to piece together a little more information. Greene's subsequent reports reveal a dawning realization of the Pyrrhic quality of Cornwallis' victory. The complete accounts in secondary sources are the result of much winnowing and comparison of reports of company commanders after the event.

84. Ward, *Revolution,* II, 788-90; Lee, *Memoirs,* p. 283.

85. Tarleton, *Campaigns,* p. 273.

86. Scheer and Rankin, *Rebels,* p. 448; Greene, *Life,* III, 199.

87. St. George Tucker to Frances Bland Tucker, Mar. 18, 1781, in Scheer and Rankin, *Rebels,* p. 448.

88. Simms, *Life of Greene,* p. 190. Washington may have taken the retreat to be that of the whole Virginia militia. Cornwallis repeatedly speaks of the thickness of the woods and the poor visibility in this area.

89. Scheer and Rankin, *Rebels,* p. 448.

90. Lee, *Memoirs,* p. 279; Ward, *Revolution,* II, 790; Lossing, *Field-Book,* II, 404.

91. *Ibid.*

92. Cornwallis to Germain, Mar. 17, 1781, Clinton Papers, WCL.

93. *Ibid.*

94. Lossing, *Field-Book,* II, 404; Lee, *Memoirs,* pp. 279-80.

95. *Ibid.*

96. Cornwallis to Germain, Mar. 17, 1781, Clinton Papers, WCL.

97. *Ibid.*

98. Lossing, *Field-Book*, II, 404; Lee, *Memoirs*, p. 280. Washington carried in the battle a small personal flag, fashioned in true knightly manner from a portion of his lady's gown. It is on display at the Guilford Museum.

99. Johnson, *Greene*, II, 21. After the battle an American soldier stole the apparently lifeless Lovell's watch and sold it to William Washington. Since Lovell was not listed in the British returns as either killed or wounded, the only possible conclusion is that the Guardsman was playing possum. His messmates, at any rate, so concluded; Lovell retired from the service under a cloud soon after.

100. Lossing, *Field-Book*, II, 404, n.; Alma Power-Waters, *Virginia Giant, passim;* Fred J. Cook, "Francisco, the Incredible," *American Heritage*, X (October, 1959), 92-95; Raleigh Taylor, "Peter Francisco" (unpublished manuscript, Guilford Museum, National Park Service National Monument, 1958).

101. Cornwallis to Germain, Mar. 17, 1781, Clinton Papers, WCL.

102. *Ibid.*

103. Colonel K. W. Treacy (personal communication) claims that he noted this smell in North Africa during World War II and says that it is something quite distinct from blood or corpses, both of which he has also experienced. He adds that one day he and one of his officers, Charles Kenniger, were on reconnaissance. They drove through a meadow all aglow with wildflowers, as peaceful a sight as may be imagined. Kenniger sniffed and remarked that there had been "a hell of a fight" in the area within the last day or two. This proved to be the case. A possible explanation may be that the release of adrenalin into the bloodstream produces some sort of odor. Medical men will deny this. Laymen with sensitive olfactory nerves (this includes primitive peoples) will not.

104. Cornwallis to Germain, Mar. 17, 1781, Clinton Papers, WCL.

105. *Ibid.*

106. *Ibid.*

107. Greene to Huntington, Mar. 16, 1781, *Battle Report.*

108. *Ibid.*

109. Lee states that he remained with his cavalry in the isolated position into which he had been forced by the Regiment von Bose after the flight of the North Carolinians. When the 71st Regiment withdrew from support of the Hessians, Lee dispatched his cavalry to join Greene on the court house hill. When most of the Regiment von Bose withdrew, Lee left William Campbell and his rifle corps to hold the remnant of the Hessians whilst he and the Legion infantry hastened to rejoin his cavalry on the Continental flank. He arrived close enough to witness the flight of the 2nd Maryland, whereupon "the corps of Lee severed from the army" (Lee, *Memoirs*, p. 281). Lee then adds that when "the contest had long been ebbing Tarleton and his horse under orders from Cornwallis charged Campbell and dispersed his few remaining men" (Lee, *Memoirs*, p. 283; Tarleton, *Campaigns*, pp. 282-83). Campbell, on the other hand, claims categorically that Lee left him without apprising him of his intent to do so and that as a result he and his rifles were swept from the field by Tarleton. Campbell immediately resigned his commission claiming that he could no longer hold it with honor (Lyman C. Draper, *King's Mountain and Its Heroes*, p. 394). On March 17 Lee wrote

Campbell praising the bravery of Campbell and his men on March 15:
"I hope your men are safe, and the scattered will soon collect [indicating
certainly that he knew little of Campbell's fate]. Be pleased to favor me with
a return of your losses and prepare your men for a second battle" (Henry
Lee, *The Campaign of 1781 in the Carolinas*, p. xvii). Campbell and his men
went home despite compliments from Green (Greene to William Campbell,
Mar. 18, 1781, Greene Papers, WCL). When Lee later refers to the "rifle corps
of Campbell" as being with him during the pursuit of Cornwallis, he can
only mean "Rich. Campbell of Taylor's Ferra," he of the phonetic spelling
(see above, Chapter 11, note 93).

110. Greene to Jefferson, Mar. 10, 1781; *TJ*, V, III; Greene Papers, WCL.

111. Greene to Washington, Mar. 18, 1781, Sparks, *Correspondence*, III,
268.

112. Ward, *Revolution*, II, 793. Cornwallis told Clinton he fought 1,360
infantry, which caused Sir Henry to inquire caustically what he had done
with the rest of the 3,000 he should have had by Sir Henry's reckoning (Clinton to Cornwallis, Apr. 30, 1781, Clinton Papers, WCL). However, the
figure 1,360 does not include cavalry or artillerists. Estimates as to Cornwallis'
total strength vary from 1,900 to a little over 2,200.

113. Ward, *Revolution*, II, 793.

114. List of Regimental Officers Killed in the Battle of Guilford, Mar. 15,
1781, Mackenzie Papers, WCL.

115. List of killed and wounded and missing Guilford, 15 March, 1781, by
Deputy Adjutant General Otho Williams, Greene Papers, WCL. Williams
expected many of the missing to rejoin. Cornwallis estimated the American
loss at 200-300. He said that his foraging parties reported farm houses 6-8
miles around full of wounded. While the British surgeons were caring
for the British injured, the Americans crawled off the field after the retreating army (Cornwallis to Germain, Mar. 17, 1781, Clinton Papers, WCL).
According to Johnson, about 300 North Carolinians had somewhat sheepishly
gathered at Troublesome Creek after the battle. Lee and the Legion marched
in at dawn wearing the short scarlet cloaks that were part of their uniform
for rainy weather. In the dim light the militia saw the red as British and
once more took to their heels (Johnson, *Greene*, II, 23).

116. Charles Stedman, *The History of the Origin, Progress and Termination of the American War*, II, 346; Greene, *Life*, III, 203; Ward, *Revolution*,
II, 795.

CHAPTER 13

1. Greene to Samuel Huntington, Mar. 30, 1781, Greene Papers, WCL.

2. Greene to Cornwallis or his staff, Mar. 16, 1781, Greene Papers, WCL.

3. Greene, *Life*, III, 207-7.

4. Lee, *Memoirs*, p. 287.

5. Ward, *Revolution*, II, 795.

6. Clinton, *Rebellion*, p. 267; Lee, *Memoirs*, p. 286; Lossing, *Field-Book*, II,
406; Greene to Morgan, Mar. 20, 1781, Greene Papers, WCL.

7. *Ibid*. The American wounded seem to have been left on the field
under the care of Dr. Wallace. There would have been no reason for Corn-

wallis to burden himself with their transport the 12 miles to New Garden. He was in no condition to hold prisoners.

8. Clinton, *Rebellion*, p. 267.

9. Stevens, *Campaign in Virginia, 1781*, I, 371.

10. Greene, *Life*, III, 209.

11. *Ibid.*, pp. 209-10.

12. Cornwallis to Clinton, Apr. 10, 1781, Clinton Papers, WCL.

13. Lee to the Commanding Officer of the militia in Roan, Surrey and Mecklenburgh counties, Mar. 20, 1781, Greene Papers, WCL. The proclamation reads in part as follows:

> My friends and countrymen:
> You have already heard of the general action between the two armies on the 15th instant. But a very small portion of the regular troops were engaged; some new raised troops behaved dastardly, which confused the regiments nearest them, and rendered it prudent to retire and postpone the decision to another day. Cornwallis is running with his broken army to some place of safety. His deluded friends, our unhappy brethren called tories, experience the imbecility of his pretenses to protect them. Come then, my friends, fly to your arms. Recollect your glorious exertion in the last campaign and let not it be said that you shrink from danger at this interesting crisis.
>
> Your friend and soldier,
> Henry Lee, Junior,

On the whole Cornwallis seems to have had the edge on Lee when it came to writing proclamations, perhaps because of his greater experience. Since New Garden was southwest of Guilford, the first impression the Americans had when Cornwallis moved was that he was retiring toward the Yadkin (Greene, *Life*, III, 210). Lee still had this impression when he wrote, for Roan, etc., lie in that direction.

14. Greene to Morgan, Mar. 20, 1781, Greene Papers, WCL.

15. Ramsay, *History*, II, 312; Lossing, *Field-Book*, II, 406.

16. Greene to Jefferson, Mar. 23, 1781; *TJ*, V, 215; Greene Papers, WCL.

17. Greene to Malmedy, Mar. 18, 1781, Greene Papers, WCL.

18. Greene to John Alexander Lillington, Mar. 26 and Mar. 29, 1781, Greene Papers, WCL.

19. *Ibid.*

20. Greene to John Baker, Mar. 22, 1781, Greene Papers, WCL.

21. Greene to Lillington, Mar. 26, 1781, Greene Papers, WCL. Deep River flows into the Haw, which becomes the Cape Fear River below Cross Creek.

22. In his letter of Mar. 23 to Jefferson, noted above, Greene told the governor that if provisions were not forthcoming, the army would have to fall back.

23. Greene, *Life*, III, 211.

24. Greene to Jefferson, Mar. 27, 1781; *TJ*, V, 258; Greene Papers, WCL; Greene, *Life*, III, 212; Ward, *Revolution*, II, 798.

25. Greene to Jefferson, Mar. 27, 1781; *TJ*, V, 258; Greene Papers, WCL.

26. Greene, *Life*, III, 213.

27. *Ibid.*, p. 212.

28. Greene to Stephen Drayton, Mar. 28, 1781, Greene Papers, WCL. The

context of this letter indicates that Drayton was connected with the partisan corps under Lillington in the Wilmington area.

29. Lee, *Memoirs*, pp. 289-90. Cornwallis gives Colonel Malmedy credit for this exploit, if credit it can be called. In Corwallis' words: "Colonel Malmedy, with about twenty of the gang of plunderers that are attached to him, galloped among the sentries and carried off three Jägers" (Cornwallis to Clinton, Apr. 10, 1781, Clinton Papers, WCL). There is a puzzling discrepancy about this matter of the bridge. Some secondary authorities say that it was destroyed; others say that it was not. Lee, as noted, says that it was not. Tarleton speaks obscurely of the "dilemma of the bridge," but fails to make clear what the dilemma was. Inasmuch as Greene did not cross Deep River for other reasons, as will appear, perhaps the matter is not of importance.

30. Greene to Samuel Huntington, Mar. 30, 1781, Greene Papers, WCL.

31. Greene, *Life*, III, 212; Gordon, *America*, III, 176. Gordon says in a footnote that he got his information from Otho Williams' papers. According to Williams, all these papers pertaining to the "operations of the Southern Army after the evacuation of Charleston" were lost at sea when Gordon shipped them back to Williams (Williams to Henry Knox [?], June 28, 1786, *Calendar, Williams Papers*, No. 353, MHS).

32. Greene to Huntington, Mar. 30, 1781, Greene Papers, WCL.

33. Greene, *Life*, III, 216.

34. Greene to Sumter, Mar. 30, 1781, Greene Papers, WCL.

35. Greene to Washington, Mar. 29, 1781, in Sparks, *Correspondence*, III, 278-79.

36. *Ibid.* Italics mine.

37. Greene to Sumter, Mar. 30, 1781, Greene Papers, WCL. Italics mine.

38. Greene to Lillington, Mar. 29, 1781, in Greene, *Life*, III, 215. Italics mine.

39. Greene to James Emmet, Apr. 3, 1781, Greene Papers, WCL. Italics mine.

40. Lee to Greene, Apr. 2, 1781, in Greene, *Life*, III, 216. The balance of this letter is sufficiently characteristic of Lee's letters to Greene and the advice contained in them as to merit inclusion here:

> This conduct [the move south] may eventually undo the successes gained by the enemy in the last campaign, and must probably render abortive every effort of his lordship to establish himself in this State. I think the following matters claim your immediate attention:—
>
> The passage of the Pedee; supply of ammunition; transported in such a manner it cannot be damaged; an extra pair of shoes per man; a proclamation pardoning deserters, pointing out the delusion of the Tories, breaking up the paroles given to the inhabitants taken from their houses by the enemy, and recommending union and zeal to all orders of people.
>
> I think it would be politic in government to attend to measures for the forming a public press, as the proper communication of events would tend very much to stir up the patriotism of the people....

Greene heeded the advice about shoes and the care of ammunition (Greene to Joseph Clay, Apr. 3, 1781). So far as can be determined he did nothing about proclamations, public presses, or propaganda. Greene's aide, William Pierce, noted that the principle behind Greene's decision was "the same that actuated Scipio when he led the Carthaginian hero out of Rome to the plains of Zama" (Scheer and Rankin, *Rebels*, 453). Alexander Hamilton later compared it to "Scipio leaving Hannibal in Italy to overcome him in Carthage" (Commager and Morris, *Spirit, '76*, II 1161).

41. Williams to Henry Knox, June 28, 1786, No. 353, *Calendar, Williams Papers*, MHS.

42. Williams to Governor Henry Lee, Mar., 1792, No. 689, *Calendar, Williams Papers*, MHS. Williams says that he sent Gordon the historian "all his notes, orderly books, muster rolls, field returns, and all his valuable collection" of which he had been "too idle" to transcribe copies. When Gordon attempted to return the material, the ship carrying it was lost. Lee wrote his *Memoirs*, in 1809 while in prison for debt (Douglas Southall Freeman, *R. E. Lee*, I, 13). The first edition was published in 1812 at which time Greene, Williams, Morgan were long since dead.

43. Lee, *Memoirs*, pp. 317-25.

44. *Idem.*

45. *Idem.* Gordon's history makes no mention of Lee in connection with Greene's decision to move south, but merely paraphrases Greene's letter to Washington of Mar. 29 (Gordon, *America*, III, 188).

46. Joseph Clay to Greene, Mar. 29, 1781; Greene to Abner Nash, Mar 29, 1781; Greene to Samuel Huntington, Mar. 30, 1781; Greene to Joseph Clay, Apr. 3, 1781, Greene Papers, WCL. Clay was in the Quartermaster Department, apparently detached at this time on purchasing missions.

47. Greene Papers, WCL.

48. *Ibid.*

49. *Ibid.*

50. Lee, *Memoirs*, p. 319 n.

51. Greene to Jefferson, Mar. 23, 1781; *TJ*, V, 215; Greene Papers, WCL.

52. Greene to Jefferson, Apr. 6, 1781; *TJ*, V, 360; Greene Papers, WCL.

53. Greene to Jefferson, Mar. 10, 1781; *TJ*, V, 111; Greene Papers, WCL.

54. Greene to Washington, *GW*, XX, 321 n.

55. Greene to Catherine Greene, Jan. 25, 1781, in Greene, *Life*, III, 152.

56. Greene to Sumter, Mar. 30, 1781, Greene Papers, WCL.

57. Charles Lynch to Greene, Apr. 2, 1781, Greene Papers, WCL. Lynch's men left in rather informal manner to the mortification of their commander:
> Sir: This morning my Men understanding they were to march to Headquarters about one hundred of them Marched off without My Knowledge and without Officers. They left all the Publick arms which I now send by my Baggage Waggon Being thirty three Musketts. and some Catrage Boxes—the Only Excuse I am able to Make for such a Piece of Conduct of My Men is, that they are Poor Men Anxious to get home.... Chas. Lynch.

58. Greene, *Life*, III, 217.

59. Gordon, *America*, III, 217. Some authorities say Apr. 6, but Gordon, who had access to Greene's lost orderly books, agrees better with Greene's letter of April 4 to Lee, saying that the army would march next morning.

60. Peckham, *Independence*, p. 149.

61. *Ibid.*
62. John W. Fortescue, *History of the British Army,* III, 403.
63. *Ibid.*
64. *Ibid.*
65. Lossing, *Field-Book,* II, 405; Greene, *Life,* III, 202; Lee, *Memoirs,* p.
281; Commager and Morris, *Spirit, '76,* II, 1160; Peckham, *Independence,* 154.
66. It had already been noted that Greene named his first child George
Washington Greene and his second (happily a girl) Martha, and that after
the war he took up the life of a gentleman planter in Georgia. In addition
he constantly sought Washington's advice in matters public and private.
Notable is that of the affair of Captain Gunn, an officer who challenged him
to a duel, which challenge Greene refused to honor, with Washington's com-
mendation (Sparks, *Writings of Washington,* IX, 20; Greene, *Life,* III, 529;
Simms, *Life of Greene,* p. 353).
67. Johnson, *Greene,* II, 456 ff.
68. Thayer, *Greene: Strategist,* 21. Greene was a student of Locke.
69. Scheer and Rankin, *Rebels,* p. 451.
70. Johnson, *Greene,* II, 448. Greene is here quoted as saying, "I am not
fit for militiary life, for I cannot adopt its maxims."
71. Aristotle, *Nicomachaean Ethics,* iii, 8, 30.
72. Clinton, *Rebellion,* 268.
73. Cornwallis to Clinton, Apr. 10, 1781, Clinton Papers, WCL. Unlike
Greene, the British did not make careful inquiry as to climate or terrain. Sir
Henry later, with great choler, asked why Lord Cornwallis did not proceed
by land down the coast from Wilmington to Charleston, apparently with no
clear conception of the rivers and swamps to be crossed in that route
(Stevens, *Controversy,* I, 66 ff.).
74. James Emmet to Greene, Apr. 2, 1781, Greene Papers, WCL.
75. Emmet to Greene, Apr. 4, 1781, Greene Papers, WCL.
76. Present population, 1611.
77. Tarleton, *Campaigns,* pp. 282 ff. Cornwallis had trouble with Tarleton
also. Tarleton wished to retire because of his maimed right hand. Cornwallis
persuaded him to remain, whereupon Tarleton began to practice writing
and the use of the saber and pistol with his left hand, with some success
(Bass, *Dragoon,* p. 171).
78. Cornwallis to Webster, n. d., in Lee, *Memoirs,* p. 292.
79. Stedman, *American War,* II, 352; Ward, *Revolution,* 797.
80. Tarleton, *Campaigns,* pp. 282 ff. Rawdon did learn from Tory sources
of Greene's approach.
81. Ward, *Revolution,* II, 797. For a critical and not particularly favorable
discussion of Cornwallis' decision see Tarleton, *Campaigns,* 282 ff.
82. Cornwallis to Clinton, Apr. 10, 1781, *Clinton Papers,* WCL.
83. Cornwallis to Phillips, Apr. 10, 1781, *Clinton Papers,* WCL.
84. In the 35 volumes of the Fitzpatrick edition of Washington's writings,
Washington makes 67 references to the interposition of Providence in
connection with the American Revolution. Anyone who has made a study of
this Revolution is forced to agree that something other than the power and
magnitude of American arms had a hand in the matter. The latter were
wholly unequal to the task.

BIBLIOGRAPHY

BIBLIOGRAPHY

PRIMARY SOURCES

MANUSCRIPT COLLECTIONS

Clinton Papers. William L. Clements Library, University of Michigan, Ann Arbor, Michigan.

This is a voluminous and varied collection which contains correspondence of Lord Cornwallis, Benedict Arnold, Lord Francis Rawdon, General Leslie, General Phillips, and others, as well as Clinton manuscripts.

Gates Papers. New York State Historical Society, New York City, N. Y.

Unfortunately the papers have not yet been published. They must be consulted at the Society, or photostatic copies of specific letters may be obtained for a small fee provided the researcher knows precisely what letter he needs.

Greene Papers. William L. Clements Library, University of Michigan, Ann Arbor, Michigan.

The 88 letter boxes in this collection contain by no means all of Nathanael Greene's papers extant. However, the coverage for the period 1780-1783 is very good. The collection includes many letters from persons other than Greene, notably Henry Lee, Otho Williams, Thomas Jefferson, Francis Marion, Andrew Pickens, Thomas Sumter, and many others great and small.

Mackenzie Papers. William L. Clements Library, University of Michigan, Ann Arbor, Michigan.

Morgan Papers. Theodore Bailey Myers Collection, New York
Public Library (NYPL).

Morgan letters and letters to Morgan from various cor-
respondents. The papers are contained in one large volume,
apparently in the order in which they were acquired rather
than chronologically. Each item is numbered. The majority
of the papers are post-Revolution.

Sumter Papers. Lyman C. Draper Manuscripts Collection, The
State Historical Society of Wisconsin, Madison, Wisconsin.

This is a vast and heterogeneous collection containing
letters from and to Sumter, nineteenth century newspaper and
magazine articles pertaining to Sumter or his men, recol-
lections of Sumter's men and their descendants interviewed in
their old age, field returns, muster rolls, sketch maps of battle
areas, and much else both trivial and consequential. As a
result it is difficult to use but on the whole rewarding. Draper
gathered the material for a biography of Sumter that he
planned to write.

PUBLISHED PRIMARY SOURCES

Blanchard, Claude. *Journal of an Officer of Rochambeau's Army
in America, 1780-1782.* Edited by Thomas Balch. Albany:
Munsell, 1876.

Blanchard made some interesting observations of the contrasting habits and motivations of British and American
forces.

Burnett, Edmund Cody (ed.). *Letters of Members of the Continental Congress.* 8 vols. Washington: Carnegie Institution,
1921-1936.

Clinton, Sir Henry. *The American Rebellion: Sir Henry Clin-
ton's Narrative of His Campaigns, 1775-1782, with an
Appendix of Original Documents.* Edited by William B.
Willcox. New Haven: Yale University Press, 1954.

Willcox's introduction is a masterly analysis of Clinton.
The work is very useful for one British viewpoint.

Commager, Henry Steele and Richard B. Morris (ed.). *The
Spirit of 'Seventy-Six: The Story of the American Revolution
as Told by Participants.* 2 vols. New York: Bobbs-Merrill
Company, 1958.

The documents deal mainly with military aspects, but there is also material on hospitals, prisons, spies, the home front, and political issues.

How, David. *Diary of David How, a Private in Colonel Paul Dudley Sargent's Regiment of the Massachusetts Line in the Army of the American Revolution, from the Originial Manuscript with a Biographical Sketch of the Author by George Wingate Chase and Illustrative Notes by Henry B. Dawson.* Morrisiania, New York: 1865.

An invaluable bit of Americana. David How was a merchant in later life and already a shrewd trader at the time of the Revolution. He was a phonetic speller, and the New England twang is evident.

Jefferson, Thomas. *The Papers of Thomas Jefferson.* Edited by Julian P. Boyd. Projected 50 vols. Princeton: Princeton University Press, 1950-.

Jones, John. *Plain, Concise, Practical Remarks on the Treatment of Wounds and Fractures; to Which is Added an Appendix on Camp and Military Hospitals; Principally Designed for the Use of Young Military and Naval Surgeons in North America.* Philadelphia: 1776.

Interesting commentary on medical and surgical practice of the time. Proof that man is an animal that can survive much abuse.

Journals of the Continental Congress. 34 vols. Washington: United States Government Printing Office, 1904-1937.

Lamb, Roger. *An Original and Authentic Journal of Occurrences During the Late American War from Its Commencement to the Year 1783.* Dublin: Wilkinson and Courtney, 1809.

Lamb, educated beyond his station in life, was an alert observer of events.

Lee, Henry. *Memoirs of the War in the Southern Department of the United States.* Edited by Robert E. Lee. Second edition. New York: University Publishing Company, 1870.

The first edition of this work appeared in 1812. Robert E. Lee as editor of the second edition corrected some of the more obvious errors in his father's work, annotated certain sections, and added a biography of Henry Lee containing letters of interest. The *Memoirs* were written long after the events described. They must be used with caution. Lee has a tendency to magnify those actions in which he personally took part. He apparently relied on memory and used little documentation in certain areas. However, he does include documents of interest and attaches a valuable appendix of thumbnail biographies of several Revolutionary officers. The book is well and dramatically written and reads like a novel. Unfortunately there is reason to suspect that, in some parts at least, it is a novel.

Mackenzie, Frederick. *Diary of Frederick Mackenzie, Giving a Daily Narrative of His Military Service as an Officer of the Regiment of Royal Welch Fusiliers During the Years 1775-1782 in Massachusetts, Rhode Island and New York.* 2 vols. Cambridge: Harvard University Press, 1930.

The careful major made a note of weather and wind direction every day. This information can be very useful in some instances. His reports of news from the Carolinas show how poor the communications were and how erroneous the information received in New York as to Greene's and Cornwallis' movements.

North Carolina States Records. 16 vols. Goldsboro: 1895-1907.

Papers of the Continental Congress, 1774-1789. National Archives Microfilm Publications, National Archives of the United States, Washington, D. C.

Scheer, George F. and Hugh F. Rankin. *Rebels and Redcoats.* New York: World Publishing Company, 1957.

Very useful primary source material.

Sparks, Jared. *Correspondence of the American Revolution.* 4 vols. Boston: 1853.

Stedman, Charles. *The History of the Origin, Progress and Termination of the American War.* 2 vols. London: 1794.

Stedman served as civilian commissary under Howe, Clinton, and Cornwallis.

Steuben, Baron de. *Regulations for the Order and Discipline of the Troops of the United States.* Part I. Tenth edition. New York: Greenleaf's Press, 1794.

Stevens, Benjamin Franklin (ed.). *The Campaign in Virginia, 1781: An Exact Reprint of Six Rare Pamphlets on the Clinton-Cornwallis Controversy.* 2 vols. London: 4 Trafalgar Square, Charing Cross, 1888.

Syrett, Harold C. and Jacob P. Cooke (eds.). *The Papers of Alexander Hamilton.* 2 vols. New York: Columbia University Press, 1961- (in process).

Tarleton, Banastre. *A History of the Campaigns of 1780-1781 in the Southern Provinces of North America*. London: T. Cadell on the Strand, 1787.

Tarleton was a competent observer and reporter, but those actions in which he had a part must be checked against other sources. He had a tendency to exaggerate his own exploits. Since he was ubiquitous, this means nearly every action of the campaign. The work contains useful documentary material at the ends of the chapters.

Uhlendorf, Bernhard A. (ed.). *Revolution in America: Confidential Letters and Journals, 1776-1784, of Adjutant General Major Baurmeister of the Hessian Forces*. New Brunswick, New Jersey: Rutgers University Press, 1957.

Baurmeister had the detachment of one not emotionally involved in the conflict.

Washington, George. *The Writings of George Washington from the Original Manuscript Sources, 1745-1799*. Edited by John C. Fitzpatrick. 39 vols. Washington: United States Government Printing Office, 1931-1944.

Williams, Otho H. *Calendar of the General Otho Holland Williams Papers in the Maryland Historical Society*. Edited by Elizabeth Merritt. Baltimore: Maryland Historical Records Survey Project, 1940.

Abstracts of Williams' papers in chronological order, 1774-1834. Most of the material is post-Revolution.

———. "Narrative of the Campaign of 1780."

Narrative may be found in Johnson, *Life of Greene*, I, 510, and in Simms, *Life of Greene*, Appendix (see below for complete reference). It is a firsthand account of the events leading up to the battle of Camden, the battle itself, and the aftermath up to and including the arrival of Nathanael Greene to take over the command from Gates. It is a pity that Williams did not continue his account of the southern campaign as he witnessed it. His style is reportorial with a minimum of bias.

SECONDARY SOURCES

BOOKS

Alden, John Richard. *The American Revolution: 1775-1783*. (*The New American Nation Series*, Henry Steele Commager

and Richard B. Morris, eds.). New York: Harper and
Brothers, 1954.

——. *The South in the Revolution* (Vol. III of *A History of the
South,* Wendell Holmes Stephenson and E. Merton Coulter,
eds.). Baton Rouge: Louisiana State University Press, 1957.

Bass, Robert D. *Gamecock: Life and Campaigns of General
Thomas Sumter.* New York: Holt, Rinehart and Winston,
1961.

——. *The Green Dragoon: The Lives of Banastre Tarleton and
Mary Robinson.* New York: Henry Holt and Company, 1957.
   Contains interesting documentary material. Most of the
book concerns Tarleton's later career.

——. *Swamp Fox: The Life and Campaigns of General Francis
Marion.* New York: Henry Holt and Company, 1959.
   Some of this smacks of legend. Bass has researched his
material, but his biographies are of the popular rather than
the scholarly kind.

Bolton, Charles Knowles. *The Private Soldier Under Washington.*
New York: Charles Scribner's Sons, 1902.
   This work contains no bibliographic references except
in inadequate footnotes. The material is interesting, the style
rather overblown. It has been frequently used by later historians, for it contains information not readily available else-
where.

Burnett, Edmund Cody. *The Continental Congress.* New York:
Macmillan Company, 1941.

Callahan, North. *Daniel Morgan: Ranger of the Revolution.*
New York: Holt, Rinehart and Winston, 1961.
   Callahan leans heavily on James Graham's 1856 biography
of Morgan but adds additional and pertinent data.

——. *Henry Knox, General Washington's General.* New York:
Holt, Rinehart, and Winston, 1958.
   Callahan says in his introduction that Douglas Southall
Freeman told him that Knox was worthy of a biography.
Perhaps he still is in the scholarly sense of the word, but this
is a very readable book.

Chitwood, Oliver Perry. *A History of Colonial America.* New
York: Harper and Brothers, 1948.

Crane, Verner W. *The Southern Frontier, 1670-1732.* Ann Arbor:
University of Michigan Press (Ann Arbor Paperbacks), 1959.

Draper, Lyman C. *King's Mountain and Its Heroes: History of the Battle of King's Mountain and the Events Which Led to It.* New York: Dauber and Pine Bookshops, Inc., 1929.

This volume was first published in 1881 in Cincinnati, Ohio. Draper was primarily interested in the heroic and the dramatic. He interviewed survivors of the battle and their descendants, and his vignettes of persons are his best contribution. The title is somewhat misleading, for in biographical sketches Draper deals with events subsequent to the battle of King's Mountain.

Duncan, Louis C. "Medical Men in the American Revolution, 1775-1783," *Army Medical Bulletin,* No. 25. Carlisle Barracks, Pennsylvania: Medical Field Service School, 1931.

Contains much valuable information on regulations for care of sick and wounded as advocated by Baron de Steuben and Dr. Benjamin Rush. It notes the most prevalent diseases of the Revolutionary Army and those most susceptible to them (country boys), hospital conditions (unsanitary), and much more. Copies are unfortunately rare and expensive.

Earle, Edward Meade. *Makers of Modern Strategy.* Princeton: Princeton University Press, 1943.

Flexner, James Thomas. *The Traitor and the Spy: Benedict Arnold and John André.* New York: Harcourt, Brace and Company, 1953.

Fortescue, John W. *A History of the British Army.* 13 vols. London: The Macmillan Company, 1902.

Comprehensive work on the history of the British army to the close of the nineteenth century.

Freeman, Douglas Southall. *Robert E. Lee: A Biography.* 4 vols. New York: Charles Scribner's Sons, 1934.

Chapter I, Volume I contains a brief history of Henry (Light Horse Harry) Lee, Robert E. Lee's father.

——. *George Washington: A Biography.* 5 vols. New York: Charles Scribner's Sons, 1948-1952.

Fuller, J. F. C. *British Light Infantry in the 18th Century.* London: Hutchinson, 1925.

Ganoe, William Addleman. *History of the United States Army.* New York: D. Appleton and Company, 1924.

Gordon, William. *The History of the Rise, Progress, and Establishment of the Independence of the United States of America: Including an Account of the Late War and of the*

Thirteen Colonies from Their Origin to that Period. Second American edition. 3 vols. New York: Samuel Campbell, 1794.

    Gordon had access to the records of Gates' and Greene's Deputy Adjutant General, Otho H. Williams. These dealt with all phases of the southern campaign. They were subsequently lost, and this material was not available to later historians except in Gordon's work.

Graham, James. *The Life of General Daniel Morgan of the Virginia Line of the Army of the United States with Portions of His Correspondence; Compiled from Authentic Sources.* New York: Derry and Jackson, 1856.

    A particularly valuable source for numerous letters of Morgan's, many of which are difficult to find elsewhere.

Greene, George Washington. *Life of Nathanael Greene: Major General in the Army of the Revolution.* 3 vols. New York: Hurd and Houghton, 1871.

    G. W. Greene was a grandson of Nathanael Greene, but he has for the most part avoided the eulogies which commonly mar the biographies produced by relatives of the subject. The work is valuable for the many documents it contains. And Greene has attempted with considerable success to follow the spirit of the lines from the *Iliad,* which he quotes on the title page:

After this manner said they, who had seen him toiling; but I ne'er Met him myself, nor saw him; men say he was greater than others.

Iliad, IV, 374

Hendrick, Burton J. *The Lees of Virginia: Biography of a Family.* New York: Halcyon House, 1935.

Herskovits, Melville. *Dahomey: An Ancient West African Kingdom.* 2 vols. New York: J. J. Augustin, 1938.

Higginbotham, Don. *Daniel Morgan: Revolutionary Rifleman.* Chapel Hill, North Carolina: The University of North Carolina Press, 1961.

Irving, Washington. *Life of George Washington.* 5 vols. New York: 1855-1859.

    Irving is famous for never letting the truth interfere with a good story, but where he can be documented he is valuable.

Johnson, William. *Sketches of the Life and Correspondence of Nathanael Greene: Major General of the Armies of the United States in the war of the Revolution; Compiled Chiefly from Original Sources.* Charleston, South Carolina: A. E. Miller, 1822.

Johnson says that he had access to a complete collection of Greene's papers through the courtesy of members of Greene's family. He includes many letters and documents in his work. Johnson was a Justice of the United States Supreme Court and something of a dissenter. In his history he is extremely critical of his sources, particularly of the *Memoirs* of Henry Lee and the *Campaigns* of Tarleton (see above for complete reference). He apparently disliked in particular miracles and flamboyant young men. He is undoubtedly biased, but it is the bias of a man accustomed to weighing evidence.

Johnston, Henry P. *The Yorktown Campaign and the Surrender of Cornwallis, 1781.* New York: Harper and Brothers, 1881.

Knollenberg, Bernhard. *Washington and the Revolution: A Reappraisal, Gates, Conway and the Continental Congress.* New York: Macmillan Company, 1940.

Lancaster, Bruce. *American Heritage Book of the Revolution.* New York: Simon and Schuster, 1958.

Profusely and handsomely illustrated.

Lee, Henry. *Campaign of 1781 in the Carolinas with Remarks Historical and Critical on Johnson's Life of Greene to Which is Added an Appendix of Original Documents Relating to the History of the Revolution.* Philadelphia: Littell; William Brown, printer, 1824.

Lee was Light Harry Lee's son by his first marriage. This book is a defense against what the son considered criticism of his father in Johnson's biography of Greene, published two years earlier. The book is carping, sententious, vituperative, and historically unacceptable. Its value lies in the numerous letters of Lee, Greene, and others contained in the appendix. A new edition has been published by Quadrangle Books, Chicago, 1962.

Lefferts, Charles. *Uniforms of the American, British, French and German Armies in the War of the American Revolution.* Edited by Alexander J. Wall. New York: New York Historical Society, 1926.

Lefler, Hugh T. and Albert Ray Newsome. *North Carolina: History of a Southern State.* Chapel Hill: University of North Carolina Press, 1954.

Lossing, Benson J. *Pictorial Field-Book of the American Revolu-tion.* 2 vols. New York: Harper and Brothers, 1850.

The order is that of a trip Lossing took to battlegrounds and historical sites rather than the chronology of the events of the war. Useful biographical footnotes on minor person-ages and sketches of sites Lossing saw. The latter are partic-ularly valuable inasmuch as many of the buildings and markers have since disappeared.

Malone, Dumas. *Jefferson the Virginian.* Boston: Little, Brown and Company, 1948.

Marshall, John. *Life of George Washington.* 2 vols. New York: 1832.

Marshall wrote this work in some haste under pressure of financial need. Should be used with caution, but contains valuable material.

Miller, John C. *Alexander Hamilton: Portrait in Paradox.* New York: Harper and Brothers, 1959.

Montross, Lynn. *Rag, Tag, and Bobtail: The Story of the Con-tinental Army, 1775-1783.* New York: Harper and Brothers, 1952.

The Continental soldier depicted in more human and favorable light than in some other works.

Montross, Lynn. *The Reluctant Rebels.* New York: Harper and Brothers, 1950. The story of the Continental Congress.

Morris, Richard B. *Alexander Hamilton and the Founding of the Nation.* New York: Dial Press, 1957.

Peckham, Howard H. *The War for Independence.* Chicago: Uni-versity of Chicago Press, 1958.

Excellent brief military history of the Revolution, partic-ularly good for the northern campaigns.

Power-Waters, Alma. *Virginia Giant.* New York: E. P. Dutton, 1957.

A biography of Peter Francisco, a Spanish waif who grew to legendary prowess in the Revolution.

Ramsay, David. *History of the Revolution in South Carolina.* 2 vols. Trenton, New Jersey, 1785.

Rather sketchy.

———. *The History of the American Revolution.* 2 vols. Trenton, New Jersey: James Wilson, 1811.

Ramsay had more material this time. He owes much to

Gordon, even to using the same phrases, but he does not acknowledge this indebtedness.

Roberts, Kenneth Lewis. *The Battle of Cowpens: The Great Morale-Builder.* Garden City, New York: Doubleday and Company, 1958.

> Roberts was primarily an historical novelist. However this is non-fiction, although somewhat fictionalized history. It contains some excellent writing and less controversy than Roberts usually indulged himself. His sources are secondary, sound as far as they go, but not recent.

Simms, William Gilmore. *The Life of Nathanael Greene, Major General in the Army of the Revolution.* Philadelphia: Leary and Getz, 1849.

> Simms used with care the sources available to him, which he names as Lee, Johnson, Ramsay, Tarleton, and others. He describes himself as editor of the work. He does not pretend to scholarship, and his style is turgid to modern ears. His facts are accurate within the limitations of his sources. The appendix is one of the few places where Otho Williams' "Narrative of the Campaign of 1780" can be found in print.

——. *Life of Francis Marion.* New York: Derby and Jackson, 1860.

> This work is in the style of the above. It suffers from the usual problem that any history of Marion is bound to be intermingled with legend.

Smith, Warren B. *White Servitude in Colonial South Carolina.* Columbia: University of South Carolina Press, 1961.

Steele, Matthew Forney. *American Campaigns.* 2 vols. Washington: United States Government Printing Office, 1935.

> The maps are especially useful.

Taylor, Raleigh. "Peter Francisco." Unpublished manuscript, National Park Service Museum, Guilford Battleground National Monument, North Carolina, 1958.

> Taylor is an historian and was superintendent at Guilford in 1958. In the museum is a shoe said to be Francisco's and a shaving set inscribed with a silver plate to Francisco from Greene.

Thayer, Theodore. *Nathanael Greene: Strategist of the American Revolution.* New York: Twayne Publishers, 1960.

> Thayer's bibliography indicates that he examined many documents in many libraries throughout the country. See

review by William B. Willcox in Mississippi Valley Historical Review.

Upton, Emory. *The Military Policy of the United States.* Fourth impression. Washington: United States Government Printing Office, 1917.

Van Doren, Carl. *Secret History of the American Revolution.* New York: Viking Press, 1941.
   Arnold's treason is the featured topic.

Wallace, David Duncan. *South Carolina: A Short History, 1520-1948.* Chapel Hill: University of North Carolina Press, 1951.

Wallace, Willard M. *Appeal to Arms.* New York: Harper and Brothers, 1951.

Walsh, Richard. *Charleston's Sons of Liberty: A Study of the Artisans, 1763-1789.* Columbia: University of South Carolina Press, 1961.
   Interesting study of a little-known subject.

Ward, Christopher. *The War of the Revolution.* Edited by John Richard Alden. 2 vols. New York: The Macmillan Company, 1952.
   Ward died before he had finished the history. Final editing was undertaken by Alden. The work is an indispensable reference for anyone engaged in the field of Revolutionary military history.

Willcox, Cornélis de Witt. *A French-English Military and Technical Dictionary with a Supplement Containing Recent Military and Technical Terms.* Washington: U. S. Government Printing Office, 1917.

Woodmason, Charles. *The Carolina Backcountry on the Eve of the Revolution: The Journal and Other Writings of Charles Woodmason, Anglican Itinerant.* Richard J. Hooker, ed. Chapel Hill: University of North Carolina Press, 1953.

PERIODICALS

Clark, Jane. "The Convention Troops and the Perfidy of Sir William Howe," *American Historical Review,* XXXVII (1932), 721-722.

Cook, Fred J. "Francisco, the Incredible," *American Heritage,* X, 6 (October, 1959), 22-25; 92-95.

Scheer, George F. "The Sergeant Major's Strange Mission," *American Heritage*, VIII, 6 (October, 1957).

Willcox, William B. "The British Road to Yorktown: A Study in Divided Command," *American Historical Review*, LII (October, 1946), 1-35.

Wright, John W. "Some Notes on the Continental Army," *William and Mary College Quarterly Historical Magazine*, 2nd series, XI, 2 (April, 1931), 81-105; XI, 3 (July, 1931), 185-209; XII, 2 (April, 1932), 80-103.

INDEX

INDEX